ENGINEERING DOCUMENTATION CONTROL HANDBOOK

ENGINEERING DOCUMENTATION CONTROL HANDBOOK

Configuration Management

For Industry

by

Frank B. Watts

EC^3 Corporation
Winter Park, Colorado

np **NOYES PUBLICATIONS**
Park Ridge, New Jersey, U.S.A.

Library of Congress Catalog Card Number: 93-26693
ISBN: 0-8155-1342-9
Printed in the United States

Published in the United States of America by
Noyes Publications
Mill Road, Park Ridge, New Jersey 07656

10 9 8 7 6 5 4 3

Library of Congress Cataloging-in-Publication Data

Watts, Frank B.
    Engineering documentation control handbook : configuration
management for industry / by Frank B. Watts.
        p.   cm.
    Includes index.
    ISBN 0-8155-1342-9
    1. Engineering--Management. 2. Configuration management.
3. Production management.   I. Title
TA190.W38   1993
658.5--dc20   93-26693
                                         CIP

Preface

Bridging the gap between design engineering and the rest of the world is a significant challenge in American industry. This book is about ways to bridge that gap and to eliminate the "throw it over the wall" syndrome. In this sense, Engineering Documentation Control is a significant company strategy. The methods for releasing a new product and its documentation, requesting changes to the product, making changes, and developing bills of material must be simple, fast, and accurate. Rules and guidelines are explained for creating world class Engineering Documentation Control processes.

The title of this book indicates that "Engineering Documentation Control" and "Configuration Management" are equivalent terms. I have taught in University of Wisconsin Seminars that they are equivalent. But are they really? The Configuration Management term has been largely usurped by the Defense Industry and the Department of Defense (DoD). The term has been used and abused so extensively by this segment of our manufacturing world that it has taken on a parochial and very complex meaning. Thus, the primary goal of this book is to keep CM simple. The basics of world-class Configuration Management will be presented from the ground up, for application in either a "commercial" or "military" kind of business.

Can CM in the Defense Industry context be made simple? Without significant reform in the DoD, the hope for military contractors is very slim. A study published in *National Defense* magazine, Sept 1992 by George Krikorian, PE summarizes the current conditions from a study, "The results revealed that the cost of a product when selling to DoD increases from five percent to one hundred percent as compared to the same or similar product cost to a commercial (non-DoD) enterprise." One of the significant reasons given is "MIL-SPECS and Standards." Configuration Management standards make up a significant portion of the total DoD Specs and Standards.

Subcontractors may be somewhat better off than prime contractors because they are "shielded" by the prime contractor, but the problem is pervasive. This is not to say that the goals of the DoD are wrong, nor that some of their standards aren't useful. As a practical matter, however, implementation of those standards adds cost and substantial time to the new product release and change processes. Those in the commercial manufacturing business can and should resist the defense department influence where it tends to complicate or slow the process.

There are some signs of improvement. There seems to be a shift toward "commercial standards" in the purchasing activity for some government contracts. This shift puts all the more emphasis on the need for a make-sense generic standard.

The typical Defense Business approach to CM is to acquire and read all the applicable Military and DoD Specs, Standards and Directives, and then design their system around them. On the contrary, every manufacturing business should develop a simple, make-sense, accurate and fast approach to Engineering Documentation Control / Configuration Management, then examine the DoD, MIL, DoE, FDA, International, and all other applicable agency standards. After careful examination of those standards, add or modify to satisfy the customer / agency specifications if necessary.

The quick release of new product documentation, and the ability to change the documentation and the product quickly are critical to a company's profitability. *Thus, the development and implementation of a simple, make-sense, fast, accurate, and well-understood CM system is an important business strategy.*

The title of this book has primary emphasis on the simpler term (Engineering Documentation Control) while recognizing the near equality of the Configuration Management (CM) term. The CM term will be used quite liberally because the basic principles of world-class CM are applicable regardless of the kind of manufacturing or the kind of customer.

Toward achieving this "make sense" approach, the following will be the guiding principles of this book:

- Develop a generic, make-sense approach which is good for commercial or agency-regulated companies. The existing texts on this subject address DoD Specifications and Standards. This work will take a generic approach.

- Take the acronyms out wherever possible! The typical text uses an index of over eight *pages* of acronyms and abbreviations. The goal here will be to only use those acronyms which are universal in the manufacturing business.

- Use the English language, defining terms as we go, as opposed to over twenty pages of glossary found in one text.

- Take the jargon, mystique, double talk, and unnecessary complexity out of Configuration Management.

- Systematically approach the discipline by using an example product—an electronic ignition, software programmed, front end loader. Develop the design documentation for this product, release it to manufacturing, change it, and close the loop by knowing when each change was made and what is in each product.

- Develop principles that are sound for any size company, while recognizing the nuances that may be present in small, large, multi-national, make-to-print, process, make-to-stock, or other types of manufacturing.

- Develop principles that are sound for any type of product, while recognizing differences in products—which vary from needles to nuclear ships—and production rates that vary from quantities per second to years per quantity one.

- Emphasize early costing of the product and changes, a generally ignored aspect of CM practice.

- Show how redundant Bills of Material can be eliminated and how to simplify Bill Of Material structuring.

- Develop generic CM processes in the form of flow diagrams and standards to use as a guide in development of your own processes. Assure that the horse (documentation) comes before the cart (the product).

- Establish methods for achieving fast processing of releases, requests and changes. The emphasis will be on speed - a long overlooked criteria that proves to be a costly oversight.

- Outline methods for analyzing an existing system and implementing a new system; methods that can be used whether reinventing the system and/or using continuous improvement techniques.

These goals must be accomplished without sacrificing quality. In fact, the quality of documentation releases and changes as well as the quality of the product must *increase* as new or improved Engineering Documentation Control is implemented.

Good CM alone will not achieve world-class Total Quality Manufacturing (TQM). However, world-class TQM cannot be achieved without world class Configuration Management—simple, fast, accurate, and well-understood Engineering Documentation Control.

Engineering Documentation Control can be a significant *business strategy* which supports TQM (Total Quality Management), JIT (Just In Time), Design Teams (Concurrent Engineering), MRP (Manufacturing Resource Planning), make-sense standards (domestic or international), and efficient manufacturing.

My thanks to the University of Wisconsin, Continuing Engineering Education program in Milwaukee, and especially to their program director, Rick Albers. His encouragement and support have been nearly as valuable to me as that of my wife, Jane. Thanks also to my mentor in the University seminars, Ray Monahan and my partner in those seminars, Grayme (Bart) Bartuli. My many customers also deserve a hearty thanks since I learn something from each of them.

Winter Park, Colorado

August, 1993

Frank B. Watts

NOTICE

Table of Contents

8   Change Control 166

1

Introduction

Why Engineering Documentation at all? Why control of that documentation? The mere use of the word *control* puts most engineers into a very defensive posture. Are we trying to stifle the engineer's creativity? What is there to *manage* about the configuration of a product?

Why do architects make drawings and specifications for a home? Does the architect do this for his own pleasure? Or for the trade magazine or show? Isn't the documentation done so that the customers get what they want? Aren't the documents for the builder who has to build the house? And for the eventual owner who will have to maintain it? Try building or maintaining a product without adequate drawings and specs. It becomes especially difficult and error prone when changes are being made. Try controlling the cost without controlling the changes. Still, most businesses operate to some extent without proper, timely or adequate control of their documentation. The symptoms are usually everywhere.

A Look at Symptoms

- Manufacturing says:

    - I don't understand what I'm supposed to build?

    - What criteria do we test to?

    - Where is the change I need to:
        Reduce costs?
        Avoid making scrap?
        Avoid making parts that will have to be reworked?

- Sales says:

    - You mean the product isn't ready for the market window?

    - Where is that new feature you promised?

- Why didn't we deliver a product with the options the customer asked for?

- Customer says:
    - I didn't get what I ordered!
    - Where is the fix you promised me months ago?
    - Where is that new feature or option?

- Dealer/Field Service say:
    - Shouldn't my documents match my product?
    - Where is the fix for this nagging product problem?

- Repair says:
    - It would help me to fix it if I knew what is in this product?
    - What changes should be incorporated upon repair?

- Quality says:
    - Is this cost in our *cost of quality*?
    - Can we treat ourselves or our customers this way?
    - How can we meet our customers' standards this way?

- Employee says:
    - I asked them to do something about this a long time ago!

Do any of these symptoms sound familiar? The cure is: simple, fast, accurate and well understood Engineering Documentation Control/Configuration Management. Good design documentation and its control is the solution for the root cause of these symptoms. Thus, Configuration Management (CM) is the medicine that cures the root cause problems, and therefore the symptoms disappear.

When CM is kept simple, it results in many benefits to the company. What are the benefits of a fast, accurate, and well-understood CM system? Take a look at the potential benefits of a carefully planned CM strategy.

Benefits

- Happier customers because they will see the change or feature they requested much quicker.
- The customers get what they ordered with fewer missed delivery commitments.

- Reduce significantly the manufacturing rework and scrap costs. Reduce the "bone piles" of down-level material. Get cost reductions implemented quicker.

- Help get new products, features and options into the market faster.

- Improve Bill Of Material (BOM) accuracy and save the corresponding material and parts waste. Make the corresponding improvement in product quality.

- Eliminate multiple Bills of Material and save the costs of maintaining the Bills, not to mention eliminating the risks associated with multiple Bills.

- Reduce field maintenance, retrofit and repair cost.

- Reduce MRP run time. Avoid weekend runs that spill into Monday mornings.

- Know exactly what is non-interchangeable in each product.

- Improve the understanding and communications between Design Engineering and the rest of the world.

- Clarify responsibilities to eliminate finger pointing.

- Save wear and tear on Configuration Managers, Master Schedulers, and all types of engineers.

- Reduce the delivery time for customized products.

- Comply with applicable customer or agency standards.

- Sort out changes that are not needed or aren't cost effective.

- Save many dollars a year in paper and copying costs alone.

- Significantly reduce the cost of quality.

- Allow the company to qualify as a world-class producer.

The ways and means of achieving these benefits is not secret, high tech, or cost prohibitive. These benefits are attainable. The following will outline the who, what, how, why, when, where, and how much is required to achieve a world-class Engineering Documentation Control System.

What is CM?

Configuration Management is the communications bridge between Design Engineering and the "rest of the world." This is the single most important function served by the CM organization.

· A BRIDGE FOR COMMUNICATIONS ·

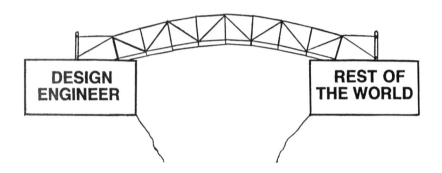

Figure 1. CM defined.

The critical nature of the CM discipline cannot be over emphasized. American manufacturing has developed a near-tradition of Design-Production / Service adversarial relationship. It results substantially from the "Throw it over the wall" syndrome—the new design release or engineering change that is done without consultation from the key people at the right time. Many CM systems are often unwittingly designed to foster that traditional kind of thinking. The enlightened CM Manager can tear down the wall or at least build a bridge over it. Lets face it, by and large, the Designers are thinkers and creators while the Operations people are movers and doers. They will naturally have difficulty communicating. The CM group can enhance communications and assure that these folks cross the bridge at the right time for necessary communications.

The CM function must assure that what crosses the bridge is: properly documented, timely, minimally controlled, distributed as needed, and that feedback is obtained as to when changes occur. All this must be done at minimum cost. All this must appear "transparent" to the creative design people and the rest of the world.

While not getting in the way of the design engineer, it must be kept in mind that the engineer's product is not just a working prototype unit. It is accurate specification and drawings for that product. The CM product is thus *Design Documentation*. The primary *customer* for this documentation is *not* Design Engineering.* It is Manufacturing,** Field Service, and your company's customer. The company's customer must be paramount among these "users" (a term that is much less acceptable than "Customer"). The vast majority of the design documents are prepared for Manufacturing and Service use. In this sense Manufacturing and Field Service people are often the most important customers.

Some of the symptoms calling for world-class CM are in every company. The benefits of having a world-class CM organization and system are a significant business strategy.

The CM Discipline

First, a definition of CM: *A simple, fast, accurate, systematic and well understood approach to planning, identifying, controlling, and tracking a product's configuration from its inception throughout its life.*

We engineers hate the word "control." Too much control detracts form speed. Notice the emphasis on speed. This is a factor missing in many companies. Also note the timeframe—birth to death of the product. Notice that the term "tracking" is used instead of the classical "Status Accounting" term. These are the traditional elements of CM—plan, identify, control, and track. The challenge for the CM Manager is to mix just the right amount of each of these elements into the CM processes—Product and Document Release, Bill Of Material, Request, and Change.

Also notice the emphasis on training—a well-understood system. In order to be systematic and well understood, it must be documented. The discipline must be depicted in a set of standards and the people trained on those standards.

"Configuration" as used herein has a narrower meaning than the dictionary definition: *Configuration is the technical description and arrangement or combination of parts and materials which are capable of fulfilling the requirements defined by the product specification, other specifications, and drawings.*

---

* In this text you can usually substitute the title "Programmer" or "Software Engineer" for "Design Engineer" and "Program Code" for "Drawings and Specifications". This will be the case as long as we are referring to *product related* software or firmware Program Code and Programmers.

** Titles vary widely. The titles used in this text are most common in industry, although not universal. The word "Manufacturing" will be used both in the larger sense as an industry and in the narrower sense as the operations function.

The discipline can be applied to companies who produce a product which is either parts- or process-driven. The product can be a building or an atomic power plant. The principles apply, with some care, to any "product."

On the other end of the spectrum, where does the Program Code fit into this definition? It is also included in the sense that the code is "assembled" onto a tape or disc which then becomes one of the "parts."

Notice the emphasis on the Product Specification. It is surprising how many companies try to get along without a product specification. Or they have one but don't release it. Or they produce or release it much later than is desirable.

The CM System

The total CM system is made up of four major processes. These are generally referred to as Product Release and Change Control. More specifically, the processes are:

Product Bill Of Material Process
Product and Documentation Release Process
Change Request Process
Design Change Process

Thus: 1 CM System = 4 major processes

The Change Request Process and the Design Change Process are often combined under one term—Change Control. This will not be done in this text for reasons which will become apparent later. The document obsolesence "process" is combined with the Design Change Process and treated as a special kind of design/document change. These four processes must cover any product from inception to obsolesence—birth to death.

There is a temptation to say that these processes occur in series. First we document the product and release the documentation, then create a Bill Of Material, etc. Although some companies try to do business "in series," it is not desirable. The processes overlap almost totally. For example: the Product Specification should be created and released very early in the product life cycle. The product specification would be put under a simplistic form of change control. Then, long lead-time parts should be released in lead time. This may well be done long before a BOM is "structured." Some documents may be obsoleted before they are released. Thus, the processes should not be "serial" but very "parallel."

In fact, trying to do these processes in series creates a problem. If, for example, we try to create all the documentation for a product before proceeding, then the need to release long lead-time items (in lead-time) creates a quandary. Shall we hold up the project until all the items are documented before releasing the long lead items? Shall we wait for their assemblies to be released? Grouping any of the documents for release creates an artificial bunching of the work. Much better to design the processes to encourage item by item release, since that is the way they are created and used.

History of Configuration Management

The real beginning of CM occurred when Eli Whitney designed and built his cotton gin with interchangeable parts. That concept of interchangeability has come to be expected in all manufacturing. Today, when industry exchanges items that are replaceable (including the end product), they are expected to interchange, or reasonable notice is required.

Many companies have CM standards and practices that date back to the early years of their conception. Industry standardization of certain CM practices began with the government during the space programs in the late 1950s. This was a necessary and natural occurrence since the assurance of interchangeability between the many contributors in a space program was very difficult. In the late 1960s, the Department of Defense recognized that each agency and branch was developing its own set of standards. They, for better or worse, brought all the CM standards under the purview of the Department Of Defense.

Almost all the existing standards and books in the field have been Military / DoD driven. It is true that the IEEE (Institute of Electrical and Electronic Engineers), SAE (Society of Automotive Engineers), EIA (Electronics Industry Association), APICS (American Production & Inventory Control Society), and ANSI (American National Standards Institute) have all made some contribution in the field. Industry, by and large, however, has been satisfied to let the DoD take the initiative. The result is an IRS like, bureaucratic maze of forms and regulations. It is time for the commercial CM world to stand up and be counted. This text will answer that challenge. To simplify, that is the goal!

The Organization

Let's examine the CM organization starting with the names it is called; the terminology varies depending upon the company. Some common names are:

- Engineering Documentation Control
- Revision Drafting
- Documentation Control
- Engineering Services
- Design Drafting
- Configuration Management

The CM title is preferred when the responsibilities are roughly as outlined in this book. When the responsibilities are broader (include functions such as Publications, Reproduction, Microfilm, etc.) then the preferred name is Engineering Services.

Presuming that your Company or Division organization is "slim" (few total levels of management) the CM function should answer to the VP of Engineering. In larger organizations there may be a Engineering Services function between CM and the VP of Engineering. If the function answers any "lower" in the organization, it will not have the necessary clout, communication of needs will suffer, and the result will be more of the "symptoms" described earlier.

Some companies have the CM function answer to QA, Manufacturing, Operations, or even to the President. If the results are very good, don't change the reporting relationship. Most companies have the function answer to Engineering, however. The question is often asked, "Isn't that like having the fox watch the chicken coop?" The answer is ; "Of course—but they're Engineering's chickens!" We are talking about *design* documentation! If Engineering has the function and the described symptoms exist, reorganization may not solve the problems. The Design Engineering management, however, runs the risk of losing the function if too many problems persist.

Large multi-plant companies should have a CM organization in each business unit or division. They should also have a corporate function to assure *minimum* standards are met. This minimum level of standardization should be based upon three criteria:

- Moving a product from business unit to business unit.
- Customers' contact with more than one division.
- Field service by a single person of products made in more than one division.

The most difficult of all worlds is confronted when Engineering is in one location and Manufacturing is in another, or several, locations. When one of the Manufacturing locations is off shore, add another level of complication. The ideal results are more likely obtained when the Engineering (or at least the "Continuation Engineering" function), Configuration Management and the Manufacturing functions are in the same location (small business unit). This is desirable regardless of the company size.

Within a small business unit, placing CM responsibilities within multiple "Project Offices" is inviting chaos. Too many groups will develop their own rules for CM practices. In large business units, it may be the only way to attain fast action. If this is done, a "corporate" type CM function will be necessary to maintain minimum standardization.

The CM Functions

As a minimum the CM Department should contain the following functions / responsibilities:
- Standardize and document the CM System.
- Train all key personnel on the basics of CM and the company CM system.
- Measure and report on the CM System.
- Assign all part numbers, change numbers, and document revision levels.
- Control master design document after the appropriate point of release (master file and "fire" file—either hard copy or electronic).
- Revision (Incorporation) Drafting / CAD update.
- Change request monitoring.
- Change control and facilitation.
- Input and accuracy of the BOM database (design information).
- Traceability and traceability reporting.
- Auditing the CM system.

If any of these functions are not included in the CM Manager's responsibilities, the results will be likewise limited. Some companies vest the CM group with other responsibilities such as:
- Assisting the design engineers in the performance of their responsibilities
- Microfilming / Digitizing

- CAD control
- Engineering library
- Product Support documentation preparation (Publications)
- Manufacturing document control
- Support document control

Placing the last three of these functions with CM should be done with care. It is far too easy to overload the CM Manager's plate with support document preparation and control of manufacturing and support documents.

Helping the design engineers with their responsibilities is a very desirable CM function. It must be chartered and staffed to be effective. It is one excellent way to have the CM organization viewed as part of the solution. It must be clear, however, that the responsibility for certain functions belongs to Engineering and not to CM or any other organization that is "helping" the engineer. For this reason, many organizations choose CAD/Drafting/Designers/Technicians to help the engineer rather than CM.

Many companies have the CM functions scattered throughout the organization. Sometimes the functions occupy fractions of people's total job. The functions need to be brought together into one group. This recognition and emphasis is the first step toward attaining world-class CM.

Organization Within CM

How does the CM Manager organize the group? After all, one group may have three and another thirty-three people! There are two basic approaches to use, as well as combinations of the two. The first is the "production line" approach. That is, each person does some steps and passes the release or change to another person, and so on, until complete. The other method is the "job-enriched" method. In this method, a person does all steps in the process. The job-enriched method is preferred. That is, one person will be responsible for all CM functions for a product, set of products, or a customer. This requires a considerable amount of cross-training.

The Manager's goal should be for every person in the group to be fully trained in all aspects of the work. This makes the people fully interchangeable. Call these people CM Technicians. Three levels of CM Technicians are ideal—entry, learned, and teacher. In this fashion, people can be assigned to a product, project, customer, or whatever depending upon the

complexity. When someone is sick or goes on vacation, the interchangeability of people avoids delay. This does require a significant amount of training.
Training is expensive. However, *if you believe that training is expensive—try
ignorance !* Training within the CM group and in related functions is the best
way for the system (all its processes) to become accepted, improved and
used.

Summary

The approach used in this book will be definition, execution, and
emphasis of the basics. We will keep it simple, but recognize and address
complexities in the simplest terms possible.   An example product—an
electronic-ignition, programmable, front end loader—will be used to build
upon these basics to develop the processes. We will develop documentation for this product, release that documentation, develop the BOM, request
changes, change the product by changing its documentation, and follow the
change to implementation in the product. We will also go into development
of the release, request and change processes with an emphasis on speed,
accuracy and training.

Figure 2. Electronic-ignition front end loader.

2

The Product Documentation

It is not the purpose of CM or this text to specify drawing standards. It is important, however, to assure that certain elements are present on drawing formats. It is also very important to emphasize that certain elements should not be on those formats.

Document Formats

Keep as few formats active as possible. A well thought out drafting standard will help in this area. Use ANSI Y 14.5, DoD STD 100, or the commercially available "Drawing Requirements Manual" (DRM) as a guideline for your own standard. Take care to assure that all the following rules and guidelines have been taken into account as well. In other words, don't just invoke one of these standards. Read and modify it according to the parts of this text which you wish to adopt.

Some general definition of the "parts" of design documents are provided below. Regardless of size, drawings, specs, lists and other documents should have a common format. They should all have a *Body, Title Block,* and *Revision Block* as seen in Figure 3.

Title Block

The typical information found in the Title Block of a drawing or specification is shown in Figure 4.

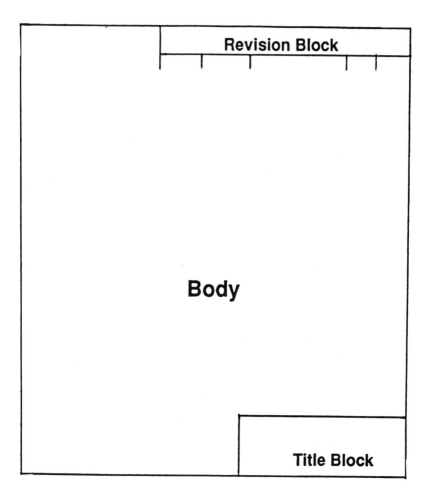

Figure 3. Terminology.

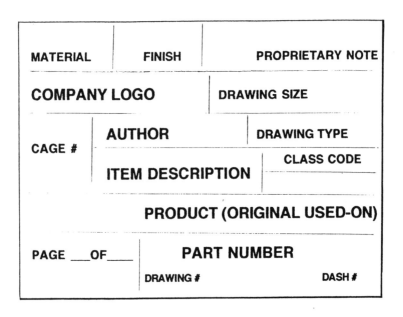

Figure 4. Title Block data.

Unique company requirements may call for more data than that shown. For example, if you're doing business with the government, a CAGE (Commercial And Government Entity) number will be required. Simplicity should be the rule, however. Thus, it is most important to cover the data which should *not* be in the title block.

Notice that the title block does *not* show the current revision of the document. Although some companies show the revision in the title block, the practice is not recommended. In one extreme, a company's "A" size drawing showed the revision in no less than four places.

Rule: Show the revision once in the Revision Block on the first page and once on each subsequent page of a document, and make sure it is current there.

Reason: Other appearances of the revision level only add work to keep them current and add risk that confusion and errors will result when they differ.

Some companies have a real need for the revision to show in the corner of a folded hard copy. If this is a worthy need, add one more appearance of the revision on the first page.

The *Original Product Used On* is shown in the title block, but no attempt will be made to keep other "Used On" information up to date on the document. A separate file (manual or computer) should be set up for maintenance of the "Used On" relationships.

Rule: Do not maintain "Used On" information on Design Documents. Set up a separate file for this data.

Reason: You may use any item over and over again in other products. It is wasteful to get the original document out and revise it each time you use the item elsewhere.

If the company doesn't currently have a computer program for doing this, as it grows it probably will, so keep the Used On information separate. This may be a manual file although most CM groups have access to a PC which can be used. Most MRP (Manufacturing Resource Planning) systems have Used On capability. If you have an MRP system, make that your *only* place to maintain it.

The material required to make the part is often shown in the title block, in a separate *Material Block,* or in the Body of the drawing. The important issue here is that it be in a consistent location to make it easy on your drawing "customers."

A simple material parts list may be in order. If you have, or foresee, problems with material tracking, inventory control, material shortages, or material formula, consider making the Part into an Assembly. That is, making the material specification(s) a call-out on the item assembly parts list.

Example: A sheet stock manufacturer wishes to control the roll stock material that a variety of sheets are produced from. This can be done by preparing a one-item parts list for each "assembly" produced:

SAE 1010 steel 1/4" nominal   x qty

Example: An injection-molding company needs to control the material content or formula of the "part". They can do so by preparing an assembly "parts list" such as:

Virgin Material   x qty

Regrind Material   y qty

Coloration Material   z qty

Whether or not this "material parts list" concept is used also depends upon how vertically integrated a company is. It should not be done without careful analysis since it adds a level to the BOM structure.

It is sometimes said that CM principles are difficult to apply to a process industry. This is often true because the company has not developed a "parts list" for their product. The materials required are not clearly specified in a separate list but are buried in the process documentation. Step one for those companies is to develop their "formula" into a parts list.

The quantities may be per piece or, in the case of a compound or liquid, a fraction of the total mixture. This allows separate control of what is normally the critical "design" aspect of process industry products. This also sets the stage for computer control of each "part" of the material content.

The *Drawing Type* is typically a alpha code that indicates whether the drawing is a:

P	=	Part
AY	=	Assembly
PL	=	Parts List
LD	=	Logic Diagram
etc.		

Some companies use this code as part of their Part Number. As a separate field, this information is more readily maintained and expanded should you not set aside enough digits in your part number. In any event, develop a standard (and keep it up to date) which spells out your acceptable abbreviations. Keep it simple—one standard covering only this subject.

Note: The term "standard" will be used in this text when one might say "policy," "procedure" or "instruction," etc.

The definition of an "Assembly" is much debated. The simplest definition is: *Any physical item with a Parts List.* It follows then that a "Part" is any physical item without a Parts List. The term "Item" can refer to both. The term "component" will also be used. Component is a general term much like "item" in that it may refer to a Part or an Assembly. If a company has a *Drawing Type* code or processes which treat parts and assemblies differently, it is critical to develop clear definitions. A definitions standard may be in order.

The *author* should be a single lettered name (signature) of the primary person responsible for the items creation. Avoid having more than one signature since at least one International Standard (ISO 9000) calls for the same signatures in the change process that originally approved the document. In order to minimize the signature gathering and to fix responsibility, have only one name here.

One "acceptor" of the document may be added to the title block. This would be the manufacturing engineer or other single responsible person who would speak for the manufacturability, testability, serviceability, etc. of the item. The margin of the document can be used in an unofficial manner for the checker, CAD designer, or draftsperson to "sign".

If computer access codes are secure, a computer-printed signature is acceptable. This single-responsibility practice is the beginning of an important concept—the responsible or cognizant engineer list. This list will be discussed later. It is kept separately from the drawing as opposed to changing the "author" name on the document. This avoids changes to documents for changing responsibilities.

Revision Block

Information typically found in the revision block of a drawing or specification is shown in Figure 5.

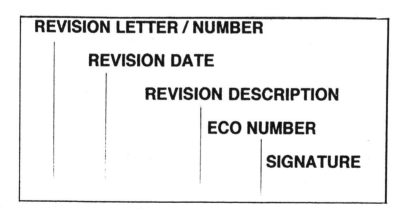

Figure 5. Revision Block data.

Note that the *Revision Date* is the date on which the change was incorporated into the document, not necessarily the date the change was written or approved.

If the *Description* of the change is short, it may be placed here. If the description is long, it is perfectly acceptable to enter "See ECO." The available space should be used to enter a minimal description of the change even if "See ECO" is used. This may avoid the step of pulling the ECO to identify what the change did.

The *ECO (Engineering Change Order) Number* should be a separate field as opposed to entering it into the Description. When it is not a separate field, it is typical to occasionally omit it. Without this number associated with the change, the traceability to the ECO form is lost; the reasons for change, other dates, change details, etc, are then not readily found. A separate field improves the chances of always having this traceability.

This *Signature* is that of the person who incorporated the change into the document. If your change system is sound, there should be no need for any other person to sign the revision block. This is to say that the ECO must be a "stand alone" document. If it is, then the person who incorporates the change into the master document or file should be the only signature required on that action. This should be a lettered "signature" to assure readability.

Rule: The signature column should be "signed" by the person who incorporates the change into the document. No other signatures should be required.

Reason: If more than one person signs, which will assure that it is right?

More than one signature also adds to the process time. The critical issue is the responsibility for incorporating the change correctly and rapidly.

Body of a Drawing

The following information should appear in the *Body* of a Drawing:

- Pictorial
- Dimensions and tolerances
- Notes and specifications

It is important to keep notes and specs short and crisp. If the *spec or note* information is long or has use on several drawings, then a separate document should be created. The "part number" of the separate spec or "detached notes" should be referenced on the body of this drawing.

An example of a Part Drawing for the Bucket of the Front End Loader is shown in Figure 6.

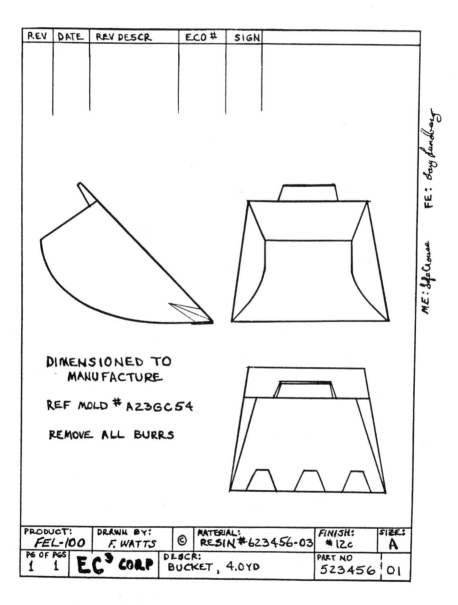

Figure 6. Piece Part Drawing.

The dimensions are left off the drawing so as to focus on the issues which are most important to Configuration Management. On a part drawing, the primary issue is reference to notes and specs. In this case, the mold to make the part is a referenced specification. It is done by referencing the mold tool number. Since the note "Remove all burrs" is short and crisp, it is shown on the body of the drawing. If the company develops a lengthy "deburr specification," then that specification would be given a separate item number and referenced on the body of this drawing.

English or Metric

If we show the dimensions on our drawing, should they be in inches, metric, or both?

Rule: Pick either the American or metric dimensioning system —do not do both.

Reason: It is *at least* twice the work to dual-dimension. Most of your parts (whereon most dimensioning exists) are made under one system. When a mistake is made and the two dimensions do not agree (this happens with high frequency), engineering intervention and probably a design change is needed.

Manufacturing Engineering can and should do the converting in the production processes when necessary. Make it as difficult as possible for foreign companies to "carbon copy" your designs. Some multinational companies have chosen to dual-dimension their drawings. Most have wished—based on informal polls taken in the University seminars—that they had picked one method.

Document Signatures

Notice that the *Author* (Responsible / Cognizant Engineer) of this document has lettered his / her name in the title block. The primary customer(s) for this document signed in the margin. This clearly separates the responsibility for the design from responsibility for manufacturability, etc. In this case the Manufacturing Engineer (ME) signed. It was also signed by the Field Engineer(FE) because it is a spared, high wear / failure part. Usually only the ME need sign in order to assure optimum manufacturability. The Manufacturing Engineer must be aware of and trained in the needs of vendors, Receiving Inspection, the production floor, Repair, etc.

Certainly no more signatures are required than the ME and FE. If you have more than these two people (three counting the author) signing your drawings and specs, it will unnecessarily delay the process. More signatures, in fact, tend to make responsibilities unclear. Thus, the more signatures, the more problems that can go undetected. ISO 9000 requires that all the functions that sign the original document also sign changes to the document. This is another reason for holding signatures to an absolute minimum.

Some companies have the ME and FE sign the release form. This is an undesirable practice since it usually places the burden for obtaining their signatures on the CM function rather than the creating engineer. It also doesn't assure that they view the drawing rather than the form. The object must be for the engineers involved in this project to converse face to face, "up front" in the development. To talk *directly* about problems, reservations, ideas, etc. The "Design Team" concept is fostered by the Design Engineer getting the ME and FE (if required) to sign the drawing. More about Design Teams or Concurrent Engineering later.

Do we print the name of the responsible person or sign? Lettered "signatures" are adequate for most companies. If you require signatures, it is best to also require a hand or CAD *lettered* name as well.

Rule: Design documents should be signed by the ME (& FE if necessary), and those signatures should be obtained by the creating design engineer rather than CM.

Reason: Engineers should be functioning as part of a "team" and talking directly to each other. Having CM obtain the signature creates a wasted and counter productive step in this process. Whenever there are questions, CM is merely acting as a "go between". Communication can be lost or misinterpreted in the process.

The ME should sign the drawing/specification rather than the release or change form since the issues of manufacturability, maintainability, repairability, etc., are on the drawings and the specifications, not on the form.

One company had a problem wherein a critical adjustment was "covered up" and a subsequent change was required to open an access hole to allow adjustment at final test. When the ME was asked how this was allowed to happen, the response was: "I didn't know that was the reason I was signing the release form!" It is also a good idea to develop a standard which crisply explains the responsibility that goes with each signature.

Specifications And Notes

If specifications and notes are brief, they are placed on the body of drawings. If they are multiple use (can be or are used on more than one drawing), or too long to be in the body, they are detached on a separate document. They are usually given a separate "part number" and that number is referenced on the drawing body. That number is also listed on the parts list of any assembly which uses the part. This is an area where using the alpha prefix to the part number has some merit. That is, the same number (different alpha prefix) can be used and the spec or detached notes more readily found. The number should still be on the body of the drawing and on the parts list however.

Body of Assembly Drawings

The face or body of an assembly drawing should contain the information shown in Figure 7.

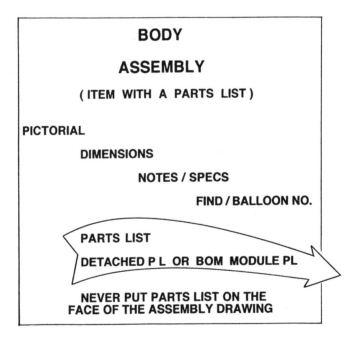

Figure 7. Assembly pictorial data.

The most prevalent mistake made on assembly drawings is putting the parts list on the body of the drawing. This is a carry over from before the advent of data processing. Prior to computers, the accepted practice was to place the parts list on the body of assembly drawings. When computers came along, they gave a powerful capability to produce detached parts lists. It was also easy to leave them on the body of the drawing. The parts list should be on a separate detached list. The "find" or "balloon" number relates the picture to the list. With the advent of data processing, the detached list can be "obtained from" CAD, MRP (Material Requirements Planning or Manufacturing Resource Planning) or another database.

Rule: Do not put parts lists on the body of an assembly drawing.
             If you have them on the body of the pictorial drawing, start
             a planned program to detach them.

Reason: As you grow, the parts list on the pictorial will be redundant
             to a parts list in a database. This redundancy is not just
             wasteful, it is dangerous as it allows a diverging design.

An exception to this rule might be for inseparable "assemblies" such as a weldment. In this case it may be best to document all parts on a multi-page drawing that shows their individual dimensions as well as the "assembled" dimensions. The Find or Balloon number should be used instead of part numbers for the pieces.

Another exception might be wherein the company has one database (such as CAD) which "feeds" the drawing as well as the other data processing systems such as the MRP. In this case the existence of one database is the desired result. At this writing, the ability to effectively "lock" CAD to MRP is nil. The conclusion therefore must be to detach the parts list and "manually" lock the databases together. Or alternately, not to develop parts lists in CAD. Much more on this subject in the Bill Of Material chapter (Ch. 4).

In start-up companies, the design assembly drawing is often used as the pictorial for the Manufacturing assembly operator. With the advent of CAD this pictorial can be three dimensional—very powerful aids to production. The Manufacturing or Industrial Engineer will want the pictorial made to best suit the operator. Difficulty begins when the production rate doubles or is cut in half. What one operator did, is now the job of two or half the job of one. Shall we run a design change to revise the picture and parts list to accommodate the new production rate? Instead of preparing and changing these pictures to suit manufacturing, give Manufacturing access to the CAD database to make production process pictorials as required.

A typical design pictorial drawing for the Front End Loader looks like Figure 8.

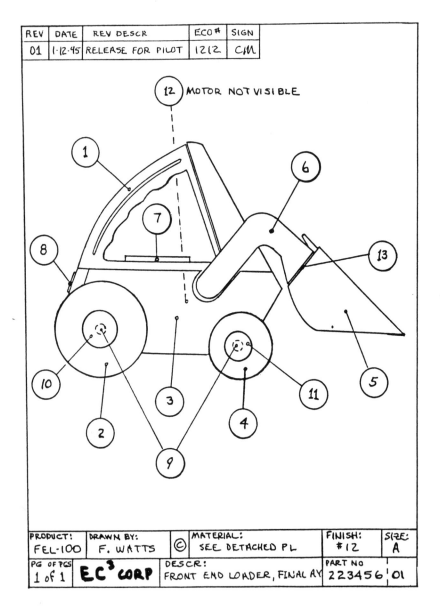

Figure 8. Assembly pictorial drawing.

The Assembly Parts List

The corresponding final assembly parts list for the Front End Loader parts list looks like Figure 9.

DATE REV 1-12-88	REV 01	REV DESCRIPTION RELEASE FOR PROTO		ECO # 1212		SIGN FBW	
ECS CORP FEL - 100		DESCR FINAL ASSEM	P / N 223456-01		SIZE A	PG 1	OF 1
FIND #	DESCRIPTION		PART NUMBER	QTY	UNIT MEAS	IN/OUT DATE	E C O
1	Motor Mount		223356-01	1	ea		
2	Tire, Large		423456-01	2	ea		
3	Frame		723456-01	1	ea		
4	Tire, Small		423456-02	2	ea		
5	Bucket, 4 yard		523456-01	1	ea		
6	Bucket Arm		823456-01	2	ea		
7	PCB, Elect Ignition		923456-08	1	ea		
8	Nameplate		323456-01	1	ea		
9	Axle		103456-01	6	in		
-	Product Spec		123456-00	Ref	Doc		
-	Material Spec		623456-00	Ref	Doc		
10	Wheel Hub, Large		113456-01	2	ea		
11	Wheel Hub, Small		121456-01	2	ea		
12	Motor		114456-07	1	ea		
13	Adhesive		115456-01	2	oz		

Figure 9. Detached Parts List.

Note: Part numbers are shown with a "-" (dash) for the sake of clarity. This would not be necessary nor desirable in actual application.

The part number of both assembly pictorial and parts list documents is identical. Notice that the find number allows easy cross reference between the two documents. The revision level of both documents is identical. Keep them that way to avoid confusion even though all changes do not affect both documents.

Some companies have chosen to make the two documents different item numbers and to cross reference by listing the pictorial number on the parts list. This is a workable scheme. It allows CM to only change the affected document and to allow their revision levels to be different. This scheme favors the CM department but not the customers of the documentation. It is better from the customer's viewpoint to spend the extra CM effort to keep them the same part number and revision level. Start up companies or companies changing their documentation system should seriously consider this issue. Established companies with a workable "two number system" should not change to a "one number system".

There are two items on the parts list that are not physical items—the Product Spec and the Material Spec. They have been entered because they are part of the design requirements for product. They have been entered with quantity "Ref" and Unit of measure "Doc" in order to flag the fact that they are only documents. If the programmable electronic ignition was at this level, the program code part number of the latest software release would be shown as a referenced document. If the code were in the form of deliverable media (a disk for example), then the disk part number would be called out in quantity one.

While in the product development stage, the designer should control iterations of the design by use of the "date" field. The "revision" field should be left blank. This leaves numeric and alpha revisions for subsequent forms of "release." In our example the final assembly pictorial and parts list are at Revision 01. As you will see later this indicates a "release" for limited quantity build (pilot production).

The revision field will be reserved solely for the use of Configuration Management. Thus, if you are using CAD, assure that the system is reprogrammed to prevent assignment of revisions by anyone except CM. This is essential to the "minimum control" aspect of Engineering Documentation Control. Unfortunately, most CAD systems do not allow such security on the Revision field. You will see this concept develop further in the chapter on release (Ch 6).

Our parts list has "in / out date" and "ECO" columns. Most parts lists produced by MRP systems have a similar "effectivity planning" capability. The use of these fields will be discussed in Ch. 8, "Change Control."

Units of Measure

The parts list depicts the items "Unit of Measure". Develop a standard on the allowable units of measure. That is, will you allow use of inches, feet, spools, boxes of ten, ounces, pounds, etc.? This must be agreed upon by Design Engineering, Manufacturing and Field Engineering. This may seem like a trivial point, however many companies have confusion and wasted effort as a result of not agreeing. Engineering specifies one unit while Purchasing would like to buy to another. Someone ends up "in the middle" converting the unit used by design to the unit used for purchase. Some MRP systems allow for a difference and do the converting for you. The CM function needs to address this issue. This is another way to bridge the gap between Design Engineering and the rest of the world.

Specification Control and Source Control Drawings

Items which are commercially available "off the shelf" are documented by a control drawing. For the Loader Company, a screw, fuse, cassette tape, etc. would all fall into this category. Some companies choose to use the vendor's catalog number and trust the vendor to maintain interchangeability. Better to specify those characteristics that are important to you. Using a vendor number also restricts Purchasing to that vendor.

These drawings are sometimes part pictorial and part specification matter. The "envelope" dimensions are shown. Critical specification matter is stated. If the pictorial is not required, the data may be all digital and placed into the database (MRP Item Master file, for example). All of these drawings have the same basic definition:

Definition: Specification Control Drawings contain critical form, fit and function design criteria that are necessary to assure that the item will consistently meet the intended purpose.

What is the difference between the "Source" and "Specification" control drawings? The body of the Source Control Drawing shows the vendor from whom Purchasing may buy the item. No vendors are shown on a Specification control drawing. How then does Purchasing know from whom to buy?

AVL - QVL

A separate listing is kept for Specification Control Drawings which show the acceptable vendor(s) for each part number. This list is variously referred to as a QVL (Qualified Vendor List) or an AVL (Approved Vendor List). Regardless of what it is called, the concept is the same. The *drawings need not be revised* each time a vendor is added or deleted.

The AVL / QVL must be controlled in such a way that Design Engineering, Manufacturing (Purchasing), and Quality Assurance (QA) all agree to any vendor changes on the list. Why bother you say? Ask your Purchasing manager what is preferred! Almost without exception they prefer Specification Control Drawings with an AVL. Their reasoning is quite simple; they can negotiate a better package for the company when the vendor does not know who the competition is.

Rule: Do not show vendors' names of the face of drawings nor use vendor catalog numbers.

Reason: Better purchasing power and fewer drawing changes.

An exception to this rule might be for a company that has made a concerted effort to adopt the "one vendor" policy such as many Japanese companies do.

The AVL/QVL is typically maintained by QA, although others can and do maintain the list. The important thing is that all three functions mentioned must agree to all adds and deletes from the list. Control problems have prompted some companies to put the AVL/QVL under CM control. I believe this is not a wise choice since it will detract from their primary mission—fast and accurate Engineering Documentation Control.

An example of a Source Control Drawing for the nameplate for the FEL-100 model Front End Loader is shown in Figure 10.

An example of a Specification Control Drawing for the Front End Loader tires is shown in Figure 11.

These drawings are frequently "tabulated." That is, a dash number which is part of the part number is assigned. In this case, two tabulations of the tire have been charted on the body of the drawing—denoting size variations of an otherwise identical tire. The question often arises; "How many variables can be handled on one document?" The answer must be made in terms of the "readability" of the document.

Guideline: Tabulations of similar items on one drawing should typically not exceed three variables.

Reason: Easy readability on the part of the drawing customer is the key issue.

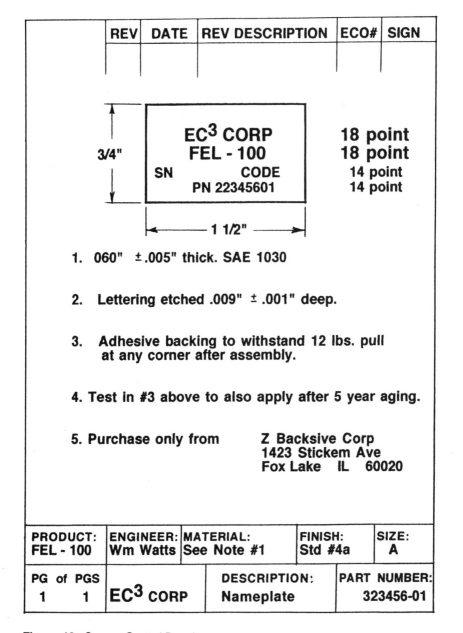

Figure 10. Source Control Drawing.

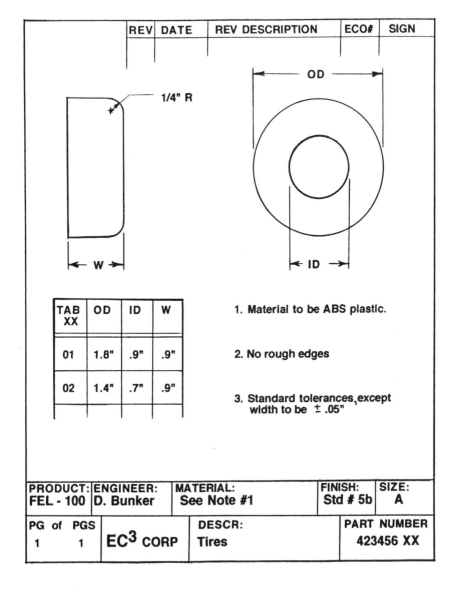

REV	DATE	REV DESCRIPTION	ECO#	SIGN

1/4" R

OD

W

ID

TAB XX	OD	ID	W
01	1.8"	.9"	.9"
02	1.4"	.7"	.9"

1. Material to be ABS plastic.

2. No rough edges

3. Standard tolerances, except width to be $\pm$ .05"

PRODUCT: FEL - 100	ENGINEER: D. Bunker	MATERIAL: See Note #1		FINISH: Std # 5b	SIZE: A
PG of PGS 1 1	EC³ CORP	DESCR: Tires		PART NUMBER 423456 XX	

Figure 11. Specification Control Drawing.

How should we maintain form, fit, and function interchangeability with our vendors? Well-engineered Specification Control Drawings are a key solution. Place all critical characteristics on this drawing and leave the vendor free to make other changes as he sees fit. Of course, if parts of a purchased assembly are to be "spare" parts, then those parts must be similarly specified.

This Specification Control Drawing concept is critical to successful Design / Purchasing / Vendor relationships, whether it is for a screw or a computer system integration. It requires well thought out criteria of mechanical fit (envelope), form, and function. It is lack of this document that causes some people to want to control the vendor's interchangeability by reviewing or approving all design changes.

Specifications

Specifications are words that describe an item. They are generally in a text format but may have text, charts, graphs, envelope drawings, or combinations of these and other techniques. They are generally prepared to describe the end product but may be defining a sub level of the product. The definition therefore becomes fairly general.

Definition: Product specifications define the critical product characteristics of a form (appearance), physical, or functional
nature.

Specification Control "Drawings" are specifications. Certain Assemblies may be described by a specification, whether made or bought. An assembly which is tested is usually defined by a pictorial drawing, parts list and specification. There is one "level" of the product that must have at least one specification—that is the end product itself.

Product Specifications

The single most important of all Design Documents is the Product Specification. It must be agreed to by key company management and your company's customer, if applicable. This agreement must occur in the quote phase or very early in the product definition phase. The key functional departments which must agree include Customers, Marketing, Design Engineering, and others as your President may designate. Our FEL-100 Product Spec is outlined in Figure 12.

Front End Loader FEL - 100	EC3 CORP pg 1 of 1	size A	by fbw	PN 123456-00

- **Four yard bucket capacity - struck level.**

- **Maximum lift height - eight feet. With special arms - 10 feet.**

- **Peak Engine RPM - 4400.**

- **Electronic ignition.**

- **Engine cannot be shut off without bucket and arms in lowered position.**

- **Minimum turn radius - 16 ft.**

- **Comes in four colors - yellow, red, white, and red & white.**

- **Electric or gas starting engine.**

Rev	date	Rev Descr	ECO #	by
	12-01 78	Development Release	2232	J Besch

Figure 12. Product Specification.

This specification is obviously very general—too general. For example, a product specification should delineate the expected Mean Time Between Failures (MTBF) and the Mean Time To Repair (MTTR). On the other hand you can be too detailed—such was the case in the seventeen page government specification for fruitcake.

A clear, crisp specification of the critical criteria is needed. However, if this is the best available definition of the product at the start of the development project, it should be put on the correct format and released. This is a numeric release which assures that all changes can reach all the people who need to know. More on release stages can be found in Ch. 6.

When several products are combined into a "system", the product specification is usually referred to as a System Integration Specification.

When companies have a customer(s) who must agree on product specifications, sometimes a Design Specification is prepared. The Design Specification is a hedge against reality. In other words, the Design Specification targets what is believed attainable while the Customer Specification has slightly less ambitious commitments. Some companies develop a Test Specification as well. This document defines how the Customer / Design specifications will be measured.

Rule: The Product Specification should be the first document released for the product and it should be released as soon as the project is established.

Reason: It is the common goal for all who work on this product. Every change to that document must be carefully distributed to all who need to know. Everyone is now "in the same church, singing from the same hymnal."

The best way to accomplish this is to release the end-product part number with a one item parts list—the Product Specification. You now have a "Top" to build under. This is the beginning of an ever-evolving product structure.

The above product specification discussion has described the "make-to-stock" environment. The Configuration Management requirements are incumbent upon the supplier / manufacturer. What is different about other types of manufacturing?

Make-to-Order Product Specifications

In the make-to-order situation, the Sales Order may constitute the product specification. Material accompanying the Sales Order (such as features and options lists) may also constitute part of the product specification. In the make-to-order environment, product specifications are often unclear. Sales Orders often, in fact, sell configurations that are not designed, tested, or even manufacturable—especially in the time frame specified.

Rule: In the make-to-order company, it is critical for the Customer, Marketing, Design Engineering, and Manufacturing to agree on the product parameters before a customer commitment is made.

Reason: Anything less than review and commitment from these functions risks late delivery to the customer, delivering something different than the customer expected, or (in some cases) not being able to deliver what the customer ordered.

One company was plagued with late deliveries of a make-to-order "customized" product. Investigation showed that frequently Sales was accepting orders for feature and option combinations which had not been *piloted* (not built and not tested). The time to do the piloting was not considered in the Sales Order. In some cases they found that they had to go back to the customer and explain that the combination of features requested was not a workable combination. Since the number of possible combinations was several thousand, they had no choice but to have Engineering examine each new combination to assure that each was a viable product. The result was more realistic delivery commitment dates.

The Sales Order and accompanying material may constitute the product specification. Some companies and / or customers insist that a specific specification be written. Whether the product specification is one formal design document or several documents, it is critical to obtain agreement before commitment.

The ideal situation is to have a unique part number (tab) assigned to each combination. A discussion of modular Bills of Material in Ch. 4 shows how this is achieved. In the make-to-order company, the supplier / manufacturer is responsible for assuring CM requirements. This starts with a clear product specification.

Make-to-Print Product Specifications

The customer print and (possibly) parts of the Purchase Order make up the Product Specification. Again, it is very important to reach agreement on the parameters before committing to the customer. Sales, manufacturing and the design engineering functions must agree on the customer requirements. The trap, in this kind of manufacturing, is that sometimes the Purchase Order contains new or changed item specifications. The company order entry process must allow for a technically competent person to watch for such nuances and to add them to the customer print. This creates a complete Product Specification.

Another specific issue that arises in the make-to-print environment is the end-item part number. Should we use the customer's part number or assign our own?

Guideline: Whenever practical, the customer's part number should be used as the end-item identifier rather than assigning your own.

Reason: Using the customer part number eliminates the need for a cross reference list and the many many references to it. This also eliminates probable error in conversion from one to the other and back again.

If a vendor has several customers who may assign identical part numbers, analysis of the occurrences as well as the pros and cons is necessary. If customers use alpha-numeric part numbers and your data processing system has difficulty handling that condition, analysis of the situation is necessary.

Design Process Specifications

When Design Engineering feels that it is necessary to control an element of the process, a Design Process Specification is required. Most of the product process and routing "design" is left to the Manufacturing Engineers. On some occasions, however, the Design Engineer feels compelled to enter this arena. In high-tech products, the Product Test (process) Specification spells out how a test is to be performed and, in some cases, what equipment is to be used. In the FEL-100, the design engineer might feel that the printed circuit board cleaning method is critical to the product performance. A cleaning spec would be written. These are examples of Design Process Specifications. They are design documents and will be treated as design documents in subsequent processes.

Document Sizes

Rule: Use multiples of 8 1/2" x 11" sizes. Use "A", "B", and "C" sizes whenever possible and avoid using larger sizes.

Reason: Reproduction of the larger sizes is difficult and expensive. The microfilming and subsequent readability and reproduction of the image is very difficult.

Proprietary Note

Place a note on drawings and specifications of your own designs to the effect that the information contained thereon is proprietary to your company. This may discourage a serious form of industrial theft.

Document Types

Group all your company's documents into three categories:

- Design Documents - Define the product or critical process elements.
- Support Documents - Support the product.
- Manufacturing Documents - Define the process.

An example grouping is shown in Figure 13.

• DESIGN DOCUMENTS

Product Spec	Process Spec
Customer Spec	Material Spec
Design Spec	Spec Control Drawing
Test Spec	Source Control Drawing

Part Drawing	Assembly Dwg / Parts List
Silkscreen Drawing	Logic Diagram
PCB Artwork	Padmaster / solder master
Cable / Harness Dwg	Schematic
Wiring from - to list	Software Program
PROM Truth Table	PROM / EPROM Spec

• MANUFACTURING DOCUMENTS

Routing / Process Sheets	Inspection Process
Illustrations for Process	CAM Programs
Tool / Fixture Drawing	Test Equip Drawing

• SUPPORT DOCUMENTS

Field Instruction / Bulletin / Kit	
Illustrated Parts Catalog	Spare Parts List
Product Description Manual	Spares Kits
Maintenance Manual	Installation Instructions

Figure 13. Grouping of document types.

It is desirable to make this simple distinction in order to determine their treatment in further processes.

Rule: Configuration Management will hold the "Master" of <u>Design Documents</u> after release. They will be released only by the company's release rules and process. They will be changed only by the change rules and process.

Reason: To assure minimum control in the CM processes.

Support Documents do not define the product. They define the information necessary to install, use or maintain the product. Manufacturing Documents define the manufacturing process.

Rule: The "master" of Support and Manufacturing Documents need not be under CM control. In fact, they may not be controlled directly by the CM design document release or change process.

Reason: These documents should be maintained by the function responsible for creating them. They are released as a <u>result of</u> a product release and changed as a <u>result of</u> a product change. The control systems (managed by the functions responsible for them) may be similar to CM's control but will probably be less stringent.

Making manufacturing or support documents part of the CM system will easily cause a distraction from, and a delay to, the Design Document processing. The argument frequently is: "They don't get changed if we don"t include them in the design change package." The question which must be asked is: "Should the process be held up while waiting for something to happen now which isn't needed until later?" The solution is <u>never</u> to hold up a product release or change to "assure" the support or manufacturing documents are up to date. Of course, the support and manufacturing documents must change as a result of many design changes. This will be controlled by the change process at the appropriate point.

This is an easy rule to violate in a small company because the same person is often designated to care for Design, Support and Manufacturing Documents. That person, however, can treat each type separately in preparation for the eventual split that should occur with growth.

The support or manufacturing documents affected must be updated as part of the change implementation. The change process developed will assure that these documents are completed before "closing" the change.

Files and Masters

This is a subset of an entire body of expertise that is generally referred to as *Data Management.* This is a subject which can, and has, many volumes written about it. The subject includes product liability implications.

The goal here will be to cover only the basic data management necessities for Configuration Management. Chapter 4 on "BOM/Databases" will also touch on this subject. The critical aspects of file and document management to Configuration Management are:

- CM must be the keeper of the Design Document "masters." The masters may take the form of the original hand-drafted hard copy. The master may be a CAD file. An aperture card, microfiche, or roll microfilm may constitute the master. An electronic image may be the master; thus, the CM master file need not always be in hard copy form. The various files must be "programmed" to allow only CM to assign revisions. CM can thus control the revision level as it is released or changed.

- The "key" to the master file must be held only by CM. In the same sense that CM manages the "Print Room," they must manage all design document masters regardless of the form. Hard copy and electronic media files must be in a locked room or locked files when not attended.

- CM must be the only group who can assign revision letters or numbers. It is by this device that they can assure that the system is being followed, "capture" a master document, file it, and assure that anyone can obtain the latest revision document.

- A "disaster file" must be kept in a physically different building. This file is necessary in case of a fire or other disaster to the master file. Its format might be any or a combination of several of those previously mentioned. In one small CAD based medical company, the Engineering Services manager took back-up disks to her home almost daily. This is also a convenient place to keep each revision level document.

- Hard-copy masters must be capable of at least two generations of reproduction. The master is used to produce a copy for redlining and a copy of the redline is highly readable. For companies using microfilm, three generations is desirable; a copy for ECO redlining can be reproduced and a highly readable microfilm copy can be obtained.

- CM must control all revision, part, document, hardware "mod"/software "release" and ECO numbers.
- The master files should include all number assignment logs and ECO masters.
- Orderly files, handling of the masters only by CM personnel, all CM personnel being familiar with the filing system, are necessities for good file management.

Now that our documents are defined—what does go on the documents as well as what does not go on the documents—let's discuss how to identify documents and product.

3

Identification Numbers

As if life in general isn't filled with enough numbers already, Engineering Documentation Control abounds with numbers: Product, Model, Catalog, Part, Item, Document, Spec, Serial, Mod, Block, VIN, Series, Release, Change, Deviation, etc.—enough already!

How in the world should this subject be approached? Trying to cover all the known numbering schemes would take a book by itself. In the interest of simplicity, the <u>necessary</u> numbers will be developed for the Front End Loader as the first product of a start-up company, a company with a fast-growing future and, hopefully, the wisdom to see what is best for the future. As this is done, variations that might be more applicable for another kind of company or industry will be discussed.

Product or Model Number

If you are a component manufacturer, or a make-to-print manufacturer, you probably don't have product or model number to worry about. Most other manufacturers do. This is the number where Sales/Marketing people usually call the shots. They pick a number (sometimes a "Name") which they believe will capture the attention of the market place: the "Whiz Bang Number". It is then Design Engineering's job to work with Marketing to place the number on the product whereever it will enhance the Whiz Bang!

The nameplate should, of course, prominently display the product number. In the case of the Front End Loader, we used FEL-100. The important point to the company and to CM people is that this number is <u>not</u> precise with regard to options, nor can it usually be changed to indicate when changes have been made. It is therefore useless to CM.

Part Number Cycle

Sometimes product numbers are used in the sales catalog—without a precise part number. Remember the Product Specification for the FEL-100 came with electric <u>or</u> gas "start" as well as other choices. If a customer orders an FEL-100, just which options does he expect to get? Any ambiguity at this stage can easily result in the customer receiving something different than expected. It is therefore <u>critical</u> that Engineering and CM develop specific part numbers for sold items. Sales must recognize those part numbers and work with the customer to sell an FEL-100 identified by the specific part number. It is by using a part number that the company can make sure that what the customer wants is what the customer gets. The diagram in Figure 14 depicts the complete part number cycle.

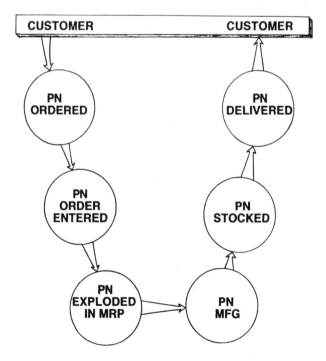

Figure 14. The part number cycle.

If this part number "cycle" is broken at any point, the likelihood of error occurring is substantial. The result is that the customer receives the product and it is not configured as expected. One of the places where the chain is often broken is at the beginning—when Sales and the customer fill out the Sales Order. If there isn't a design document which helps Sales translate the options into a specific part number, breakdown will occur. That is, when the Order Entry Department tries to convert the Sales Order to a specific part number, they can easily make a bad assumption about what the customer desired. This design document might be a matrix or a "selected" number that does define the specific configuration.

If the Product number (or catalog number) is a precise and unique, it should not be necessary for Engineering to assign a part number. The catalog number should be brought under CM control and used as the top level part number.

The other place where this chain is often broken is upon making a functional non-interchangeable change. Regardless of the level or place in the product that a <u>functional</u> non-interchangeable change is made, interchangeability rules will require CM to "roll" the part number change up through all replaceable levels. Some companies even change the part number of the end product. After all, it too is functionally not interchangeable. Interchangeability rules and issues will be discussed later, but in the meantime consider the affect of changing the end-item part number. It breaks the chain every time a functionally non interchangeable change is made. This creates havoc if you have very many non-interchangeable changes.

We need to know if the change is or is not present, but frequent changing of the part number of end items drives the Master Scheduler into orbit. He or she just got done negotiating run quantities and rates between Sales, Materials, and Manufacturing based on end-item part numbers. Does Master Scheduling now have to go back and reschedule old and new part numbers based on the probable effectivity of the change? Then reschedule it again because the effectivity plan changes? This is why many companies do not change the end-item part number. They prefer other ways to <u>modify</u> the top level part number. For most companies, it is best not to break the part number chain.

Rule: Do not break the part number chain.

Reason: We want zero unhappy customers and zero product return or replacement. Breaking the part number chain increases the risk of sending the customer something different than was expected.

End-item "Mods"

Process-oriented companies generally use a "date code" which they can change (or record) each time they make a non-interchangeable change. Automobile manufacturers generally use a part of the "VIN" (Vehicle Identification Number) for this identification. Software people use a "Release" number for this purpose. Some manufacturers have an identifier which they call a "Machine Level Control" (MLC) "Series Code" or " Mod." High end manufacturers (low volume, high product cost), usually choose to trace changes to the serial numbers and not have a "modifier" (and do not roll the end-item part number).

The modifier also allows batching or blocking of changes. The software "Release" modification is typical. This is an economical approach with software because of the extensive testing that is required for each release. Be cautious before using the "batching" technique with hardware changes however. The most economical point of incorporation (effectivity) of a hardware change seldom matches the next (or the prior) hardware change.

This "modifier" discussion raises the question "If I trace my change effectivity to Serial Number (and don't change the end product part number), why do I need a "modifier." Answer; if you have a serial number and no modifier, and it works for you—leave it alone. *If it ain't broke—don't fix it !* In fact, this is a simplistic and therefore an excellent method of tracing changes.

Some companies find it more simplistic to be able to identify the version of the hardware as well as the version of the software. If your production operations tend to recycle units and therefore mix the units with and without a non-interchangeable changes, the resulting effectivity looks like this:

Change "A" - effectivity: Serial Numbers 122, 125, 126, 129, 131, 132, 135 & up ,

The complexity of this condition increases with:
- Earlier assignment of serial numbers.
- Higher numbers of non-interchangeable changes.
- Higher production rates.
- The fact that engineers think up changes in a different order than they may best be incorporated in.

You may thus want to consider a "modifier." In it's simplest form, the above units containing change "A" might be marked with a "01" modifier on the nameplate. The next non-interchangeable change "B" would be "02", and so on. Modifiers can be assigned for units that have change "A", "B" and "D" but lack change "C". One company designed an alphabet "matrix sticker". The changes were assigned a letter and the letter was "scratched" if the change was present.

Traceability

The significant CM issue with Product Numbers, end-item Part Numbers, Modifiers, and Serial Numbers is traceability:

- What is the exact content of each product with regard to non-interchangeable changes?
- What is the approximate content with regard to interchangeable changes?
- Precisely how can it be known that a unit is under warranty?

If you can answer these questions, your "traceability house" is probably in good order.

Serial Numbers

A serial number is a number assigned to each individual product in order to distinguish that product from all others. They are usually assigned in sequence per product or product family. Manufacturing normally assigns the serial numbers to each product.

As companies grow, they may decide to build products in the same family in more than one plant. At this point the blocks of serials used by each plant must be controlled in order to avoid duplication. CM should control all serial numbers. The best method is to do it with a released document. CM must assure that all necessary parties agree to and are aware of the assignment of the blocks. An alternate method is to have each plant prefix the serial with a letter assigned by CM. This letter should be reflected on a released document. This document could be the nameplate drawing or a separate document referenced on the nameplate drawing.

Serial numbers are typically assigned by Production Control at some point near the end of the production line. The shipment date of each serial number must be captured by manufacturing for warranty purposes. Manufacturing must also track non-interchangeable changes to the Serial Number(s) they actually affect (actual effectivity).

Rule: If you serialize, make sure you know the date shipped for each serial and the actual effectivity by serial number(s) for non-interchangeable changes.

Reason: Why else have a SN? This is the essence of Configuration Management traceability (Status Accounting) requirements.

The manufacturing organization may have to assign a control number to each product in order to trace non-interchangeable changes to a serial which is assigned later in the production process. There are several trade-offs that CM and manufacturing need to consider and agree upon with regard to when the serial number is assigned—early or late in the manufacturing process. All the factors discussed need to be considered as well as other factors such as tying test data to an individual unit, etc. Analysis of the best point in the manufacturing process to assign serial numbers may lead to:

1. Early assignment and use of a modifier to overcome the serial number effective "mix" problem.
2. Use of a Manufacturing Control Number with later assignment of the serial number. This method is used with or without a modifier.

Part Number

These are the numbers we associate with parts, assemblies and product in order to precisely identify them. The term "item number" is probably the more expressive term, but "part number" is more universal. The terms can be used interchangeably.

Since the Front End Loader Company is a start-up company, the company has a choice, therefore the part number "system" will have minimum significance.

Rule: Put as little significance into the part number as possible.

Reason: Because significant numbering systems tend to break down. No matter how good you are at anticipating the number of digits you will set aside for a given characteristic, at some point it won't be enough.

With the advent of low cost computing, it is far better for a start-up company to set up a database with those characteristics that might be put into a significant part number. More on how to establish a database in Ch. 4.

The temptation to use a significant part number is high. The significant part number helps us to find similar parts. If we don't have significance in the part number, how do we search to find similar parts? How do we avoid reinventing the wheel? A group technology or class code system is the answer.

Classification Coding

This technique classifies items by their principal characteristics. There are basically three methods for doing this.

1. Purchase a packaged system. There are several packaged systems on the market which have served companies well.

2. Make sure that "Descriptions" and "Name" on drawings are done with considerable discipline. Then, when purchasing a CAD system, make sure the CAD has the ability to do "key word" search. The result is a crude classification system.

3. Devise your own class code in your database. Set aside a separate field for each element that is a significant item characteristic. This will require report programming to make it useful. This should be done only after carefully considering purchase of a packaged system. Designing your own class code is a very difficult project to accomplish for all but the simplest of products.

The intent of any coding/classification system is the same—to aid the company, especially the engineers, in four ways:

- Allows the Design Engineer to "avoid reinventing the wheel." That is, to use an already-designed item. Without a classification coding system, the engineer may well conclude that it is easier to create a new part than to try to find an existing one.

- Similarly it allows the company to "standardize." In other words, to sort through similar items and to designate only certain ones to use in future designs. Other items would be obsoleted.

- Engineers can more easily find similar items for possible substitution. This is very helpful to manufacturing when a critical part shortage arises.

- Allows the Industrial or Manufacturing Engineer to utilize "Group Technology" to produce similar items in manufacturing "cells". It can also help in the machine loading of molding machines for example.

A good starter reference on this subject is an article titled "Group Technology" by Frederick Ingram in the fourth quarter 1882 *Production and Inventory Management* (Journal of the American Production and Inventory Control Society, Inc.)

A good place for a young company to start is to write and follow a standard for noun name and descriptions. Standardizing terminology makes sense anyway. It will help a little until the need arises to choose or devise a better classification coding system. This standard will describe the nomenclature method and give sample document descriptions.

Example: Standard says to always start with the Noun Name, follow
with Modifiers, then the Value of the item.

Resistor, Carbon, 20 ohm, 2%

Bucket, Front End, steel, 4 yard

The trick is to develop a method that will be most helpful for your company until the need is apparent for a bona fide classification coding system.

Preferred and Alternate

Some companies struggle with their parts lists and / or the MRP system to try to inject "preferred" and "alternate" part numbers into their Bill Of Material.

Rule: Put the preferred item in the parts list and BOM. Let your classification coding system find the alternate(s).

Reason: You normally want the best for your product. When alternates are necessary, there are probably several choices. Engineering intervention is normally advisable in these situations.

A standard may be required to indicate which engineering function can make this decision, whether or not a deviation is required, etc.

Significant vs. Non-Significant Part Number

Many companies have a significant numbering system. Some have a significant number for Specification Control Drawings and a non-significant system for their own designed items. Many companies have mostly non-significant numbers. The pros and cons of each are shown in Figure 15.

SIGNIFICANT   VS   NON SIGNIFICANT

Significant		Non Significant
Describes Part	·	No Significance
Is a Class Code	·	May need Separate Class Code
Must Publish Code Book	·	No Code Book (or Code Book in CM)
Misinterpretation Likely	·	Eliminates Interpretation
Security May Be Breached	·	Security Better
Often Variable Length and Alpha Numeric	·	Uniform Length Numeric
Less Compatible with MRP / Info Systems	·	More Compatible with MRP, etc.
Check Digit Use Not Practical	·	Lends Itself to Check Digit
Longer Harder to Memorize	·	Shorter Easier to Memorize
More Error Prone	·	Fewer errors
Probably Separate Document Number	·	Document Number Part of the Part Number
Categories Usually Breakdown - Limited Life	·	No Categories Lasts Longer

Figure 15. Significant vs. nonsignificant part number.

The most critical of these issues is that, over time, the significant numbering systems tend to break down. Companies with more simplistic products take longer to breakdown than those with more complex products. Companies with simple "commodity" products often make significant numbers work well. Significant part numbers often work at the end item or product level. As time passes, variations arise which were not foreseen. One digit was set aside where two are now needed. Significant numbers thus tend to loose their significance. They no longer do the classification coding function intended by their inventors. This is the prime reason for recommending as little significance as possible.

Recommended Part Number

The recommended (minimally significant) part number system is shown in Figure 16.

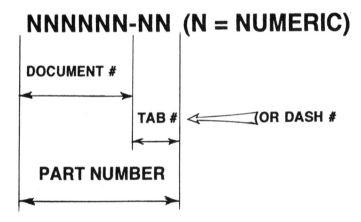

NNNNNN-NN (N = NUMERIC)

DOCUMENT #

TAB #   **OR DASH #**

PART NUMBER

TAB SIGNIFICANCE:

- **IF DOCUMENT ONLY 00**

- **IF TABULATED DOCUMENT... XX**

- **FIRST ITEM (TABULATED
  OR UN-TABULATED) 01**

Figure 16.   Ideal part number (minimum significance, document number embedded, and tabulated).

Notice that this part number has the Document Number "built in."

Rule: The document number should always be incorporated into the part number.

Reason: Avoids making and maintaining a cross reference list. Avoids making repeated reference to the cross reference for all time to come.

Most CAD, MRP and other automated systems have a limit on the digits allowed for a part number. Combining the document number with the significant number therefore becomes a problem. Companies with significant numbers generally have a separate document number and a cross reference. Every cross reference is difficult to produce and maintain. They also waste a little bit of time every time a person has to make a cross reference—for ever. They also introduce another possibility for error.

The "Tab" (sometimes called a "dash number") is a form of significance—but minimal. It is used to delineate similar items on the same document. It saves documenting time during product development. It also makes similar items easier to find (a form of classification coding). If you remember, both of the Front End Loader <u>tires</u> are documented on one tabulated drawing. Similarly we can tabulate assemblies and end products. This is also a portion of the part number that will change on non interchangeable changes. This will save making a new document each time we change part numbers.

Rule: Always tabulate the part number. If you have an existing system that does not include this feature, <u>add it as soon as possible</u>.

Reason: Saves significant amounts of labor to prepare documents and to revise them.

Document Numbers should be assigned by CM. Have a document number log which has the document numbers previously listed. Assign the numbers one at a time, capturing on the log:

- Document Number
  - Project # / Product # (FEL-100)
    - Engineer Assigned to
      - Date Assigned
        - Document Title
          - Kind of Document (part, spec, assem, etc.)

This is an excellent automation application. If your automated database has this ability, use it. A simple PC spread sheet also works well. If your database has a "status field," show the status as "PN Issued" or an equivalent code. If it doesn't, add "status" to your log. You will see how status coding works when we get into the product release process in Ch. 6.

It might be more practical to assign document numbers in a "block". This is less desirable but still manageable. Your assignment log should capture enough information to "recover" part numbers should you need to in the future. Assign in the smallest blocks possible.

As the document number is assigned, give the engineer your written rules on tabulation: only two digits allowed, 00 = document only, XX in the title block to indicate that the drawing is tabulated, 01 = first part, etc.

Changing the Part Numbering Method

Again, "least significance' is the best method for a start-up company. It can also be used when an existing significant numbering system breaks down. Some companies design a totally different numbering system for Specification Control Drawings. Since there appears to be no particular advantage in doing this, use the recommended part number universally. This would also be an excellent method for a company which has gone through several acquisitions and needs to consolidate into one numbering method.

Changing from one numbering method to another is not an easy matter. Those who have gone through the change-over report that considerable planning is required:

- Research the alternates, and plan the number.
- Plan the change-over and all its ramifications.
  - New items as designed?
  - Cold turkey on active items?
  - Cold turkey on every item?
  - Combination?
  - Plant shutdown or long weekend?
  - Affect on MRP, warehouse, vendors, shop floor, etc.!
- Look out for documents "referenced" in the body of drawings and specifications!
- Trial run the proposed number in parallel with existing method!

- Train necessary people!
- Cut over, debug, and refine!

Reports indicate that the lack of planning, testing and training are the problem areas to be avoided.

Revision Numbers and Letters

The revision letter or number is the change status or level of the <u>document.</u> The revision is for changing the document to reflect interchangeable changes to the item <u>or</u> changes which do not affect the item—only the document.

Rule: The Revision is <u>not</u> part of the part number.

Rule: Revision is <u>never</u> marked on the parts.

Rule: <u>Never</u> stock by revision level.

Reason: If your company's system is causing you to do any of the above, it is probably because it does not have clear, crisp, or correct interchangeability rules. If it did, then the part number would change for non-interchangeable conditions. The revisions of a part can therefore be intermingled. This is the only mode of operation that the father of interchangeability—Eli Whitney—will allow.

The revision level of the document should appear in the document revision block <u>and</u> in your database. The revision level of the assembly document would be the only revision shown on the parts list.

Rule: The revision level of the component parts should <u>not</u> appear in the Engineering Parts List.

Reason: The revision level relates to the *document,* not to the parts. The revision level's appearance on a parts list implies that it is the latest level. To assure that the latest level is shown, one would have to revise every "using assembly" when any document representing a part thereon is revised. Doing this is a waste of energy.

Example: Frame PN 723456-01 used in the FEL-100 (see Figure 9) may be a frame made from any revision-level document. The revision level relates to 723456-00 the assembly document. Any assemblies made from this document must be interchangeable.

Rule: The revision level of parts should <u>not</u> appear in support documents. Parts Catalogs, Maintenance Manuals, etc. should not refer to the revision level of the document depicting the item.

Reason: Items of the same part number must be interchangeable. Showing revision levels would (at least) confuse the issue.

Of all good CM practices, the above rules are the most often violated The result is a significant contribution to the widening of the gap between engineering and other groups. Sometimes revisions are interchangeable and sometimes they are non-interchangeable! The MRP system doesn't treat the revision as part of the part number! Manufacturing doesn't want to stock by revision level! Publications job is complicated! The Field Support people order, stock and think part numbers! More on interchangeability and part number changing later in this chapter.

Revision Levels

The question arises, when does the revision level change?

Rule: Every time a change is made to a released document, the revision level must be increased. These may be interchangeable changes to the part represented thereon or document-only changes.

Reason: Changes made to documents are important. It is therefore necessary for everyone using that document to know that changes have occurred. If the part is affected, the production people or the vendor must be notified to implement the change.

It is also important to have a source for determining the latest revision level of any released document. To satisfy this need, the revision level must be kept in your database. This might be a manual file or data processing file but <u>not</u> both. MRP systems (part information file) require a revision level. If you have MRP, keep it there and only there. Many companies have implemented an MRP system but CM is still maintaining a card file with the latest revision level for a document number.

Engineering, CM and Manufacturing all using the same database bridges the gap between Engineering and the rest of the world.

Page Revision Levels

When design documents are more than one page long, a decision must be made. Will all the pages of the set be kept at the same revision level or will each page be allowed to remain at its current level if it is unaffected by the change? In the later choice, a matrix must be added to the document (generally on the first or last page) which shows the correct level of each page. Thus, in either system the "customer" can tell, given the latest revision level, if they have an up-to-date set.

Both systems work. Some companies use one or the other and some both. Typically the "page matrix" method is used for very long documents. This writer prefers to keep every page of the set at the latest revision level. This costs CM a little extra work but is easier on their customer.

Change Identification Number

Each change should be identified by a unique number. This is the change number or ECO (Engineering Change Order) Number. This ECO # should be:

- Assigned by CM
  - Sequential numeric
    - The number by which the change is filed
      - Logged. The log should contain at least the following:
        - ECO Number
        - Date Assigned
        - Primary part number affected
        - CM Technician name

The log is another good automation application. Use your PC spreadsheet if nothing else. This will fit into the ECO tracking that we will talk more about later. The ECO Number is the "common thread" for change tracking and change traceability. It is the Social Security Number for the change. It appears on:

- Drawing Revision Block
  - ECO Form
    - Database (Item master)
      - Configuration Tracking Lists and Reports

As stated before, the ECO number should be a separate field in the drawing revision block. If your company has multiple divisions, each with design responsibility, the Corporate CM function should assign prefixes (probably a letter) to each business unit. Each division of the company can then assign its own ECO Number.

What Gets a Part Number?

Many companies assign part numbers to anything that is movable and some even to fixed objects. If your product is a power plant this may be wise. A product company assigning design part numbers to desks, chairs, and pads of paper is at least wasteful. Not only wasteful of the numbers but of CM time. Time spent to release, file, control, and change the document representing the item can be better used. What should get a design part number then?

Rule: All design documents should be assigned a part number (document number included).

Rule: Support documents which ship to a customer should get a part number.

Rule: Documents which represent items that are not shipped to customers should <u>not</u> get a part number unless they are critical to the field support or maintenance process.

Reason: It takes time to process each document. CM should not spend their resources processing other documents.

Packaging material would be documented with part numbers by this rule. Publications which ship with the product would also be assigned part numbers. Publications which ship separately (from the product) to customers, should therefore be assigned a part number. If a tool is critical to the manufacturing or field support process, it should be assigned a part number.

This does not mean that the manufacturing people cannot assign "part numbers" to fixtures, jigs, and test equipment. The CM manager should work an agreement with manufacturing to use a prefix(s) that identifies the "part number" as "NOT A CM PART NUMBER". If a piece of test equipment or a fixture is to be sold or shipped to a customer, it should then be released and given a CM part number.

Rule: Just because it has a part number assigned to it, doesn't mean that you need to put it under CM change control.

Reason: Let manufacturing set up its own change control system for Manufacturing Documents. This will free CM time to improve the CM processes.

Does this mean that Manufacturing cannot identify its process and routing documents by the engineering part number? Of course not! They can, and probably should identify by the engineering part number. The <u>same</u> part number can identify more than one document. This is done on formats (process sheet, route sheet, etc.) that are <u>not</u> design documents. Thus they should <u>not</u> be under CM change control. Manufacturing must control that document to assure that it reflects the proper design of the product.

In companies regulated by the FDA there is a great concern for "the process". The necessary concern for the drug/process manufacturing has carried over to the medical products. This still doesn't mean that FDA requires CM change control. FDA requires all the same "traceability" of process changes but doesn't dictate who does it.

Every process company needs to be concerned about the "traceability" of process changes. This is especially true because the formula or mix of the product is sometimes embedded in the manufacturing process. Some process-oriented companies have solved this problem by creating Bills of Material for their formula. This makes the mix "design" controlled by making it a design document. It would be similar to making the iron, molybdenum and carbon for the axle in the Front End Loader a parts list.

Bottom Line - the fewer things you put a CM part number on, the fewer you will need to release, change control, file, etc.

Item Marking

Some believe that if a part number is assigned to an item that it should be physically marked with that part number. This is a trend that is very wasteful!

Rule: Avoid physically marking parts and assemblies whenever possible.

Reason: Part marking is expensive. What does it buy? Won't you have an parts catalog (or illustrated parts catalog) that gives the right part numbers for replaceable items? Might the latest replacement item be a different part number than was in the customer's product?

"It only costs a quarter" some say. "Doesn't it simplify the spare item replacement?" If you look closely, you will find that you will still need the spares catalog. Every replaceable item at a quarter apiece! Would you want it to be your quarters?

What happens when the part design changes non-interchange-ably? If the part can be reworked, there will then be a need to rework the part marking. With most kinds of part marking, this is no easy task. Now it is a quarter to "erase" the marking and another quarter to remark. What happens after the product has been in service for a while? Much of the marking can't be read anyway. Then the part number changes and you want the customer or field service people to order the new part number. Will they take the part number from the old part or will they read the parts catalog?

Take a close look at some assemblies and try to figure out which part number refers to which part or assembly! It will cost more than a quarter when the wrong part is ordered. Also pay another quarter for every part that is rejected only because you can't read the marking.

While on the subject of marking, lets talk about <u>labels</u>. This is a costly trend in American industry. A friend just bought an outboard motor. He counted no less than *fourteen* labels on it. A lawyer must be running this company! The punch line, however, was that the information needed most frequently—the oil and gas mix—was not on any of the fourteen labels! This "wallpapering" of the product may not be under the direct control of the Configuration Management function, but CM can exert some positive influence.

The Printed Circuit Board (PCB) is also infamous for being plas-tered with <u>marking</u> of various kinds. The part number of the assembled board, the part number of the raw board, revision letter of the artwork or silkscreen, the connector part number and then throw in the board "Type" number. Could this be a bit of overkill? It might make good sense to examine these historical practices. Manufacturing makes some very complex mechanical devices without numerous markings—why not a PCB too? As for the argument that "If it's in the artwork it's free!"—file that with the "free" lunch. Would you take a nickel for every board rejected because of bad marking? Also the PCB real estate is typically very valuable, so why waste real estate with unnecessary marking.

A better alternative to the PCB marking is to assign a board type or function acronym to each board. For example, the electronic ignition PCB might be an ALTZ board. This identifier can then be used on the artwork (and thus appear on the board). It would be used on the schematic and in wiring lists. The ALTZ acronym would also appear in the parts catalog with the proper part number(s). This acronym would not change unless the function of the board changed.

The Front End Loader Company will mark only the final PCB assembly and only with the board type letters. The part number will be used in the parts catalog, on the box or tag. The PCB acronym will also be used where appropriate. If a customer or field service person reads the acronym and looks in the parts catalog, they will find the proper part number for their unit. If they order that part number, the odds are very high that they will receive that part number. Since the revision level refers to the design <u>document</u>, we will not mark revision level on the board.

In any event, if spares catalogs are not kept up to date and distributed to customers, it will be necessary to send the customer the latest part number—regardless of what they order.

Interchangeability

Ever since the cotton gin was invented, customers have come to expect interchange of replaceable parts. If parts are not interchangeable, customers expect fair warning (usually in their parts catalog) to tell them which part number to order.

On the other hand, if an item is made up of inseparable parts (referred to as an inseparable assembly), then its parts cannot be interchanged at all. Interchangeability of the parts, therefore, becomes a moot point.

Examples: Weldment, Molded Assembly, Riveted Assembly, etc.

If your car windshield wipers are designated to be replaceable only as an assembly, then all you expect is the assembly to interchange with the mating car part. The company made a conscious decision to spare the assembly, not the parts. If you are the production department manufacturing the parts and assemblies, you are concerned with the parts and the assembly. If you are the factory repair center, you may also have still different expectations.

Interchangeability Defined

How do we sort all this out? Lets start with a time-proven definition:

Definition: Interchangeable:

- Two or more items are considered interchangeable if, in all applications, they are:

1. Of an acceptable form (appearance) to fulfill all esthetic requirements per the Product Specification.

2. Of a proper fit (physical) to assemble with other mating items.

3. Of a proper function to meet the Product Specification.

- Items meeting these criteria are completely interchangeable, one for the other (both ways) with no special adjustments, modifications, or alterations to the item or related items.

- Items which meet some but not all of the above criteria are not completely interchangeable and are therefore considered *non-interchangeable.*

Notice that the definition refers to "all applications." Let's say we have several Front End Loaders, each with a different size bucket. If we made a change that would not allow exchange of the Bucket Arms between any one bucket, the Bucket Arms would not be interchangeable. In order to analyze this, however, we need a way to know what applications the Bucket Arms are used on.

Rule: Configuration Management must maintain a manual or computer "Used On" database (sometimes called "Where Used").

Reason: In order to test interchangeability of parts in all applications.

Remember, this data is kept in a database, not on the face of drawings. The Used On format will show (for the desired Part Number) the next assembly(s) by part number and preferably next assembly description(s).

Example:

Affected item		Next assembly	
Part Number	Description	Part Number	Description
121456-01	Wheel, small	223456-01	Final assembly

Another kind of Used On format might show the next assemblies and the product Part Number/Product Number in a single look up. This is to save time by avoiding the necessity to step up through the structure, one assembly at a time, in order to find the Product Used On and thus the responsible engineer and or the customers involved.

Also note that both <u>form</u> and <u>function</u> statements refer to the "Product Specification." In other words, the criteria to be used is not what the engineer or anyone else "thinks", but rather what the Product Specifications "say." Many, many hours are spent debating the form and function interchangeability. The best way to eliminate these debates is to invoke the Product Specifications.

Examples To Ponder

Lets take some examples from the FEL-100, referring to the Product Specification in Figure 12:

Change: The outside diameter of the rear tires is increased in order to improve the performance and appearance of the machine. The machine will still meet the maximum lift height requirement of eight feet.

Discussion: Nothing said about being required to meet product specifications! What if the spec had a requirement that the Loader move at x feet per minute in first gear? Might this change be improving performance toward meeting that spec?

Conclusion: The change must be considered *interchangeable* unless the Engineer is willing to include a product spec change which adds a specific criteria which the change is being made to satisfy.

Change: The frame (previously untreated) is now to be cleaned and painted black.

Discussion: If we again examine the FEL-100 Product Spec, we find no reference to frame paint in the color choices. We find no reference to corrosion resistance for the frame or any other part.

Conclusion: The change must be considered *interchangeable* unless the engineer is willing to add the treatment of the frame into the Product Spec.

Change: The tire ID of the front tires is decreased 1/2" and the front wheels are also decreased in OD by 1/2".

Discussion: With these mating parts, it is difficult to imagine either new part being exchanged with the old design and fitting.

Conclusion: The change must be considered *non-interchangeable.*

Change: The fuel injection port sizes are increased in order to increase peak engine performance to 4400 RPM from 4390 RPM.

Discussion: Notice that our Product Specification committed 4400 RPM.

Conclusion: This change must be considered *non-interchangeable.*

Change: The fuel lines and fittings have been "beefed-up" in order to prevent breakage when an operator or maintenance person uses them to pull themselves onto the machine.

Discussion: This would seem to fix an obvious safety hazard, both because of a possible fall and possible fire. Examination of our spec reveals that nothing was said about these safety criteria.

Conclusion: If the Engineer is <u>not</u> willing to add the safety requirement to the product spec (and call the change *non-inter-changeable),* take this one "up the chain of command" for resolution!

Change: The seat material is changed from vinyl to leather in order to improve the functional life and operator comfort.

Discussion: Examination of the product spec reveals no requirement for seats to last for a prescribed period nor that they be leather. Sales Management has heard about this change and wants to advertise the leather seat. Engineering Management doesn't want to commit to leather in the Product Spec. This change may be a candidate for the "don't do" basket.

Conclusion: This change must be considered *interchangeable.* It is up to the Sales Department to take this issue "up the chain of command" if they feel strongly enough about it. The Company should also have a policy that Sales can not advertise criteria that are not in the Product Specification.

These examples reveal one very significant rule about the process of determining whether or not a change is interchangeable.

Rule: If a criterion isn't in the Product Specification, then it cannot be used as a reason for form or function (including "safety") non-interchangeability.

Reason: Without a Product Specification, or without using it for this purpose, endless debate results. The responsible design engineer must put form and function (including safety requirements) into the Product Specification.

As you read these examples, you no doubt made your own analysis. You may have tempted to reach a different conclusions. Read over the examples again and ask yourself on which examples you might disagree with the conclusion. You will probably agree with the "fit" issues and tend to disagree with "form" or "function" issues. Discussion of similar examples in the University seminars yields very few "fit" interchangeability debates. Most of the "form" and "function" issues arise from unwritten or implied specifications. In this case, our Product Specifications were very minimal, thus bringing on debate.

Rule: Product specifications must be considered a dynamic document which must be changed or added to when the conditions warrant.

Reason: The alternative is to ignore the specification and have the Engineer, CM, or a committee interpret the change / specification. The alternative leaves the same issues to be discussed over and over again as subsequent changes or product "spinoffs" use the same Product Specification. Fine tuning the specifications narrows the gap between Design Engineering and the rest of the world.

Make sure that your system requires that the Product Specification be revised with the change which is said to be "non-interchangeable" (when the form or function criteria cannot be found in the Product Specification). If the responsible Engineer isn't willing to do this, your policy should make the change <u>interchangeable</u>.

It is interesting to note that the process was held up while settling the safety issue, but not held up for Sales on the leather seat issue. It isn't necessary to hold up the process in either case, but CM Management certainly needs to diligently follow up on safety issues to assure proper resolution.

Interchangeability Test

Interchangeable changes are done by a revision change to the document. Most manufacturing systems (MRP, etc.) assume that the part number will change on non-interchangeable changes. A very good test to assure interchangeability is to ask: *"Can the old and new design parts be intermingled in the same stock bin?"* Include the requirement that the material handler or the assembly operator pulling the item is blind and the bin is identified only with the part number in braille!

Part Number Change Logic

Now we have a grasp of what is interchangeable and not interchangeable. So what effect does that have on part number changing? The general "rule" is shown in the logic diagram in Figure 17.

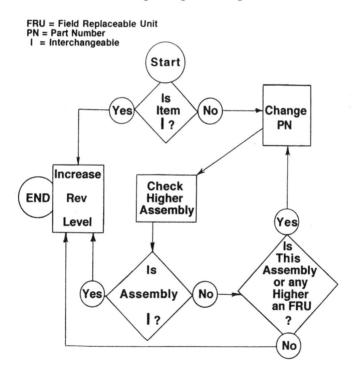

o **Consider all applications (all used on).**
o **Top assembly will not change PN.**

Figure 17. Part Number change logic.

Examine the use of this diagram in the example of the tire / wheel change just discussed. If we use the diagram for the tire and wheel separately we get the same answers:

- Is the item (tire or wheel) interchangeable? Answer - NO! Therefore change part number.
- Check the higher assembly. Is the assembly inter- changeable? Answer - Yes! Therefore increase the revision level (of its document). END (of process).
- Result: the part numbers of both the tire and the wheel must change. Since the tire and the wheel were on tabulated documents, all that is necessary is to add tabs to those documents for the new versions. The next higher Assembly would also have to be revised. That would be a deletion of the old tire and wheel and addition of the new tire and wheel. This would be done by increasing the revision level of its parts list (and the pictorial drawing if it is the same part number)!

The question arises in this and other "fit" non-interchangeable changes: "How do I tell by looking at the product / nameplate, that a non- interchangeable change has been made?" Answer: you can't since we didn't change higher level assembly part numbers. Take the serial number from the nameplate and refer to the parts catalog. It should have the old and new parts listed with the effective Serial Number(s). If you decide that this is not sufficient, then a "Modifier" should be considered. In this example, the Mod Level would be increased for those units containing the change. The modifier would be on the nameplate.

The physical fit criteria are relatively easy conditions to analyze. The dimensions and tolerances on drawings generally answer the inter- changeable questions. If they don't, the following rule should apply:

Rule: If physical fit interchangeability is not obvious from the drawing dimensions and tolerances, added and / or changed dimensions are required.

Reason: Fit criteria must be on the drawings—not in someone's head.

The example that increased the engine RPM to spec (4400 rpm) was noninterchangeable. If we apply the part number change logic, we would change the engine part number. Then we would go to the final assembly and ask if it is interchangeable? Answer: No! Thus we are also tempted to change its part number. Either that, or a Modifier (if you have one), or have a company policy that says the end-item Part Number will not be "rolled".

This kind of change—functional to meet specs—raises another issue: "Do I need to revise units in the field? This question raises many issues. Are customers who have the old design likely to be unhappy? Do we have contracts that require us to *retrofit* the field units? How many old design units are there? How expensive will it be to retrofit some or all units? What are the liability issues? Etc.

These are all questions that need to be addressed—but not as an early part of the ECO process. They need to be addressed as a result of the ECO, in a Field Change Order described later. The key is not to hold up the change while solving all the related "field" issues. There is no reason to hold up the change. There are several reasons for making the change in manufacturing quickly—not the least of which is to produce fewer units that may require retrofit.

Notice that the logic diagram and the discussion has assumed that the items which are "Field Replaceable Units" (FRU) are identified. They should be coded in the database and "listed" in the spare parts catalog. By doing this we can minimize part number "rolling":

Rule: Assemblies that are not field replaceable need not change part numbers when they are "next higher assemblies" in "form" or "function" non-interchangeable change.

Reason: "Rolling" part numbers is expensive, delays the needed change, and is unnecessary. CM, Manufacturing, and Field Service functions are able to handle the "fit" noninterchangeable change without changing higher assembly numbers, then they can also handle the "form" and "function" noninterchangeable changes without rolling all levels of assembly.

Assemblies which are not field replaceable should not be displayed in the parts catalog. One more anomaly regarding non-interchangeable / part number changing:

Rule: Part numbers need not change on non-interchangeable change of any type if:

- all parts affected are under factory control, or

- if no parts have been made.

Reason: Speeds up the change process and saves some work.

These rules need to be addressed in the company CM standards. CM and manufacturing should agree on the precise definition of "under factory control" and write it into the standards. For example, the definition might be that "Production Control decides."

PCB Interchangeability

There are those who believe that Printed Circuit Boards (PCB) are a special and different case. The argument is: "Any change to a PCB is a functional change and therefore it is noninterchangeable." This misconception sometimes spills over into any predominately electrical assembly. It is just plain wrong! In the first place there are mechanical changes to a PCB: connector changes, access holes, solder path spacing, etc. More importantly, the same interchangeability and part number change logic should be applied to the PCB change. Are the functional changes required to meet specs or not? If the change is to improve over and above the Product Specifications, isn't it interchangeable?

The question also arises as to the interchangeability of reworked boards. There are two issues involved (assuming the old and the reworked boards are fit interchangeable):

1. The first issue is the "form"—the cuts, adds, and "piggy backs" make the board look different. Since boards are not visible in the finished product, the appearance is generally not considered an item to put in the product specification. Many companies have a limit on the number of cuts and adds that they will tolerated before embedding the changes. This is a quality and workmanship issue—not an interchangeability issue.

2. The second issue is the "function" of the reworked board. Is the functional change to meet Product Specifications? Yes! = non-interchangeable. No! = (improvement over product spec) = interchangeable.

It follows then, that the part number of the embed should be the same as the reworked version. How should the rework be documented? The same as any rework—as part of the ECO which directed it. All these issues should be addressed in the company interchangeability standard.

When In Doubt

Having and following crisp interchangeability and part number change rules will go a long way toward bridging the gap between Design

Engineering and the rest of the world. Even the best rules leave some gray areas. Therefore, one last rule:

Rule: When in doubt—change part number!

Reason: Items that are not interchangeable must be of different part numbers. The revision level changing must be an indication of interchangeability.

This last rule must not be used as an "excuse" to throw out any or all earlier rules and logic however.

4

Database/Bill of Material

A *database* sounds like something only a big company would have, not something needed in a small start-up company! Actually it is important to any size company. A small company may want to keep it on a PC. A larger company may have networked PCs or have a main frame database. As we talked about earlier, some companies try to keep too many data elements on their drawings. The Front End Loader Company will keep most elements off the drawings, on a PC. The reason for this is that we hope to grow and want to plan for growth. The data can be more easily converted to a data processing system (such as MRP), if it's on a PC.

The product database is concerned with data that is document or part number related. There are three groups of this kind of data. The groups relate back to our document groups. There are three different functional groups who should be responsible for this data:

Data	Responsibility
• Design Documentation	• Design Engineering and CM
• Support Documentation	• Field Support
• Manufacturing Documentation	• Manufacturing

In some companies the organizational responsibility may differ from the above. If that works, don't change the reporting responsibility. On the other hand, if there are operational problems relating to the documentation or data, one of the first things to look for is "responsibility."

Example: Who should be most interested in having up-to-date publications ship with the product? Answer: Field Support! If the publications aren't up to date, and they are produced by Design Engineering, consider moving the responsibility! On the other hand, if they are always up to date and ready to ship when the product ships, don't change the reporting chain.

Some companies are too small to even have a Field (or Customer) Service organization. Its functions are done by Design Engineering and Engineering Services. That's fine, but still group the data as described above because it is wise to plan for growth. This separation also allows for separate treatment of the data in the release, request for change, and change control processes.

Data Dictionary

It is most important that the database be carefully conceived, grouped, and executed. The definition of each element of data, its source, and the functional group responsible for entering it into the database must all be addressed. Whether the data relates to the document or to the part also needs to be determined. This basic information related to each element of data is referred to as a "Data Dictionary."

Example: Data dictionary

> Data Element: Item Weight
>
> Source: Release Document / Drawing
>
> Entry: CM
>
> Character Definition: 5 digits NNN.N (N = Numeric)
>
> English Definition: The weight of the part in pounds and tenths of pounds. Not required for assemblies. Not required for documents unless they are shipped with the product.

Next, carefully decide which data elements belong in which group. We will do this with some examples (not meant to be a complete list).

Design Engineering Data

Element	Comment
Part Number	Primary data element. (Also used in the Support and Manufacturing databases.)

Document Number	00 tab of every part number represents the document
Description	Per Standard: Noun Name, Modifier, Value, etc.
Cognizant Design Engr.	Relates to the document
Type of Document	Per Standard: Assembly, Part, Doc, PL, etc.
Size of Document	Per Standard: A, B, or C
Item Weight	Relates to parts only: pounds
Unit of Measure	Only one per PN (the same for any "used on")
Assembly(s) Used On	Multiple entries possible

The last entry above (Used On) is the source of "all applications" for interchangeability logic. With most MRP systems, the "Item master file" is a database. The "used on" is typically maintained as parts list data of parent-component data. If you have an MRP system, don't create another database.

Front End Loader Example

A partial database for the Front End Loader Company design data might look like this (not intended to be a complete database):

PN	Description	Engineer	Item	Size	Lbs	U/M	Used On
121456-00	Wheel, Small	P Rushmore	Doc	B	NA	NA	NA
121456-01	Wheel, Small		Part		14.2	Ea	223456-01
							223456-03
123456-00	Product Spec	J Byers	Doc	A	NA	NA	223456-01
223356-00	Motor Mount	H Peak	Doc	C	NA	NA	NA
223356-01	Motor Mount		Part		22.8	Ea	223456-01
223456-00	Final Assem	L Crouse	Doc	A		NA	NA
223456-01	FEL-100		Asy			Ea	Top Level

Several interesting things are visible from this database. The Small Wheel has two "used on" assemblies—surprise! If we make any changes to the Small Wheel, we will have to check the interchangeability in both applications.

Notice that the Responsible Engineer and the Size of Document relate only to the document. If we had included the Revision Level in the database, as we should, then it would only relate to the Document.

Discussion of the "Responsible Engineer" concept will come later, but for now it is the only person CM will accept a release or a change from.

The database can now be used to retrieve information about the Design Engineering and CM business subset. How many assemblies in a product? How many parts? How many documents? What is the "Used On" for any part? What size is the document? What is the combined weight of an assembly? What is the weight of the product?

The entry of the drawing size replaces the need for a manual card file often maintained in the print room (to allow retrieval of the drawing since they are normally filed by size). You can begin to see the power of a database. It is a powerful source of facts about this subset of your business. If you had a Classification (Group Technology) Code, it would be added to the database.

Parent-Component Relationship

The assembly parts list is the parent-component relationship. If you have an MRP (Manufacturing Resource Planning) data processing system, the Parts List (parent-component relationship) would be entered into the Bill Of Material file. That is, for each assembly, at least the following data would be entered into the MRP assembly (parent) file for each item (component) on the parts list:

Data	Comment
Part Number	Of each component called out
Quantity Per	In each specific assembly
In date	Release date or date added by ECO
Out date	Date deleted by ECO
ECO #	The change number related to the add or delete

The "description" and "unit of measure" are not repeated again since those elements are in the part related file.

Without an MRP system, the parts list data (Quantity Per, In Date, Out Date, and ECO #) would be maintained manually on the parts list or in the CAD file. Changes would be maintained in the ECO file. That is, a marked-up copy of the parts list must be kept in the ECO package. This will show what changed on the parts list for posterity. The marked-up parts list in the ECO package is a good idea even if you have an MRP system.

The Marked-Up Parts List

This technique can save many hours of drafting time, as well as reduce drawing and Bill of Materials (BOM) errors. An example of this useful method for the Front End Loader product:

Example: In a change discussed earlier, the front (small) tire and wheel changed by making both non-interchangeable. The resulting mark-up of a parts list would look like Figure 18 (underlining denotes delete).

DATE REV 1-12-88	REV 01	REV DESCRIPTION RELEASE FOR PROTO		ECO # 1212		SIGN FBW	
EC3 CORP		DESCR	P/N	SIZE	PG OF		
FEL - 100		FINAL ASSEM	223456-01	A	1 1		
FIND #	DESCRIPTION		PART NUMBER	QTY	UNIT MEAS	IN/OUT DATE	ECO
1	Motor Mount		223356-01	1	ea		
2	Tire, Large		423456-01	2	ea		
3	Frame		723456-01	1	ea		
4	Tire, Small		423456-02 423456-03	2	ea		
5	Bucket, 4 yard		523456-01	1	ea		
6	Bucket Arm		823456-01	2	ea		
7	PCB, Elect Ignition		923456-08	1	ea		
8	Nameplate		323456-01	1	ea		
9	Axle		103456-01	6	In		
-	Product Spec		123456-00	Ref	Doc		
-	Material Spec		623456-00	Ref	Doc		
10	Wheel Hub, Large		113456-01	2	ea		
11	Wheel Hub, Small		121456-01 121456-03	2	ea		
12	Motor		114456-07	1	ea		
13	Adhesive		115456-01	2	oz		

MARK UP IN RED PEN

Figure 18. Marked-up parts list.

This marked-up parts list gives adequate data for the traceability of changes to the effective date. Non-interchangeable changes must also be traced to to serial number (or date code, or mod, etc.). The marked-up parts list is an ideal tool for input to the BOM database. The deletes and adds are easy to identify.

Configuration Management should also keep an ECO database, which will be discussed as part of change control.

Manufacturing Data

Manufacturing should keep this database. It would have elements such as:

- Make / Buy code
  - Lead time to buy or build
    - MRP codes
      - Cognizant Manufacturing Engineer
        - Cognizant Industrial Engineer
          - Cognizant Test Engineer
            - Fixture number
              - Cost: Material, Labor, Overhead

If your company has an MRP system, manufacturing would "call up" the part number and add this data to fields allowed (or established) for them. If you don't have MRP, manufacturing should set up a PC database.

It is important that the information contained here be available to Design Engineering, CM, and others. Availability of each database to other groups is necessary to avoid redundancy and to answer their needs. Availability of this data will answer questions such as: Who are the people Design Engineering should put on a "Design Team"? Which ME does Design get to sign a drawing? What is the cost of an item? Notice that the databases and the access to them helps to close the gap between Design Engineering and the rest of the world.

Not all database elements are clearly for Design, Manufacturing, or Support. For example, many MRP systems contain a code that is critical to the program functions. The code is called by different names in different MRP systems. For this discussion, it will be called an MRP Code. An example of MRP coding is shown in Figure 19. A "set diagram" defining the code is also shown. Notice the similarity to CM's "Document Type" code. The MRP codes should have the same meaning as CM codes or, if there are differences, the CM Manager should understand why they are different and reconcile the differences, if necessary.

P = PART   V = VENDOR ASSEMBLY

B = BURDEN   N = PHANTOM ASSEMBLY

D = DOCUMENT   A = ASSEMBLY NOT SCHEDULED

T = TOP ASSEMBLY   S = SCHEDULED ASSEMBLY

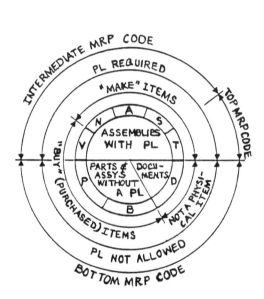

Figure 19. MRP coding (sample).

Field Support Data

Field Support should enter elements into their database such as:

- Field Change Order number
  - Field effective date / SN (CM entered)
    - Field Bulletin number
      - Illustrated Parts Catalog PN
        - Maintenance Manual PN
          - Repair (Field, Repair Center, Manufacturing)
            - Cognizant Field Engineer
              - Cost to Repair

Note that the field support people must capture the date and SN of any change installed in the field and feed that information back to CM.

Data Element Criteria

The data should be established and maintained by some common criteria:

- Notice that no data element is entered more than once. If it appears more than once (with the exception of the Part Number) it is wasteful and probably indicates some confusion about responsibilities.
- The Data Dictionary should be a Company Standard that all necessary parties agree to.
- Access to enter, add, delete elements should be limited (secured) to the functional groups indicated.
- Make the data available to all who need to know on a read or report basis.

CM should probably co-ordinate the establishment of all three databases since they will be responsible for the design data and there is need to avoid redundancy and clarify responsibilities.

Purchasing A Database

This topic is a subject of considerable complexity. Things that are critical to the CM strategy will be covered once lightly.

If your Company is planning to write its own MRP or other database system, it needs to be pointed out that there are many systems on the market that are time-tested and relatively inexpensive; that is, inexpensive compared to designing and programming your own system. Your Information Systems Group may want to write the program for a unique system to cover your company. That isn't surprising because, after all, they are programmers and they like to program. Some support will come from various quarters because people believe that the company products, organization and methods are unique.

The "we're unique" argument is often used but is very weak. Take an objective look at what is available on the market. Also look objectively at the real cost of designing, coding, testing, and debugging your own programs. The purchase cost will appear minor alongside a realistic "do it yourself" estimate. Your product and people are unique, but the basics of efficient manufacturing are very common to all manufacturers.

If your company is purchasing a new MRP or other database system, the CM Manager should be part of the team working on that task. If you are the CM Manager and haven't been invited, talk to the chairperson, go to their next meeting, and invite yourself in. It is <u>critical</u> to the CM function to be part of that activity. From a CM standpoint, the major features you need to look for are:

- Compatibility with your CAD. That is, can you "down load" CAD parts list data into the Bill Of Material module? Is, or will, an interface program be available?

- The Bill Of Material module is made up of at least two "files," Part Information and Assembly Information. Is a method of checking transactions to both files available on line or (at least) over night?

- Is a "Used On" capability included which:
    1. Is easy to use, on line—no overnight wait for a report?
    2. Shows next assembly PN and top level PN without "rolling" up through the structure?

- Are all the data elements present that the CM is responsible for? Are there also "expansion fields" available to add other "new" elements?

- Will the system print out a report that looks like a design engineering parts list or can the MRP be easily programmed to print the parts list?

Avoid the temptation to buy a system from the marketplace and tailor it to fit your way of doing business. It is actually much better to change your way of doing business to fit the system. The changes required usually make sense from a business standpoint anyway. Experience has shown that successful MRP system implementation is done with no more than a half dozen program modifications. This does not count programming of unique reports. Realize that this advice "flies in the face" of major consulting firms advice. They do business by selling tailored MRP to companies that believe they are different.

Plan to streamline your manual systems which interface with the MRP. Probably do this before you implement. For example, the engineering change system should be functioning fast and accurately, or else the new MRP system will appear to be malfunctioning.

Don't automate any process unless you are prepared to spend the necessary time and dollars to plan, test, and train before you implement.

Hundreds of companies are changing MRP systems. Many in the same kind of business are "trading" systems. That is, Company A is throwing out system X for system Y while Company B is throwing out system Y for system X.

The reasons given for throwing out the old systems usually come down to:

- Tailored the system until the vendor wouldn't support it
- Tailored the system until it did exactly what we used to do (didn't improve anything)
- Implemented without planning, testing, and/or training

The implementation of an MRP system is a huge undertaking and needs to be carefully planned and executed. It is the latter point which seems to be the most prevalent reason. Plan, Test, Train, Replan, Retest, Retrain, etc., etc.; then implement.

Part of the planning process must be to plan the relationship between Design Engineering and Manufacturing. Too often Design has it's CAD and Manufacturing has it's MRP and the gap between them widens.

Bills Of Material (BOM)

The Bill Of Material is the heart of most manufacturing organizations. Whether they are MRP-oriented or JIT (Just-In-Time)-oriented or a combination of both (American JIT), the BOM is still the heart of the process. In fact, no manufacturing system that man has invented can operate well without an accurate BOM. Engineering parts lists "are the BOM" or "feed the BOM," depending upon whether or not you have a manual or computer database.

"Engineering worries about the CAD and Manufacturing worries about the Bill of Materials." This is the most prevalent negative mind set in American industry. It is wrong! It's a mistake! It widens the gap between Engineering and Manufacturing! It creates major redundancies and waste! The result of this historical monster is two, three, and often more Bills of Material in many companies. The solutions are fairly easily described, but very difficult to implement. But before getting into solutions, let's lay some groundwork.

Parts List and BOM

The engineering parts list is a single level BOM. All the parts lists for a product, entered into a database (just covered in the last chapter), is a BOM. Other data is added by CM, Manufacturing, and Field Service as discussed. Industrial Engineering adds cost related data and Accounting adds rate information.

From the database (usually an MRP system), we obtain a multitude of "Bill Of Material" reports. Many of these reports contain more than parts list data. Some of these reports are:

- Indented   - Parts Only   - Used On
- Costed   - Lead Time   - Assembly Only
- Pick List   - Indented By Lead Time

The more reports the better—as long as we are talking about availability, and not printing out tons of paper. One company had twenty-seven different reports available. Fantastic! Reports are not the concern. It is the redundant input and maintenance of the databases (plural) that is the concern.

BOM History

Go back in time prior to computer drafting days. The assembly pictorial drawing was prepared and the parts list for that drawing was placed in the corner of the drawing. Some drawings got so complicated, the idea of detaching parts list came along. Also, MRP systems came about, and it was more convenient to have the parts list detached so as to use it for the "input" to MRP. CAD provided for putting the parts list on the face of the pictorial or on a detached list or both (it wasn't until recently that exploring the ability to "down load" from CAD to MRP began). The result is that many companies have ended up with *multiple BOM databases*. The diagram in Figure 20 pictures the numerous BOM databases that are being kept at many companies:

- The parts list on the face of assembly drawings is a BOM database.

- The detached design parts list is a BOM database. This is the parts list that Design Engineering created and which CM usually hands out if asked for an assembly parts list.

- If you make and maintain family tree drawings—another BOM database.

- The MRP system is still another BOM database.

- Multi-plants building the same product with different MRP—more BOM databases.

- The CAD is a BOM database if the parts list data is developed there.

- Publications people often create their own BOM database.

- Manufacturing Engineers often create their own BOM database.

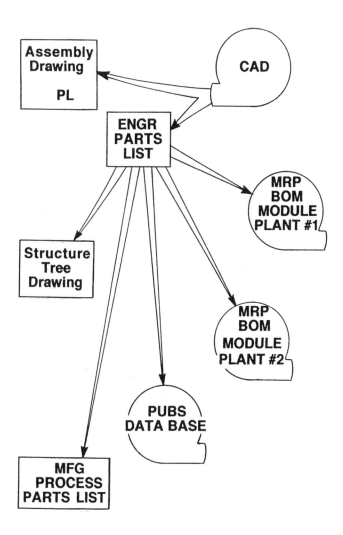

Figure 20. Multiple BOMs (multiple input).

Could there be waste here? In my University of Wisconsin Seminars I tell the story about a Company President who heard that an Industrial Engineer (IE) could save him some money. He decided to hire one and started to interview. An IE came to interview. The President told him he was going to take him down the assembly line, and if he saw any place where he could save some money, to speak up. A little way down the line there was a man sitting and watching the line. The IE asked "What does he do?" The President checked, came back and said, "Nothing!" The IE didn't say anything, so they proceeded down the line. Further down the line, there was another man sitting and watching the line. The IE asked, "What does he do?" The President again checked, came back and said, "Nothing!" The IE said: "Ah ha! Redundancy!"

In American industry the redundancy of databases in general, and Bills of Material specifically, is ludicrous.

One BOM Database

More than *one* Bill Of Material database is redundant. A waste! Worse than redundant—it allows for diverging designs! When manufacturing has a problem, shall they be allowed to create their own fix? This is an easy trap to fall into if manufacturing maintains the MRP design data! Shall each plant devise their own fix? Which design is the best? How do we get out of this very costly and risky situation? Take it a step at a time (refer to Figure 21).

- First, easiest but probably most painful, is to erase the parts list from the pictorial drawing. Do this after comparing the MRP parts list to the drawing parts list and resolving any differences. Manufacturing must be included in the planning since they make substantial use of the drawings as they are.

- Second, if you have MRP, don't make Family Tree Drawings - use the Indented BOM report. If you have tree drawings, get rid of them. If you don't have MRP, tree drawings still do not need to be released unless they are your only "used on" record. Tree drawings may help in the product development phase but should not be released or maintained.

- Third, decide that since you have it, and manufacturing is dependent upon it, you are going to use the MRP as the single BOM database. If it doesn't already exist, program a parts list "report" from the MRP that is in the exact format that Design Engineering wants. Double space this parts list because it can be more easily marked up for subsequent change. For guidance, use the FEL-100 format.

- Fourth, compare every MRP Engineering Parts List to the "input" Engineering Parts List. Reconcile all differences and throw away the "input" parts list. When anyone approaches the print room for a parts list, CM gives them the MRP parts list.

- Fifth step is applicable only if you have CAD. If it isn't too late, and you do have an MRP system, avoid using the CAD to create parts lists. Otherwise, place the CAD Revision Block under security that allows only CM access. Require that any parts list produced from CAD carry no revision level (date control only). Thus, if copies are printed out, it will be obvious that they are not released documents. CM will assign the proper revision number or letter upon "release."

- Sixth, purchase or modify your MRP system to allow "Multi-plant" mode. That is, the same database allows different change effectivity in different plants. This allows each plant to make the change happen as fast as possible for their conditions (inventory, WIP, lead times, etc.).

- Seventh, require Publications and Manufacturing to use the MRP BOM module rather than creating their own BOM database.

If you have CAD and MRP, you should strive for the ultimate in single BOM / parts list processing. Link the CAD to the MRP such that the Parts List can be down loaded from CAD to MRP. This should be allowed to occur only through CM, because only CM should assign revision levels in order to exercise minimum process control. The CAD revision field should, therefore, be secure to CM. The diagram would look like Figure 21.

Getting from where your company might be, to a single database, is easier to write about than to accomplish. The potential rewards are significant, however. This multiplicity of BOMs is a significant contributor to the gap between Design Engineering and the rest of the world. Getting to one BOM is "step one" toward Bill of Material accuracy. With this approach, 100% BOM accuracy can be obtained.

Rule: One BOM database.

Reason: Avoid redundancy, avoid multiple designs, avoid many
            problems resulting from multiple databases.

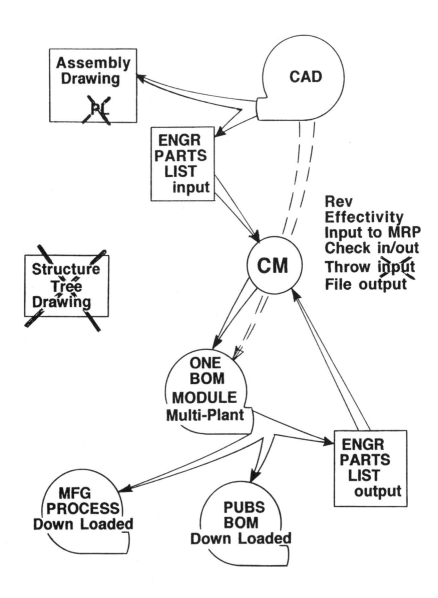

Figure 21. One BOM database.

100% BOM Accuracy

Now that you have only *one* BOM database, it will be easier to make it accurate. Following the process above will eliminate many BOM inaccuracies. The other steps are relatively easy:

- Make *CM responsible for BOM accuracy.* Design data elements only.

- Make CM responsible for all *design data input.* Check the input (normally by obtaining an output report and comparing the two). If input errors are found, make sure the error is corrected by the person who made it. *Design data* includes both the parts list input and the engineering parts data file as previously discussed.

- CM initiates an *audit of the product* and the product documentation with the Quality Assurance Group. If QA is not able to help, do it alone. Pick a simple product to start with.

  1. Compare the Bill of Material from the database with the pictorial drawings. Note and resolve every discrepancy.
  2. Compare the drawings to a finished product. Resolve every discrepancy.

Resolution of discrepancies must mean that the root cause of the problem has been identified and fixed. Now tackle your most important product. Keep going through all your active products.

In order to assure that this auditing occurs, it must be planned, scheduled, and executed on a regular basis. Every product should be audited, probably once a year, until the problems found with the parts list information has reached zero. Now that you have attained World-Class BOM (singular), what else is there? Before a company can have a World-Class BOM *process,* we need to resolve some nagging issues that are typically ignored.

What Items In the BOM?

What items should be put into the Parts List and therefore into the BOM? Many companies find this to be a significant issue. Does the packaging (box) material go into the BOM? Are fixtures and tools included? How about specifications? Labels? Literature? Burden Items? Raw material?

Process consumables? Remember, just because you put a part number on something, doesn't mean it has to go on the BOM. For the purposes of this discussion, we need to make a distinction between the database and the BOM. As discussed earlier, it is desirable to put important data elements into the database. Much of that data is related to the item part number. Much of it to assembly part numbers. However, that doesn't mean that these items must be on a parts list.

Rule: Design Engineering, Manufacturing, and Field Service should agree on what goes into the BOM (parts list). That is, they should agree on a set of rules that CM should arbitrate and document in a standard. Then every product will be done per the standard.

Reason: This is one of the issues that causes conflict between Design Engineering and other departments. To eliminate the "Throw it over the wall" syndrome, this issue must be settled.

Why is being consistent from product to product so important? If the BOM on the FEL-100 includes the product packaging, then an FEL-200 is designed and released excluding the packaging, what might happen? The company can complete the build of the FEL-200, have the product on the dock ready to ship and guess what—no package to ship it in! This wouldn't be the first company that this happened to.

A well-thought-out and agreed-upon standard serves to remove one of the significant barriers between Design Engineering and the rest of the world. Instead of debating these issues over and over, people can now spend their energy on making it correct. They can also easily identify cases where exception to the standard should be taken.

It is very difficult to address each issue and to develop a standard for all companies. For example, one company may <u>include</u> burden items ("C" items in the ABC inventory analysis), and the next company might <u>exclude</u> them. Both companies could operate without problems on burden items.

One company—a submarine valve manufacturer—had a system set up for packaging that worked well. They were a contract job shop. Each time a contract came in, the Contract Administrator completed a packaging form. They sent the form down to Emanuel who managed the shipping function. Emanuel always had packaging material ready for shipment. He didn't have big inventories, and packaging problems were nonexistent. When Emanuel was on vacation the packaging department still functioned smoothly. Should they be advised to change that system? Of course not.

There are, however, some general guidelines that we can develop. They can be treated as rules for many companies:

Guideline: Include any item that is part of the product or defines the product. This would include any item defined on design documentation.

Examples: Burden items, raw material, schematics, specifications, product labels, nameplate, etc.

Reason: These items should show up in the proper assembly "Used On". If you have MRP, most systems allow items to be coded as "burden" or "document". This coding yields simplistic treatment of the item—such as min-max inventory control. Some of these items may not be properly included in the product cost if they aren't in the BOM.

Guideline: Include any item that ships with the product.

Examples: Packaging cardboard, tape, address label, warning labels, publications, literature, etc.

Reason: The company cannot get paid until it ships the product. It is impossible to ship without these items. The damage in shipment is typically a significant problem and packaging costs are often very high. These items should therefore be scrutinized the same way the product is.

Guideline: Include any item that is critical to the support process. Such an item should be referenced on the applicable assembly parts list.

Examples: A unique adjustment tool that is needed in the field replacement of an item but is not shipped with the product. A specific and unique test device is required in order to assure the product is performing to specifications. A unique cleaning fluid is used that is critical in Manufacturing and Field Service.

Reason: It is critical that the field support people be aware of those requirements. Inclusion on the assembly parts list will assure this.

Most process consumables, fixtures and test equipment used in manufacturing, would *not* be included or referenced in the BOM. They *would be* referenced and included in the manufacturing routing or process description. They might well be entered into the part information file of the manufacturing database but not into the parts list.

Remember that the above is guideline, not rules. It is important for each company to carefully work out its rules and document them with an agreed-upon standard.

Structuring the Bill Of Material

Every product is made up of parts, structured or grouped into assemblies. The grouping can be, and often is, quite arbitrary. Design Engineering, Manufacturing, Field Service, Accounting, and other people all have an idea as to what the "best" combination or grouping is. This is another area that is often a sore point between Design Engineering and the rest of the company. Consider the FEL-100 structured the way that Engineering designed it.

Engineering Structure

The design and development people get together early in the project life and decide which engineer, group or department will contribute portions of the design. The classic way of doing this is to draw a product tree or family tree drawing. This is a very good way of pictorializing the responsibility for pieces of the product.

Note: Use of an MRP indented bill or a family tree early in the development project is encouraged. It helps engineers, CM, and others to agree on a common structure. Do not release or maintain the family tree, however, as it then becomes a redundant BOM.

In this case, Design Engineering did not include Manufacturing in this early structuring discussion. As they saw it, the meeting was only to outline the responsibility for the design. They assign design tasks as follows:

Final Assembly and Project Engineer	Crouse
PCB Programmable Ignition	Kramer
Motor Assembly	Watson
Motor Mount and Frame	Karnick
Bucket Assembly	Radacovich
Wheel Assemblies	Peterson

As this is being done, Crouse draws the tree as in Figure 22.

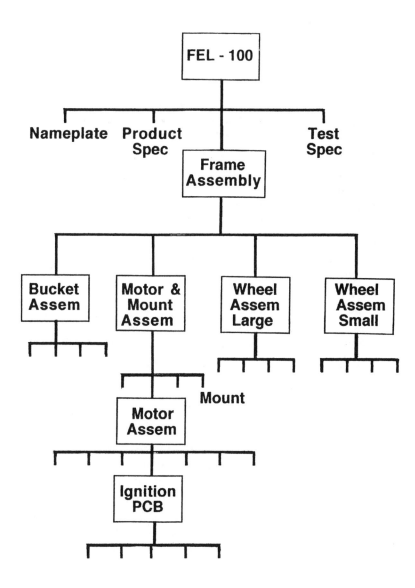

Figure 22. BOM structure - Engineering.

Each of the engineers can now do their designs without duplicating work and without forgetting any elements of the product. Should any of them have questions about mating, interface, specifications, etc., they know to consult with Crouse. They created a five-level structure. It made sense to them. At this stage, it would seem to make sense to any casual observer. As development of the product progresses, a new viewpoint arises.

Manufacturing Structure

At some point the manufacturing people get involved. The manufacturing people have their own idea of how to structure the BOM. The Industrial Engineer wants to assemble wheels and axles to the frame and put them onto "tracks" that will become the main assembly line. They will do the frame assembly early in the production line, but without the motor. After adding bucket arms and bucket, they will add the motor. The motor, however, will be an assembly less the Printed Circuit Board (PCB). They plan to test the motor with a known good PCB. The PCB will then be added near the end of the line. The tires will be put on at the end of the line just before final test and preparation to ship.

As a result of this plan, the Manufacturing people want the structure as in Figure 23.

The Industrial Engineer may want to use the assembly pictorial drawing as an operator aid in their process. In fact, to obtain simplistic pictorial drawings, they may want them prepared for very small groupings of parts. This can mean even more structure levels.

Materials and Accounting Structure

Other departments enter the structuring issue. The materials people want a part number on anything put in stock or shipped between buildings. The buyer often requests restructuring to aid in purchasing an item from more than one vendor. Guess what—more levels in the BOM.

The Materials and/or Accounting people have divided the production operations into "cost centers." In fact, it seemed like such a good idea, lots of cost centers are created. Then, in order to get the right parts issued to the right cost center, the structure of assemblies needs to match the cost centers. This may add several levels of assembly.

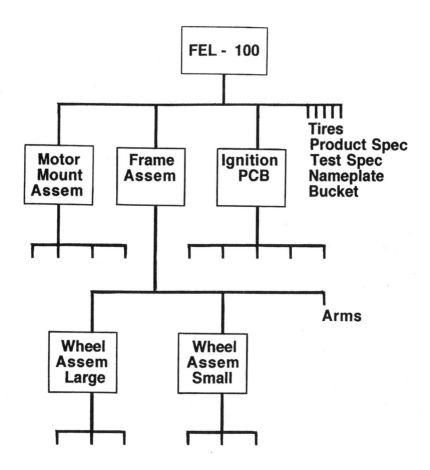

Figure 23. BOM - Manufacturing.

Field Support Structure

The Field Engineer enters the picture. The Field Support people want to spare the windshield wiper assembly without a wiper blade. Another level of assembly? Actually, the field people would really like to have the blade and the wiper assembly each made into another assembly with a box and instruction. Now Manufacturing and Field Support are at odds because Manufacturing does not want the box and instruction in "their" structure. In fact, Manufacturing makes the wiper assembly in a different building than the final assembly, and they want to ship it as a wiper assembly with blade. Sometimes companies resolve this kind of problem by adding levels to the structure.

MRP's Solution

The MRP system "operates" on each level of assembly. That is, the MRP takes the schedule and *explodes* it against the BOM to develop material requirements in lead time. The MRP run produces purchase orders, shop orders, pick lists, etc. It starts with the top level and progresses down the structure to do this at every level of assembly. Orders and reports are produced. This is a time-consuming process—even for high powered computers.

Most MRP systems have developed the "phantom" designation in order to minimize this process time problem. The designation of an assembly as a "phantom" tells the computer to pretend that the assembly isn't there for some of its operations. Thus, the "phantom" designation is "pretense" that the assembly doesn't exist. Every level of assembly that the system can ignore means less MRP process time. This solution has limitations, however, which vary from MRP system to system. As a result, the company adds levels faster than MRP can ignore them.

Common Industry Problem

Industry tends is to treat each of these individual requests as reasonable and to add assemblies to the structure. The growth of BOM structures is a significant and continuing problem in American industry. Many companies develop BOMs that have six, eight, ten, or more levels. There is a significant amount of work to create them as well as to maintain them.

The work involved is no surprise to Configuration Management Managers. Much of their time is spent creating, recreating, revising, and changing documents and part numbers in these multi-level BOMs. They do such a good job of it, most other functions do not realize the work involved.

Those companies that have MRP, usually see a symptom of the problem. The data processing department wants to get a new computer:

Symptom: "We need a new computer because it takes the whole weekend to run MRP !"

Come Monday morning, the system is "not available." When it does "come up," it is slow—it seems to take forever to get a report. Running of an "explosion" (MRP) or "implosion" (Used On) requires significant amounts of computing power. The real need is for shallower BOMs, not bigger computers!

Unstructuring The BOM

It should be obvious by now that the fewer BOM levels, the better. But how does a company achieve this goal? Let's examine each request for a new assembly level and seek alternatives.

Field Replaceable Items

Situations like the wiper blade, and the wiper assembly without blade, are common occurrences. Especially when the box and instructions are included in the problem. First of all, does the Field Support request seem reasonable? It certainly is something companies face every day. Structuring with box and instructions would allow proper costing of each field-replaceable item. Proper costing will lead to proper pricing. OK, it's reasonable! Then structure an assembly for the unique field requirement. For example the FEL-100 Printed Circuit Board assembly for the field might look like Figure 24.

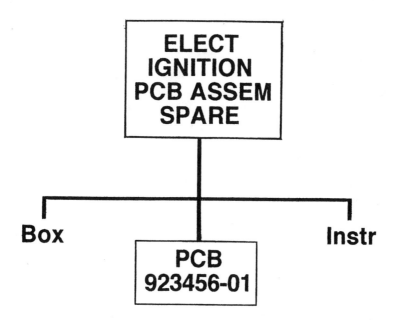

Figure 24. Unique spared assembly.

The unique spared assembly is thus properly documented. The assembly can now be ordered by the field, manufacturing can build it, and it can be packaged for the field as desired. It can be costed and priced as the unique entity it is. If we enter this item into our database, it will be part of our Used On relationship. The PCB assembly spare (822334-01) should also be coded in our database as a Field Replaceable Unit (FRU). In this way the interchangeability of the item can be maintained.

This unique assembly should <u>not</u> be put into the design/manufacturing structure however. Create a separate list for all the FEL-100 field replaceable Items—a spares BOM. Some call it the FRU (Field Replaceable Units). This BOM will contain parts and assemblies designated as "spares".

Assign a document number (tab 00) to the list. Reference the spares list on the parts list for the end product, FEL-100. This will allow anyone who has the product part number to find the spare items list.

Guideline: Structure field needs on a referenced spare parts and Field Replaceable Units Bill Of Material. Include required field-unique assemblies on that list.

Reason: It satisfies the field needs without adding structure to the product BOM.

Design Engineering and the Field Engineering should agree on which items are to be field replaceable. The design engineer and the field engineer are the minimum (perhaps the only) signatures required. These documents should be released and under CM change control.

Now we have satisfied the legitimate needs of the field without adding levels to the product BOM. We end up with a two level spares BOM. With some careful programming you can add data elements as needed to make the list most usable for the field support documentation people. For example, the parts list portion of the spare parts catalog can be created from this BOM.

Manufacturing Unstructuring

There are those who say; "Structure the BOM however Manufacturing wants it". This is a gross oversimplification of the problem. "Aren't drawings made for manufacturing?" you ask. Yes, part drawings are for the purpose of manufacturing. Structure and assembly drawings are a different issue however. They are made for manufacturing only to the extent that the structure is good for the company. Examine the issues.

Cost Centers

Too many cost centers create more problems than just adding BOM levels. Each cost center begets cost reports, inventory tracking reports, MRP output reports, etc. Piles of paper that no one reads. Errors increase while reporting labor or material usage. Journal entries to correct errors increase. When costs get out of line, the accounting solution may be to add Cost Centers. This adds to the complexity of doing business and doesn't get at the root cause of the problem(s):

Guideline: Cost centers should correspond to the management structure. They should normally be at the shop superintendent or the second level production manager and in no case less than the first level shop manager.

Reason: Smaller breakdown will add cost, not help reduce costs. If you have an MRP system, adding cost centers probably means adding BOM / assembly drawing levels.

Pictorial Drawings

Consider this situation. Design Engineering makes pictorial drawings called assembly drawings. The Manufacturing Engineer or Industrial Engineer makes a series of pictorial drawings to accompany the process / routing instructions. The Field Support or Publications Department makes a series of exploded views for parts catalog, maintenance and repair.

This is a situation that is all too familiar. Is there a pattern of redundancy here? Yes—but each pictorial has a specific purpose in mind. The process pictorials are best in step-by-step detail, while the ideal Field Support pictorial should focus on the replaceable items. If you have CAD, other departments should be allowed to "use" the CAD database. The manufacturing and publications people can use the CAD to develop their unique pictorials. If your CAD doesn't lend itself to secure files with other "user" access, it should be modified to allow access. If you don't have CAD, you should expect the other groups to cut and paste, trace or otherwise make use of the design pictorial assembly drawing.

Why shouldn't the process pictorial be the design pictorial? When the production rates are very low, this can work effectively. The design pictorial may be very close to the work performed at a single work station. As the rates increase, however, the same pictorial is now used at several work stations. It begins to become difficult for operators to pick out the portion of the pictorial that relates to each work station. This is why the ideal processes have step-by-step detail with mini-pictorials referring to just that step. Then as the rate changes up or down, the process (with mini-pictorial) can be "broken down" into the appropriate number of work stations.

Rule: The determination of assembly structure should not have any relationship to the manufacturing work station.

Reason: The make up of the work station is dependent upon the production rate, and is therefore far toodynamic to be a structuring criteria. Avoid frequent engineering changes for restructure due to production rate changes.

There are obvious exceptions to this rule. If you are building ships, your rate is probably always going to be low and relatively fixed. In one instance, a locomotive refurbisher first identified the workstations and then structured the assembly pictorials to match. If their rates doubled or were cut in half, they doubled or halved their work force and the people moved among the work stations. In this company, the work stations, and thus the assembly drawing structure were very fixed.

Stock An Item

The request frequently is made of CM: "We want to stock this assembly and need to have a part number to do that!" If the request is to add the assembly to the field-replaceable list, it should come from field support. If the request comes from manufacturing, it must be suspect.

Rule: Requests to add structure to allow in-process stocking of an item should be refused. A comparison of the costs of alternative fixes to the root-cause problem are needed.

Reason: Adding an item to "stock" will normally add to inventory quantities and value. Inventory carrying costs are variously estimated from eighteen to forty percent per year. The root-cause problem should be identified and fixed. One of the alternatives considered should be some form of Just-In-Time (JIT) manufacturing.

Buy An Item

The buyer who feels that a level of "assembly" is needed to buy an item from more than one vendor must be similarly challenged. This is not to say that there are not exceptions to the rule. But following the rule will assure that costs are properly identified for all alternatives and that the best one for the company is chosen. Many, many companies are blessed with buyers and systems that allow them to handle this problem without more part numbers and assembly levels.

Ship Between Buildings / JIT

Manufacturing has established a production facility in a separate building to build motors. The motor plant makes motors for several Front End Loaders. Shipping between buildings normally requires a part number. JIT purists believe that they don't need a part number for this item. They will however, have some means of specifically identifying the unique motor, so it might as well be a part number. If you have JIT and are getting along without part numbers for these items, don't add them because you read it here. In this case, the need for a part number and assembly level seems legitimate.

The purest JIT structure is a single-level BOM as shown in Figure 25. It is a condition that some companies have attained and are successful with.

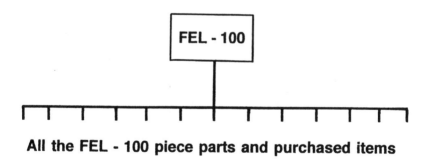

All the FEL - 100 piece parts and purchased items

Figure 25. One-level JIT BOM.

One Product Structure

We have now minimized cost centers, separated the spares BOM, and completed all the other steps possible to minimize levels in the BOM. But our original problem is still there! Design Engineering made a structure that was significantly different than Manufacturing wants!

Look at the design structure and ask why and when it was done. Examine the manufacturing structure and ask why and when it was requested. The two BOMs are not very similar. This situation is not unusual. When the structure-related activities are done independently, the choices are:

- Tell Manufacturing to live with what Design did.
- Restructure (redo assembly pictorials and parts lists) to suit Manufacturing.
- Design some kind of hybrid structure that "kind of" satisfies both.

All the options are poor ones. Of course, we should have done it right the first time. Easy to say but hard to do. At this stage, what is the best choice?

Guideline: If all of the above logic and rules have been applied- then the differences are in the "order of assembly." The product should be restructured to suit the order of manufacture. This assumes that manufacturing management is *committed* to the process.

Reason: We should have done it right the first time, but better late than never.

Structure Right The First Time

The root-cause problem stems from the failure of Engineering and Manufacturing to get together to agree on the structure. In our case, we could say that engineering didn't ask manufacturing what their plan was. In the next case, we might ask manufacturing and they wouldn't be prepared to address the issue. In another case, manufacturing might give some thought to the issue but change their minds one or more times during the development process.

Yes, there will be changes in the manufacturing plan. Yes, there will be changes in the design. But these facts should not preclude early planning, understanding of each issue, and development of *one structure*. This too, is easily said but not so easily done. It requires dedicated manufacturing people, preplanning the manufacturing process and intense discussion between all the key parties involved.

Modular Design, Build, and BOM

All designers are aware of the huge benefits in "modular design." Properly done, their designs can be used over and over in similar product designs. For example, if the FEL-100 bucket arm design is done properly, it might be very cost-effective to use the same arms in the FEL-200, etc.

But are all designers aware of the great advantages in designing for modular build and BOM? This concept has to do with planning the design to anticipate features and options, and designing them to be "modular."

Definition: Modular feature and option design, is to design all parts that are variable with a feature or option, so that they are in the top of the structure. Thus, they can be assembled on the end of the production line.

Manufacturing generally assembles from the bottom of the structure "up." So when we say "in the top of the structure", it is the same as saying "on the end of the production line." Examine some examples of feature- and option-modularity.

Example: The FEL-100 is specified to have either electric or gas starting. That is to say that either a gasoline engine or battery / starter can be ordered for starting the loader motor. If all of the parts unique to either the gas or electric versions are in the top of the structure, then the design is feature- and option-modular—because the feature and option parts can be assembled on the end of the line.

Example: The FEL - 100 specification said that the company would paint the loader red, yellow, white, or red and white. If the frame (assembled early on the line) was designed to be painted the option colors, the design would *not* be modular. If the frame was painted black regardless of color option, then the design would be modular.

Example: If our motor RPM adjustment feature is a screw on the motor and the screw is covered by the PCB when assembled, this would not be a modular design.

The idea is simple. Allow manufacture of a maximum portion of the product in an identical process. This also allows a maximum portion of the product to be structured only once. Look at a tree drawing of a modular FEL-100 in Figure 26.

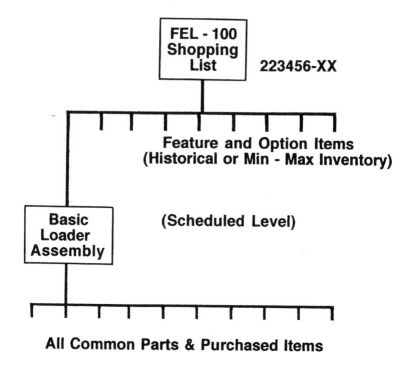

Figure 26. Feature and Option modular BOM.

Modular Parts List

The "shopping list" or modular parts list would be a matrix that looks like Figure 27.

Notice that the "basic loader" is used in every tabulation of the product. The basic loader is all the parts (and assemblies, as necessary) that are common to every product. The feature and option "choices" are designed and structured in the final assembly. They are listed in the basic assembly. The customer must choose either gas start or electric start. Thus the 01 tab is a gas start while the 02 is an electric start, etc. The features and options may be parts or they may be kits of parts and assemblies.

Not all features and options need be "either / or" conditions. For example, the "lights feature" is the quantity of lights desired. A note appears that says: "Multiple of 2's, 10 maximum." Since our design featured a programmable PCB, the switch settings / programmable chip on the PCB might be an option.

FEL - 100   PN 223456-XX

FEATURES & OPTIONS XX ⇒	01	02	03	04
BASIC LOADER	1	1	1	1
GAS START	1	1		1
ELECTRIC START			1	
1/2" WHEEL/TIRE KIT	1	1		
3/4" WHEEL/TIRE KIT			1	1
STD ARMS	2	2	2	
SPECIAL ARMS				2
RED PAINT	1			
YELLOW PAINT				1
WHITE PAINT		1		
RED & WHITE PT			1	
QTY OF LIGHTS *	2	4	2	8

*Lights come in multiple of twos, ten max.

Figure 27. Modular Shopping List drawing / matrix.

Rule: Do not attempt to document all <u>possible</u> combinations. Only list those combinations that are <u>built and sold</u>.

Reason: The possible combinations tend to boggle the mind, while the "real world" combinations are more manageable. Only document the combinations that have been tested, costed, priced, etc.

Modular Document Benefits

This document must be precise and void of "ifs", "ands" or "buts." It puts together a specific set of features and options. This document serves several needs.

- *Avoids many nearly redundant structures* by having only one basic Assembly.

- Allows the Industrial Engineer to *easily cost* each specific product. This, in turn, allows Marketing to *price* each specific product.

- Tells the sales people which specific combinations *are available.* By omission, it indicates which combinations *aren't available.* Thus, a special procedure will have to be followed in order to *add unavailable combinations.*

- Provides a tool for the salesman to use when closing the deal with the customer. The precise customer needs are now in the form of a *unique part number* (unbroken part number cycle is now possible).

- Increases the odds significantly that *what customers' order is what they get.*

- Allows manufacturing to *schedule and build* the Basic Assembly

- Allows Sales to forecast and Manufacturing to schedule at the Basic Assembly level.

- Significantly reduces the order-to-delivery response time.

Modular Scheduling

Most MRP systems do not have the ability to produce this kind of matrix document. This is probably fortunate because it tends to discourage the scheduling of each unique product.

Rule: Do not schedule unique end products. Schedule the Basic Assembly. Put all feature and option items under "Min-Max" inventory control.

Reason: Allows the Master Scheduler to keep his or her sanity. The features and options can be scheduled (or min-max controlled) on the basis of history. Once the feature and option "mix" is handled in this fashion, sales forecasting attention is focused on the most significant issue—how many FEL-100s will we sell? This is much more reliable than attempting to forecast each flavor of the product.

Manufacturing can now build the Basic Assembly on an identical assembly line. The features and options can be assembled at the end of the line. The time from customer order to delivery can be significantly shortened in this manner. One high tech company cut its time to "customize" its product significantly by using these modularity concepts. Their delivery time was reduced from about sixty days to twelve days.

Modular structuring is another significant way to close the gap between Design Engineering and the rest of the world. This tool is so powerful that it should be considered for existing product lines. Look especially at product lines where the BOMs are numerous, but are known to be the same basic product. A Basic Assembly and shopping list document can be prepared even though the products were not designed to be feature- and option-modular.

Feature and option *modular design and structuring* is a key element in making CM a significant company strategy.

The Perfect BOM

Although the Bill of Material will be different for different industries, and even different companies, there are some attributes that are common. Let's summarize the eleven most significant attributes:

1. Singular - one database.
2. Must be 100% accurate.
3. Contains part and document numbers required by the BOM standard, and no more.
4. Design engineering data is input by CM, manufacturing data by Manufacturing, and support data by Field Support.
5. Is feature- and option-modular, if the product has features and options.
6. Has at least two levels (if feature- and option-modular), and no more than four or five total levels.
7. Contains the database elements (defined in a "dictionary") for Design, Manufacturing, Field Support, and Accounting (labor and overhead rates).
8. Has date effectivity ability and historical record ability (discussed more under Change Control, Ch. 8).
9. Has ability to produce the Used On assembly part number(s) and the corresponding Used On product part number(s) and model numbers.

10. Will produce a variety of reports on demand. One of these reports must be a double-spaced Engineering Parts List. Various cost reports are included.

11. Has been jointly developed by Engineering and Manufacturing.

Some of the attributes are a function of the BOM module design (8, 9, and 10), and some are a function of our use or "management" of the BOM Module (1 through 6), or both (7). As mentioned before, when purchasing an MRP system, look for capabilities 7 thur 10. The last (11) is a function of a world-class Configuration Management organization.

These are only the attributes which are most important from a CM standpoint. There are other criteria that Manufacturing or Accounting or Field Support would add to the list. The inclusion of cost information is critical to the design management. It is important to them that the cost data is developed from the BOM and done in a disciplined manner.

There is a trend to use the BOM for developing reference document lists for other than design specifications. Some people are adding manufacturing referenced documents to the BOM. Some add contract deliverable documents. Their goal is to develop a "Bill Of Documents". These unique uses must be carefully analyzed and modeled. Can it be done in your MRP system? Can it be done without cluttering the parts list with non-design documents? Will doing it require more cross reference lists? Can the same results be obtained by numbering manufacturing processes with the design part number? Can the data be added to the database but not to the parts list? Caution needs to be exercised when considering addition of other than Design Engineering data to the parts list

BOM Evolution

The perfect BOM doesn't happen in the first day, week, or month of a project. It evolves. The first day of a project, the top level part number should be assigned and the product spec released. This forms the framework under which the BOM will develop.

As the design team does its work, they will release more pieces of the BOM. The next most significant event in the BOM's life is the long lead-time items release. These long-lead items need not be released under the assembly that they will eventually be part of. If more time is needed to develop the structure, release the long-lead items under the final assembly.

The next release might be standard assemblies, standard parts, or single drawings with or without their "home" assembly. As completed or needed, the documents are released. All the parts must be present and accounted for by time of release to pilot production. The "final" structured BOM probably won't be released until release for full production. Thus, the ideal BOM evolves, with the design team making constant progress.

The evolution of the "perfect" BOM is pictured in Figure 28.

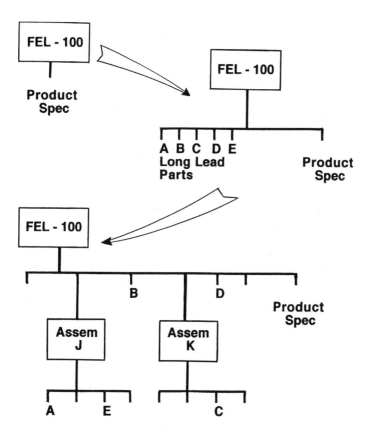

Figure 28. BOM evolution.

If a company has many similar BOMs or many features and options, they should analyze the power of the modular BOM. Whether or not the modular BOM concept is used, however, the BOM and its structure should evolve during the development and pilot production of the product.

5

Potpourri

Before launching into the heart of Engineering Documentation Control—release, request and change control—it is necessary to discuss several related issues.

Design Teams

In order to have the most efficient release and change processes, the use of Design Teams is a necessity. Design Teams (sometimes called Concurrent or Simultaneous Engineering Teams) must be established very early in a development project. They are also need to function early in the change process.

Rule: Institute Design Teams at the beginning of the project, coupled with regular management reviews.

Reason: The team approach should improve both the documentation and product. The team concept is difficult to get started, but the alternative is to continue some form of adversarial relations.

How early to start in a new program development? Planning the team (a management function) should start the day after the program is approved. The first team meetings might come a week to a month into the program. Design Engineering must be encouraged to concentrate on functional layouts and specifications in the early development. This leaves assembly structure and other manufacturing issues until a little later in the project, when design teams are functioning. Manufacturing then has a some time up front to do their planning.

Management must make sure that appropriate manpower is dedicated to the project. It is especially important that Manufacturing *commits* manpower to the development project early on.

Note: The word "committed" is used as opposed to the word "involved." There is a difference. We want *committed* as in "ham and eggs." The chicken was involved and the pig was *committed!*

Regular meetings are required both for the Design Team itself and for the entire Design Team with the management. CM acts as a "quality assurance" function during the team process. They make sure that management is aware of any short-comings in the team process. Are meetings held? Has a leader been established? Are the right people present? Is management doing its part? Etc.?

Team Make-Up

Design Teams must be broad-based and well led. Representatives from other engineering functions should be on the team:

Manufacturing Engineering

Industrial Engineering

Test Engineering

Field Engineering

Sales Engineer

Other functions should also be represented on the team:

Configuration Management

Production Control

Purchasing

Publications

Marketing

The make-up of a Design Team at any particular company might vary from the above. At some companies, Quality Assurance has the Receiving Inspection, Reliability Test, and other functions which would require their participation. The key element is that they be "broad-based."

The team should be physically located together. This will help create the trust and teamwork that is required. It also makes communications easier. Any representative that is (more than half time) dedicated to the project, should be physically located with the team.

Do broad-based teams work? R. D. Garwood, in a white paper titled "New Product Development," states: *"Broad Based Teams surface problems early in the process. A widely quoted study points out that a change could cost up to:*

$ 1,000 in the design phase
$ 10,000 in pilot testing
$ 100,000 in process planning
$ 1,000,000 in production test
$ 10,000,000 in production / field"

This is often referred to as *"the rule of tens."* Finding or fixing a problem one stage later than it might be, is ten times more expensive to fix. It also reinforces the need for concurrent engineering. For example, if the "process planning" is done during the design and pilot phases, how much cost would be avoided?

Team Responsibility

The team must not be a "committee design" team. The members are there to offer alternatives, present trade-offs, and to listen to others positions. The final responsibility for the design, however, must be with one person:

Rule: The Project Engineer must be responsible for the design
of the product.

Reason: Committee designs are almost never on target.

All members of the team must be made aware of their responsibilities. A standard may be in order. They must also be aware that the final responsibility for the design of the product lies with the project engineer.

If a Design Team does not do "team design", what do they do? They consider alternatives in areas such as:

- Customer Specifications, Reliability, Safety, Performance, Form, etc.
- Design Specification
- Testability - Test Specification
- Manufacturability
- Maintainability

- Minimum Assembly Structure
- Time-To-Market
- Product Cost and Project Cost

Notice that there must be emphasis on cost. This is why the Industrial Engineer is involved. The IE should calculate the costs of alternatives as requested by the chairperson.

The roll of the Configuration Manager in the Design Team can be pictorialized as shown in Figure 29.

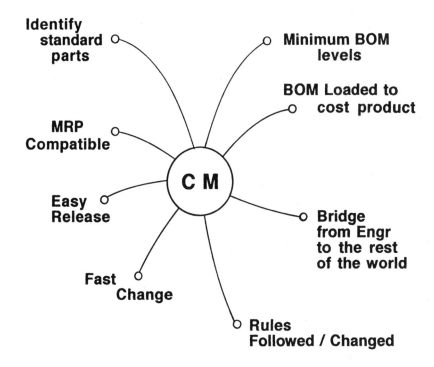

Figure 29. CM's role in the Design Team.

Team Meetings

The effective Design Team should function throughout the definition, development, pilot, and production phases. For released products, meetings might be less frequent, but they should still be held. This is one way of curbing ongoing changes to a mature product. There are other methods that will be discussed later.

Notice that these meetings do *not* constitute a Change Control Board (CCB). They are, however, a prerequisite to elimination of the CCB. Discussion of all technical aspects of each product under development and of each change to a product should occur in team meetings. This is the time (up front in the process) for technical and cost exchange.

The meetings should *not* try to set the effectivity of a change. They should *not* be for sign off of the Engineering Change Order. They *should be* for the sign off of any new or marked-up design documents (ME and FE).

The Project Engineer might chair this kind of meeting. The design manager might act as chair person. CM might act as chairperson. Group dynamics might reveal a natural leader. If the leader is not the Project Engineer, then the leader must be careful not to usurp the design responsibility. Training for team leaders and members is advisable. Figure 30 shows the kinds of functions represented and the frequency of the meetings diminishing through time.

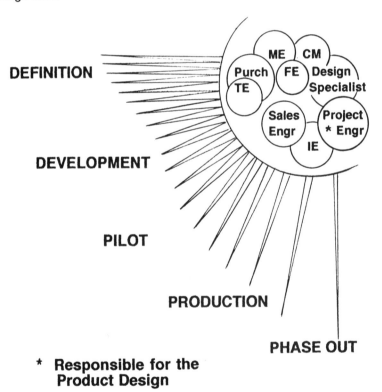

DEFINITION

DEVELOPMENT

PILOT

PRODUCTION

PHASE OUT

*** Responsible for the
    Product Design**

Figure 30. The Design Team at work.

Meetings should be held regularly at a set time and place. However, they need not be in a conference room every time—the layout table, the lab, over the prototype unit, at a vendor, in front of a CAD terminal—are all effective places to meet.

Minutes should *not* be kept. Who said what to whom is not critical. Action item lists *should* be kept. What are the technical concerns, who is to resolve them, by when, and what was the resolution? The following format works for keeping action items:

HEADINGS FOR ACTION ITEMS LIST

- Concern Number (never repeat a number)
- Concern (brief description of the problem or concern)
- Action Required (brief) (reference change request # if applicable)
- Person assigned to take that action
- Committed Completion Date
- Number of times the Commitment changed
- Actual Completion Date
- Resolution

The CM representative might well keep the action items list. This is a very good way to help in the process.

All the members need not be at every meeting. The people who have action items due should be at that meeting.

Rule: The action items list should be hand carried to each team member the day after a meeting.

Reason: Reduce the time-to-market by demonstrating a sense of urgency.

The Project Engineer and the Manufacturing Engineer should be at every meeting. The meetings should be short. The agenda is the action items list. Items that have actions due in the meeting week should be covered. Review that list crisply. See if there are new items to be added to the list. Don't try to solve problems in the meetings.

Team Success

Management needs to make it clear that every team will be measured for success. The criteria should be established and it should be the same for every team. One criteria for measuring success:

- Fast development (elapsed time to get the product released, piloted, and produced).
- The shallowest BOM (fewest levels).
- Meet targeted product cost (decrease design change activity).
- First units meet product specifications (reduce changes to meet spec).

The first criteria is the primary reason most teams are established. The goal is to speed up the process of development and release in order to beat the competition to the market. Shallow BOMs keep the structure simple and therefore help speed the process. To be sure that the product cost is on target, the team should develop a costed BOM.

Management is looking for the advantages that the team can produce by "concurrent engineering." In effect, the various engineering functions are working in parallel, rather than Design Engineering getting the documentation "done" and "throwing it over the wall" to Manufacturing.

Team Measurement

Each of these criteria is measurable. The measurements that are possible and relevant are stated above in parentheses. Perhaps CM should be given the responsibility to measure the results (except for cost) and to report to top management. After all, *measurement in and of itself, tends to improve performance.* Besides, without measurement, how can anyone know if conditions have improved.

The measurements (except cost) can be presented in a simple chart. First pick a product recently put into production without a Design Team. We will call that our "Baseline" product. Measure what happened on the FEL-100 development, and add what is happening on the FEL-200 development. See Figure 31.

If all criteria are not improving, then the teams are not functioning as well as they should. Top management needs to review these criteria frequently.

Each team will develop a character of its own. This is a natural process. The successful team will have a "garage development attitude." They will all be pulling in the same direction because they are all part of, and aware of, the whole picture.

	Baseline	FEL-100	FEL-200
From project start to all docs released to pilot	4.1 mo	3.5 mo	3.0 mo
From pilot release to pilot units completed	4.3 mo	3.1 mo	2.2 mo
From pilot units completed to production release	5.0 mo	2.3 mo	
From production release to first production unit	3.5 mo	2.0 mo	
Structure levels	7	5	4
Design Changes/ week	14	8	

Figure 31. Measuring the Design Team.

Design Responsibility

There are Project Engineers, Component Engineers, Power Supply Engineers, Manufacturing Engineers, Industrial Engineers, Agency Coordination Engineers, Test Engineers, Quality Engineers, Software Engineers, and Systems Engineers. Oh, yes! Mechanical Engineers, Electrical Engineers, Chemical Engineers, etc.

Who is responsible for the design? Who should CM accept a release from? Who is a request for change given to? Who is invited to the Design Team Meeting? Who is responsible for the changes? All legitimate questions! It is surprising how confusing the issue is in many companies. CM people are wandering the hallways trying to find out who is responsible for a particular assembly or part. Some organizations solve the issue by having the Project Engineer be the responsible engineer. As often as not, the Project Engineer becomes a bottle neck in every process. Even if all he or she is doing is delegating the issues to the correct engineer, the bottle neck remains.

As companies grow, the problem becomes more and more apparent. The printed circuit board change may affect the Component Engineer, Software Engineer/Programmer, and Agency Coordinator. Shall we have CM carry the change to each of them and get their approvals? Some companies do this. The CM Technician walks the change between and among the various engineers. When one asks a question that another must answer, the CM Technician goes from one to the other relating who said what to whom! Another bad solution.

Have Design Teams, let the Engineers talk there and sign off there! But do we need each of these engineers at every meeting? How about the concern that looks too important to wait for the meeting? If we wait for the meeting that is now held once a week, it will add two and a half days on average onto the process time.

There has to be a better way, and there is.

Cognizant Engineer List

Develop a list that depicts the name (and perhaps the phone number) of the responsible or "cognizant" engineers. The Project Engineer is still responsible for the overall design. If Cognizant Engineers have questions or doubts, they must consult with the Project Engineer or other engineers as needed. This places the burden for technical communication where it belongs.

The Cognizant Engineer will consult with the Component Engineer, Software Engineer / Programmer, Agency Coordinator, etc., in order to optimize the design decision. Now the process is engineer talking to engineer without a "middle man." The responsibility is clear. The Cognizant Engineer need *not* get signatures of other engineers in order to make a release, reject a request, or make a change. The standard that covers the Cognizant Engineer list must make that clear.

Rule: The Cognizant Engineer is designated only by the Project Engineer or the Design Management.

Reason: Since Design Engineering is responsible for the design, only they can delegate that responsibility.

Rule: Configuration Management should prepare and maintain the Cognizant Engineer list. This is done per the Project Engineer's direction.

Reason: CM will be the principal user of the list and therefore has a vested interest in seeing it prepared, maintained and distributed.

The list can be prepared in various kinds of detail. It might be simplistic or in part number detail. The important criteria is to remove all doubt as to who is responsible for the design. The list for the FEL-100 started out looking like this:

Final Assembly and Project Engineer	Crouse
PCB Programmable Ignition	Lawrence
Motor Assembly	Watson
Motor Mount & Frame	Karnick
Bucket Assembly	Radacovich
Wheel Assemblies	Peterson

For small companies, that may be all that is needed. As the company grows, it will be necessary to add more detail. A Component or Specification Control Drawing (SCD) Engineer may be added to the staff. At some point the Project Engineer may choose to add the Component Engineer to the list:

Components or SCD documents	Maday

Some companies put the Cognizant Engineer's name in the database for every part number. As companies grow the tendency should be in this direction. Certainly the small company should allow for this possibility when they design their database.

Other Functions Engineers

Who is responsible to sign a drawing for Manufacturing? Who for Field Support? Who is the release package sent to? Who will approve changes? As the company grows, the issue becomes more troublesome! It may even become unclear as to which CM Technician is responsible for a product/part of a product. The simplest solution—expand the list:

COG ENGR	DESIGN	ME / IE	FE	CM
Project Engineer	Crouse	F. Peterson	Cross	Pierson
Final Assembly	Mathews	"	"	"
PCB	Lawrence	Shumar	"	"
Prog. Ignition	Black	"	"	"
Motor Assembly	Watson	"	"	"
Motor Mt & Frame	Karnick	Ford	Jacobs	"
Bucket Assembly	Radacovich	Sjhig	Hankins	Martin
Wheel Assems	J. Peterson	Ford	Jacobs	"
SCDs	Maday	"	"	"

This is certainly a simple enough concept. It requires some work on the part of the CM Manager. The preparation and maintenance effort will be saved many times over, however. CM people are often found chasing engineers, being middle man, getting unneeded signatures, etc.

Responsibility

The Cognizant Engineer Standard should spell out responsibility and perhaps what each engineer signs. Chances are, people may be signing things and not even know why! An example of a signature standard:

- Design Engineer - Responsible for the design of the product and its documentation. Signs the documents, all release forms, all request forms, and all change forms. Must consult, as necessary, with all other engineers prior to signing.
- ME - Responsible for the manufacturability of the product and the process. Signs the design documents. Must consult with all other manufacturing technical people and vendor technical people, as necessary, prior to signing.
- FE - Responsibility for the maintainability of the product. Signs design documents of field replaceable items. Signs change forms of changes that are to be installed in the field or upon repair. Must consult with all field support people, as necessary, prior to signing.

Notice that the responsible engineers are the "hub" of technical people in their organization. The responsibility statements for any company should be just as short, clear and crisp as the above. If the responsibilities aren't clear, confusion will exist or a committee will become involved in the CM process.

Delegated Design Responsibility

The Project Engineer often delegates portions of the product design responsibility to other design engineers. Some companies delegate the entire product design responsibility to a Continuation Engineering group after some period of production. Some delegate portions of the design to Manufacturing Engineering.

I first ran into this concept as a young Engineer doing pilot processing on the first "single sideband" airborne radio. The Quality and Workmanship

Manual was very clear about service loops and connections. The actual length of a wire could vary depending upon the operator technique. The production people were constantly asking for wire length changes in the wire harnesses. I, in turn, would ask the design people to change the wire lengths. One day the Design Engineer added a note to the wire lists. It said that all wire lengths could be determined by Manufacturing Engineering. From that point on, I was able to control the lengths by the process instructions. The number of change requests and change orders declined and we were able to shift our efforts to other matters.

This delegated design concept is often used by the design engineer in the quantity column of the assembly parts lists. The "convention" is to enter AR (As Required) when the designer knows the requirement is not critical. This is OK when the item is in the burden category (costed as part of the material overhead rate). If not, it leaves a part of the product cost in limbo.

The responsibility should be delegated by note, standard and/or the Cognizant Engineer List. The Manufacturing Engineer can then assure that the proper quantity is entered.

Another application is to design a "weldment" as a completed "part." Delegate to the Manufacturing Engineer the design of the pieces to be welded into the "part'. In this way the ME can design the pieces based on the fixture, shrink, tools, etc.

Rule: Allow for and encourage the concept of *delegated design.*

Reason: It is the most cost effective way of achieving quality product design in many cases. It also can reduce the number of changes that the system must deal with.

When a company has a meaningful Quality and Workmanship Manual, this concept becomes easier to do. The Design Engineer will relinquish the responsibility more easily if the criteria that manufacturing will use are clear.

Since many design changes are for cost reduction purposes, logic favors making manufacturing responsible for significant portions of the product design.

This concept is one that the design management and the manufacturing management need to foster. Careful review of several months of changes will show likely areas for delegation.

The effect of delegation from the CM perspective, is simply to place the Manufacturing Engineer's name in the design column on the Cognizant Engineer List. The ME now has the responsibility to discuss the proposed change with any other affected engineer. Another effect is to eliminate many change requests.

Change Control Boards

The Change Control Board (CCB) is an outgrowth of Military and DoD specifications. Those specifications recognize the need for releases, change proposals, and changes to be reviewed by the affected parties for technical issues, impact, etc. This need is exactly the same as the needs discussed in the Design-Team–Concurrent-Engineering topic. The typical CCB meeting is held <u>after</u> the design engineer says, "Here is the change, I'm done." The proper point in time for such discussions is, however, "up front" in the process. The design changes should be discussed very early in the process—at design team meetings.

Rule: CCBs are typically held too late in the change process. They should be held "up front," before the development of a fix for a problem.

Reason: The team needs to discuss technical and other aspects of the problem, and the potential fixes, prior to development of a solution.

Properly implement the Concurrent-Engineering–Design-Team, and part of the need for CCBs will go away. If necessary, call the design team meeting that deals with changes "the CCB". Thus, after the design team has done the discussions, analysis, cost estimate, etc. there will be no further need for meetings.

"But CCBs do more than that," you say! Yes, they often do several other functions:

1. A rare CCB calculates the cost of the change.
2. Set effectivity / disposition parts.
3. The place where signatures are or aren't obtained.
4. Talk about implementing the change.
5. Add emotion to the process
6. Substitute for a process.

The usual CCB is a large room full of people, some of whom do not even know why they are there. Typically several manufacturing people, several design engineering people, and several others are present. Most have not analyzed the change before coming to the meeting. Many have not even read it. The design engineer that developed the fix thought he or she was done with that problem. They don't even want to come to the meeting since they have moved on to another problem. People question the "proposed" fix. The emotions run high. Someone that needs the change wants to get it signed right now. Those who haven't done their homework ask questions or divert attention to other subjects. Verbal battles result, name calling, even worse.

Some of the people involved feel comfortable with the group signing. Safety in numbers. People think, "They can't fire all of us!" If something does go wrong, the stock answer is: "Gosh, I thought Charlie worried about that!"

Rule: Have precise placement of authority and responsibility. CCBs are typically a substitute for a process. Better to have a process for limiting signatures by establishing precise responsibilities and assuring communications within a functional area through a single person.

Reason: The CCB got started because: design teams didn't exist, it is easier to start than a process, and the DoD encourages them.

This is an area where the DoD influence should be resisted. Examine the functions that CCBs perform. Look at each objectively and ask what is the best method to fulfill that need. Move the CCB up front into a Design Team format. Then look at the four other useful functions earlier identified:

Cost of the Change. Few companies formally estimate the cost of changes. Most design engineers have an idea of the development cost and some feeling for the product unit costs. A few engineers have a feel for the one-time implementation costs. The key issue with regard to CCBs is the timing. The cost should be estimated up front in the process. The design team should have a person—probably an Industrial Engineer—who is responsible for estimating the cost. When a cost estimate is needed, the IE can project the effectivity of the change and estimate the implementation cost accordingly.

Some design functions hold the Cognizant Engineer responsible for the cost estimate. Regardless of who does it, the time to do a cost estimate is very early in the process. Perhaps the solution that first comes to mind is not the most cost effective. Thus, the estimate should be done as part of the team action items.

Set Effectivity of the Change. Someone in the CCB has typically taken it upon him/her self to set the effectivity and disposition old-design parts. Everyone else usually accepts this. It is never quite clear, however, as to who on the committee will follow up on the change to make it happen or to change the effectivity plan when necessary. This is left up to "the computer" or "the group."

The setting of the effectivity is sometimes dictated by the customer. When it is not dictated, several forces are at work. Among the effectivity "drivers" are:

- Lead times of make parts, buy items, assembly, test, etc.
- Work in process, at vendor, etc.
- Time to rework, scrap, etc.
- Lead time for tools, test equipment, inspection devices, etc.
- Lead time for process documentation, programs, etc.
- Schedules, schedule changes, etc.

Certainly no one person can be "all knowing" with regard to which item is the longest, or which costs are the greatest, etc. However, far better than having a committee (CCB) performing this task, look to a single manufacturing representative to be totally responsible. Pick a manufacturing function that is already deeply involved with many of the effectivity "drivers."

Rule: In most companies, Production Control is the most logical function to co-ordinate the analysis of the change impact and effectivity analysis.

Reason: Most design changes are driven by schedule and material factors.

Of course, a committee can do the function. When a CCB is used, however, one other thing happens. The typical meeting is held once a week. The typical change thus waits two and a half days before CCB. Then someone finds a problem with that change or raises an issue which needs investigation. The result? Another week to see it again at the next CCB. Then another issue is raised. Another week! The process is so slow that someone invents a way to make fast changes—another method to make changes—sometimes two or more methods.

Rule: CCBs tend to become a way to let the documentation catch up to the real world (or to use when there is no hurry).

Reason: The process with a CCB is so slow that other method(s) of making changes are devised.

A few CCBs do function adequately, particularly in small companies where very few people are involved. These companies typically meet several times a week at a regularly appointed time and place. Small companies have a tradition of growing, however. It is for this reason that even the small company needs to find a better method.

Obtaining Signatures. The design team has done its job. The Design Engineer and the Manufacturing Engineer sign the marked or new drawings at the team meeting. The impact analysis has been done and the effectivity set. What other signatures are needed? The Field Engineer, if affected, should sign. If the cost policy requires, the proper level of management should sign. Since these are both "sometimes" signatures, the CM department should know the rules as to when they are required, and should obtain their signatures.

Implementing the Change. This is certainly not a job for a committee. Every function affected by the change needs to take proper implementation action. Their action should start with the design team and progress from there. Details on implementation will follow. The significant element to this discussion, is that conditions frequently change. As a result of changing conditions, the effectivity plan often changes. Production Control must be the focal point for this responsibility as well.

It has been said that a committee set out to design a horse—and a camel resulted! As constituted in most companies, CCBs are committees. They are, therefore, usually a symptom of a failure to address the gut issues involved in CM.

Process Documentation

Process documentation may be either design documentation or manufacturing documentation. When the design engineer feels the need to specify a particular process, he or she typically does that with a Process Specification. That specification is treated as design documentation. All other process documentation is typically manufacturing documentation.

The manufacturing process documentation is made up of many different documents. Tool drawings, test equipment drawings, inspection procedures are some of these. The documents are also called by different names at different companies. To process a part in a fabrication environment, "route sheet" is common terminology. An assembly shop may refer to "assembly procedures." These are all process documentation, and for simplicity, will be called "process sheets."

Process sheets are produced as a *result* of a new product release. They should be produced concurrently with the design documents because manufacturing engineers were part of the Design Team. However, the product release is not held up if process documents are not complete, nor will the changes be held up waiting for the process documents to be marked up or revised.

Start-up companies tend to use the engineering drawings instead of having assembly procedures. Large "high end" companies (like a shipbuilder) do the same thing. The typical company, however, has someone in the manufacturing group producing process sheets. This "someone" is usually a Production Engineer, Industrial Engineer, or Manufacturing Engineer. Hopefully they will be using the CAD file that Design Engineering did. They will access CAD to produce what is best for fabrication and assembly—tiny steps and tiny pictorials to go with each step or a few steps.

This step/sequence detail is the most efficient way for the production operator to learn the task. The process sheet also allows the time standard to be properly "engineered." This results in improved product labor costs. When changes are made in the process or to the design, the change of process sheets is the most effective way to change the production operator's method.

Many customers are rightfully concerned about process control. The FDA is acutely concerned about process control. Process companies are keenly concerned about process control. If the manufacturing process control isn't part of the CM system, then how is the required control attained?

Process Document Control

The control of the manufacturing process documentation is challenge similar to design documentation. ISO 9000 recognizes that fact. So do the FDA and others. However, this is still not reason to place it under the control of the CM Department.

Rule: Manufacturing should be responsible for doing release and change control of process documentation.

Reason: Keep the responsibility and authority together and in the department (Manufacturing) that is responsible for producing that documentation.

The control might be done by each department that creates the documentation or it might be done by a single function. Manufacturing could control the unique part numbers that may be required for tools, fixtures, production equipment, test equipment, etc. They might even assign unique document numbers to process procedures, but that practice is wasteful.

Rule: Identify process sheets with the corresponding design document part number.

Reason: If unique numbers are used, cross reference lists are usually required. Up-keep of, and reference to, these lists is wasteful.

Rule: Manufacturing would maintain each process sheet with its own revision control. They must record the relation of each revision to the design document change.

Reason: Changes can occur to process sheets for many reasons other than the change of design documents.

Perhaps the best way to understand this concept is to take some examples:

Receiving Inspection Process Sheet. It would be identified by the design part number because that is what the vendor is building and shipping to the Receiving Department. The process sheet would explain which dimensions to inspect and with what frequency. The process sheet would state which purchase-order–design-changes should be incorporated in the incoming lot. The process sheet would instruct the inspector as to sample sizes, process control charts, etc. The entire package would be filed by the design part number. Changes would occur to the process sheet for a variety of reasons—change in sampling technique, for example. The revision level of the Inspection process sheet must therefore be relatable to, but not the same as, the CM assigned document revision. Date revision control is often used to accomplish this. When applicable, the corresponding ECO (Engineering Change Order) number is referenced in the "description of change" column of the process sheet revision log.

Test Process Sheet. The Test Engineer would identify the test process sheet for an assembly with the design part number. The TE could maintain a separate revision assignment and log. Revision numbers might be used that are relatable to the assembly drawing (CM revision) only through the log. This allows the TE to make process changes without a corresponding change order.

Fixture Drawing. This drawing might be assigned a manufacturing "Tool Number." It would have a revision block just like a design document but need not be revised by ECO. The description of change would spell out the details necessary to trace the change to its "cause." If an ECO did cause the fixture change, the ECO number would be referenced.

Process Control Summary

Other manufacturing process documents can be treated as described above. Require the level of control (to the entire process documentation set) which is necessary in your kind of business. Are you FDA regulated? Is Lot Control in order? Do any of your parts have a "shelf life" requirement?

In the extreme, the manufacturing process control can be as stringent on process documents as CM controls are on design documents. A separate "MCO" (Manufacturing Change Order) may be required. The master drawings may be removed from the engineers hands upon release, placed under a Manufacturing Engineering administrative control. Companies that are FDA regulated have usually controlled the process documentation in this manner.

In smaller companies, the process document control may be made a CM responsibility. This is a most critical time. The CM Manager must take all possible steps to keep it separated from the design documentation. Release or change the process documentation as a result of design document releases and changes (and other change "causes"). As the company grows, this will make it easier to spin off the responsibility and give it to manufacturing.

Lot Control

Lot control is the traceability of the content of a product by an identifier. Certain materials, parts, assemblies are specified to require lot control. They are specified in customer contracts, agency standards, or company standards. Why is lot control important? This is typically required because of the critical nature of the item to the function of the product. Since processes have some tolerance they work within, and since the process control may not be precise, lot identification and tracking is sometimes required. This may be true whether the item is produced in batches or continuous flow.

Several methods of identifying lots are used in industry. Date coding or lot numbering are typical identifiers. The date code or lot number must be changed when ever a significant change is made to the process sheets.

The date code or lot number must then be tracked through subsequent "mixing" or assembly. This is done by "attaching" the code or number to each subsequent mix or assembly until the final product is completed. The lot or date code(s) in the product are recorded. The end product serial number (or mod or date code) is thus traceable to the exact lot for each required item.

The items which require lot control must be carefully sorted out and noted. The best way to identify them is in the database. A code would be entered to note each item requiring this treatment.

Rule: If Design Engineering is involved in the decision as to which items are lot-controlled, CM should maintain the database. If not, Manufacturing should maintain the database.

Reason: Keep the responsibility and authority together.

The responsibility for lot tracking should be a manufacturing responsibility. Answering customer lot-control questions, hosting agency audits, etc. should be a joint CM and Manufacturing responsibility. CM might coordinate the customer or agency visit, but manufacturing should answer lot control questions.

The manufacturing control number previously mentioned, is a lot number for a lot size of one. Manufacturing must also be responsible for the tracking of this number to the end item.

Shelf Life

The longer you live, the shorter your remaining life! That makes sense. The same sense applies to some of the items in our products. "O" rings are a prime example. You or your customer may require that no ring be assembled with an effective life of less than two years. Your vendors identify and ship you rings that have an effective life of three years or more. The problem, then, is to identify the rings as to their effective life and to trace the product content of "O" rings.

Typical shelf life identification is handled like the grocery store. The vendor is requested to identify the "expiration" date. Identification would usually be by the "bag and tag" method.

As manufacturing assembles the rings, the process sheets should instruct the operators to tag the product with the expiration date. Manufacturing must design a tag(s) which allows traceability of the "O" ring content to specific locations. The tag would have the serial number added and a copy of it stored in either Quality Assurance or CM. The customer would be made aware of this information as the contract requires.

Drawing Proliferation

The appearance of "down-level" (old revision) drawings on the production floor should be of serious concern to any manufacturing person. The product must not be built from down-level prints after the effective date. ISO-9000, FDA, DoD, and most product companies are all rightfully critical of any drawing distribution process which allows this to happen. The best cure is an ounce of prevention. Don't allow design drawings to get onto the manufacturing floor in the first place.

Rule: Drawings should be sent to the manufacturing process sheet writer. They should give the production floor a process sheet. The process sheet includes mini-pictorials, as required. They should review subsequent design changes and make the required process sheet changes.

Reason: Keeps the design drawing file in the hands of a single control function.

Incorporation of design changes into the process sheets is done by the process sheet writer and the process sheet is placed on the production floor on the effective day. If drawings do accompany the process sheet, the old revision level is removed on that day.

It is typical manufacturing practice (and most productive) to have process sheets. But what about the start-up company or the "high end" manufacturer of products like locomotives? They use drawings on the production floor. It is then necessary to purge the drawings from the floor on the effective date. Have someone in *manufacturing* responsible for placing the design drawings on the floor and removing them. This assures that the old drawing is retrieved before putting the new one out. They must also assure that this is done on the effective day or at the effective Serial Number. Production Control may be the logical function to do this.

Drawings are also distributed to Purchasing and Receiving Inspection. Purchasing should also be charged with the responsibility to place the revised drawing with the vendor. Receiving Inspection (or Quality Engineering) would control the receiving inspection process sheet and the drawing. At the correct point in time, they would replace the inspection process sheet and the drawing.

By this method, CM has a limited number of changes and drawings to distribute. The control of down-level prints is then done by the people closest to the production operations. This requirement should be written into the company standards. Each controlling group must destroy the down-level prints on the effective day.

On Time Publications

Many companies suffer from, "We're ready to ship the product but the publications aren't ready." The same thing happens with the revised product. Why can Manufacturing order parts, make parts, buy parts, assemble product, test product, while a few revised sheets of paper cannot be done in the same time? In this case, there is probably a "management problem", not a CM system problem.

The Management must be made aware of the condition and take appropriate action to fix the problem(s). This condition existed at one high tech computer company—the publications were never ready to ship with a new or revised product. After asking a few questions, it was clear that the responsibility for their publications was with another division, across the city. This other division built another product line. You can guess who's products had up-to-date publications! The responsibility was transferred to the producing division. It was surprising how fast the problem cleared up. The management must assure that the publications function is organized by product and located with the producing plant.

CM managers are often burdened with the management edict: "Don't release another change until the publications have been revised". This is a bad decision! Hold up the fix for a serious problem while waiting for publications? Build more scrap or rework while waiting to update the publications? Hold up a cost reduction while waiting for publications?

Address the root-cause of the problem! The publications people aren't brought into the process early enough. Usually the publications people are the last to find out that a new product is being developed or that a change is being made. Get them into both processes early. They should be part of the design team in both the new product release process and the change process.

Publications people can also do many things that will assure the publications are ready to ship when the product is. Some of the actions are:

- Say it once with as few words as possible. Most manufacturers have gone from little or no support literature to far too much. When the pile of paper exceeds the size of your product, something is wrong.

- Don't try to cover all possible combinations of features and options. Cover those that have been sold, and add others as sold.

- Don't try to cover all possible failure modes. Add failure mode data as the frequent failures become apparent.

- Don't hard bind the manuals. Use three-ring or equivalent. This is especially effective when changes are to be incorporated. Thus, replace only the affected pages when a change occurs.

The most significant thing that the management can do is to expect/ demand that the publications be ready when the product is. They must never use the release or change processes to "fix" the problem—it must be addressed directly.

Non-Conforming Material

CM is not normally involved in the non-conforming material process. However, since that process can produce design changes, it should be briefly discussed. Usually a company has a discrepant material form. All items that do not conform to the drawing/specification are tagged and a form completed. A Material Review Board (MRB) is formed of a Design Engineer, Quality Engineer and a Manufacturing Engineer.

All non-conforming material is reviewed daily and dispositioned - return to vendor, rework, scrap, etc. MRB members must treat each problem as importantly as the next. They identify the root-cause of the problem and address the proper fix for the problem. Sometimes a change in design is called for. Usually this is because of a repeated problem with a disposition of "use as is." The above is a condensed version of the normal MRB process.

One company added a wrinkle that is worth considering. A copy of the discrepant material report was sent to CM whenever the decision was made to "change design." This allowed CM to assure that the clock started on that change when the report was dated.

Field Support

The continued trouble-shooting, repair, and maintenance of a product is one of the most difficult and high customer visibility tasks in the manufacturing business. Whether it is done by dealers, your own service people, or the customer himself, this is: "The Customer Satisfaction Test".

The field service is embodied in:

- The people who perform the task.
- The training they receive and give.
- The publications (Maintenance Manual, Illustrated Parts Catalog, Spare Parts List, etc.).

- Field change orders and kits.
- Traceability (Status Accounting) Reports.

The last three are of significance to CM. The field people have an adage—all serious problems occur when the factory is closed. Their dependence upon the publications, field change, and traceability reports is critical. The Publications and traceability reports are discussed elsewhere. The field change order and kit is of special significance to CM.

Field Change Order and Kit

Field Change Orders almost always are a result of a design change to fix a safety problem or to meet product specifications. The FCO is a separate document and originated because an ECO so directed. The ECO should not be held up waiting the FCO. Here are some other "rules" about FCOs:

- Only a class I ECO (non-interchangeable) should be a candidate to result in an FCO.
- Not all class I ECOs need to become an FCO. One company saved over one hundred thousand dollars a year in field change cost by eliminating a "rule" that said: "if the change is class I, an FCO is required."
- The Field Support group should sign all ECOs which "direct" an FCO.
- The Field Support function should write all FCOs and originate a kit of parts for each. People who have done field repair are in the best position to write them. Detailed instructions for incorporation of the kit and subsequent testing are needed.
- The CM group should furnish standard marking / sticker information if identification is required.
- The CM group should furnish a simple, self addressed post card for feedback of the unit serial number (or code) affected.
- The FCO should reference the kit part number. The FCO document should be assigned a part number and that number should be referenced on the kit parts list. The FCO document should thus be included in the kit.

- FCOs might be called "mandatory" (do to all units) or "on failure", however, the Field Engineer is most likely to treat all FCOs as "on failure".

- All FCOs should be modeled and tested. A person, different than the writer, should get a production kit and install it into a production unit and test per the instruction. That person should identify the unit per the instructions and fill out the postcard. A complete "modeling" of the field change is the best way to assure the field people of a quality field change.

Many companies do not have a field change problem. Those that do have many problems in this area that might be solved by taking some or all of the above steps.

ISO 9000

The International Standards Organization has done an outstanding job of writing make-sense, minimum logical requirements for a quality operation. An excellent overview, analysis and perspective of ISO 9000 can be found in the April 1993 issue of *Tooling and Production* magazine in an article by the senior editor, Donald R. Stovicek.

It is significant to note that the vast majority of the 9000 - 9004 series of standards are Engineering Documentation Control / Configuration Management kinds of requirements. Seminar attendees report that a majority of the "gigs" received upon ISO audit are for documentation control issues. This is international recognition of the significance of Configuration Management.

Since most of ISO 9000 requirements are for make-sense engineering documentation control, those requirements will not be repeated again. For example, ISO rightfully places high emphasis on the product specification. The key nature of product specifications is discussed throughout this text. They are also very concerned about down-level drawing proliferation. That issue is covered elsewhere in this text.

ISO also says "the supplier shall establish and maintain procedures to control and verify the design of the product in order to ensure that the specified requirements are met". Since the ISO requirements and many product specifications are very general, a company can choose to do the minimum or choose to do something more. In that process, a significant issue remains. What is currently being done in any given company may be ill-conceived, slow, wasteful, and even counter-productive. ISO doesn't care about such issues as long as the requirements are met. Thus, there are three ways that ISO certification can be approached:

- Document minimum requirements without seeking improvement, and then seek certification.
- Document minimum requirements, seek certification and pursue improvement afterwards.
- Pursue improvements as the documenting is done, then seek certification.

Each company launching into this venture needs to make a conscious decision as to which course it will follow.

6

Product and Document Release

As previously discussed, the release of the product and its documentation should be an evolutionary process. Concurrently, the manufacturing support planning and process development should take place. Design Engineering is developing the product, Manufacturing is developing the production process, and Field Support is developing the service and maintenance plans and process. Each is communicating its needs and plans to the others through the Design Team. Each is presenting its needs for the drawing, specification, and BOM. The Design Team is costing the alternatives, and settling individual issues as they occur. They meet with the management to review progress on a regular basis. When a single drawing is agreed upon, it can be released. This is evolution of the product and its documentation. It is the fastest approach to new product release.

Life Cycle Phases

As this process takes place, the management (or your customer) will impose certain major milestones to pass. These milestones (or baselines as they are more frequently called) divide the project into phases. These phases are called by different names at different companies. Our Loader Company will use the D^2 - P^3 terminology pictured in Figure 32.

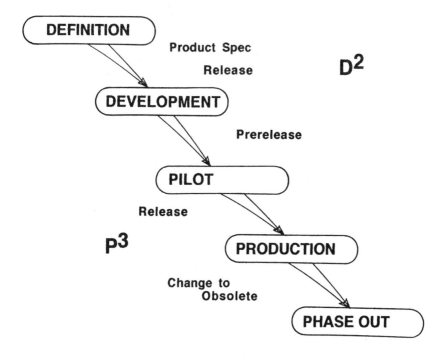

Figure 32. Product/documentation release phases.

Some companies choose to have more or fewer than five phases, although five is most typical by my experience. Some companies have a field operation phase. Some treat obsolesence as a separate phase. The DoD defines the line between phases as baselines—Functional, Allocated and Product. Commercially the phases are divided by "releases," or in the case of obsolesence, by a document(s) change. The distinguishing "event" (Product Spec Release, Prerelease, Release, and Obsolete Change Release) between phases, in a commercial environment, is also shown in Figure 32.

Rule: The phases and baselines to be used at your company need to be defined and agreed upon.

Reason: This is a matter of defining communications and management expectations. The people in a given company have come from different experiences and tend to use different terminology. However, they may or may not mean the same thing. Communication barriers start to come down with the definition of common terms.

Documents Tied To Release Phase

These are product *and document* life cycle phases. Since the product is defined by its documentation, it is necessary to tie these phases to the documentation. Since the development of the product is evolutionary, it is necessary to be able to look at any single document and tell which phase it "represents." This is sometimes done by stamping the document. For example: "OK for Pilot Build." More often, companies use the revision block to indicate the applicable phase. The diagram in Figure 33 indicates how the product and its documentation are "tied together" by use of the revision.

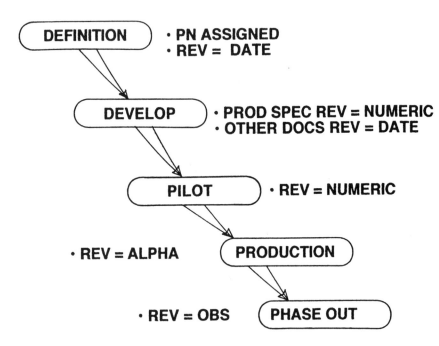

Figure 33. Release Phases and Revision Levels.

In this case, a blank or dash in the revision field indicates that the document is in the "definition" phase. This means that the designer will need to use the "date" field to keep track of the changes. In the "development" phase, also use a blank or dash revision. This choice is made purposely— to reserve the revision field only for CM use.

The Product Specification is an exception because it was prereleased (revision number control) the day after the project was started. In the pilot phase the documents will be a numerical revision. In the "production" phase, use the <u>alpha</u> revision. When it is determined that an item will no longer be produced, place a notation of "obs" in the revision field.

Rule: A standard is needed for a company which defines how to relate the revision block to the development phases.

Reason: It should be apparent by looking at a document, which phase it may be used in.

It must be kept in mind that the above refers to documents developed uniquely for this program. The program will use other items already released. Those items remain in a released condition. Sometimes companies reverse the roll of the alpha and numeric. That is OK providing they are consistent. In no case should a drawing or specification that is under the engineer's control be done by revision letters or numbers. The engineer-controlled drawing should always use date control.

The Revision Block

As a result of these rules, the revision block on a particular document could, over time, look like Figure 34.

Life Cycle Phase Issues

It is also necessary to resolve several other issues in respect to the development phases:

- Location of, and control over, the "master" drawing.
- Whether or not the drawing will be microfilmed, digitized, etc.
- Formality of the change control process.
- Associated MRP codes.
- Names to call the units built during that phase.
- Budget responsibility for the units built in that phase
- Kind of test that will be required to progress to the next phase.
- Kind of management and / or customer review required.
- Management and / or customer approvals required to proceed.

REV	DATE	DESCRIPTION	ECO	SIGN
_	3-21-94	drafted	_	engr
_	3-29-94	redraw	_	engr
1 *	4-12-94	Released to Pilot	248	CM
2	4-17-94	Changed orientation	283	CM
3	4-20-94	Finish note added	280	CM
A **	4-27-94	Tested & Release to Prod	302	CM
B	5-11-94	Changed front tire O D	324	CM
C	5-30-94	See ECO	352	CM
D	4-20 95	Changes material	589	CM
OBS	8-04-02	Not used for new designs	2040	CM

* **Move Master Document from Engineering to Master File and Start Informal Change Control**

** **Start Formal Change Control**

Figure 34. Document Revision Block.

Baseline-Phase Relationships

These phases need to be company / business unit decisions. That is, each product/project within the business unit should not make independent decisions. Allowing each program to develop its own rules invites chaos. The best way to develop these "release rules" is to write a standard which includes a relationship chart such as that in Figure 35.

Rule: Every company should have a standard on "Product and Documentation Release" which includes a chart that crisply defines these relationships. The chart must be devoid of lines/arrows crossing baselines. The standard and the chart must also be free of "ifs," "ands," or "buts."

Reason: The terminology and the tie between the product and its documentation must be clear. It represents the manner in which the evolutionary design process is to be monitored. Communications are much clearer.

PHASE	UNIT NAME	CHANGE CONTROL	REV	DWG
DEFINITION (Concept)	Breadboard or Development	Engr	Date	Engr
PRODUCT SPEC BASELINE / PRELIMINARY DESIGN REVIEW				
DEVELOP-MENT	Prototype or Development	Engr	Date	Engr
DESIGN BASELINE / CRITICAL DESIGN REVIEW				
PILOT	Pilot Prepro Qual	Informal	Number	CM
PRODUCTION BASELINE / QUALIFICATION TEST REVIEW				
PRODUC-TION	Production	Formal	Letter	CM
PHASE OUT (Obsolete)	NA	No Longer "used on" any application	OBS	M'Film

Figure 35. Baseline / Phase relationships.

It is important to note that "passing a baseline" doesn't mean that all the product's drawings and specifications need to be pulled and identified with a common date or stamp or ECO number. This is a waste of time if the suggested rules are followed.

Product Definition Phase

In the Front End Loader Company, the standard which describes the Definition Phase will address:

- The kind of testing that the breadboard model will be subjected to.
- That change control is in the hands of the responsible designer.
- That revision control will be only by date.
- The master drawing will be under the Cognizant Engineer's control.
- Prerelease of the Product Specification immediately after the project is approved.
- A meeting(s) of the Design Team with the top management (Preliminary Design Review) to examine the:
  1. Latest Product Specification.
  2. Test results and the breadboard model.
  3. Product cost estimates, pricing, contracts, etc.
- If the management (and the customer if applicable) approve, the Product Specification will be "released" (rev "A" and under formal CM change control).

Note that progress from the Definition Phase to the Development Phase is marked by two milestones—completion of the Preliminary Design Review and revision of the Product Specification. Successful passing of these two milestones constitutes passing the Product Specification Baseline.

Rule: When the management (and customer if applicable) determine that the Preliminary Design and Product Specification are acceptable, the Product Specification must be released or revised if it has already been released. The reason for and description of change is the "completed preliminary design review."

Reason: To document the fact that the Product Specification is agreed to and the date the agreement was accomplished. Track specification changes.

Notice that the Product Specification has "skipped" the Development Phase. This puts the document under formal change control and assures that Manufacturing and others are involved in any further changes.

Product Development Phase

The company standard for the Development Phase will describe that phase by addressing the following issues:

- The kind of tests that are required for the prototype unit(s).
- That change control will still be with the responsible designer (except the Product Specification).
- Revision control will continue to be done by date only (except Product Specification).
- The drawings remain in the designer's hands (except the Product Specification).
- Item-by-item prerelease is encouraged. At prerelease, the revision changes to numeric (Rev 1 description of change = "pilot prerelease"). The drawing is now under informal change control. The master drawing goes to CM control.
- The designer and the field support person will make a prereleased spares item list.
- A meeting of the Design Team and the top management to examine;
    1. The latest Product Specification.
    2. The Prototype Unit and the test results.
    3. The evolving costed BOM, pricing issues, etc.
- If management (and customer if applicable) approves, the remaining drawings and specifications must now be prereleased.
- The Product Specification must be revised (next letter) because: "critical design review is complete." This should be done whether or not there are changes to the specification.

Note that progress from the Development Phase to the Pilot Phase is marked by three milestones: completion of the Critical Design Review, prerelease of the remainder of the drawings and specifications, and revision of the Product Specification. This constitutes passing of the Design Baseline.

Rule: When approved to pass the Design Baseline, all the master drawings and specifications must be in CM. *Informal* change control will now be administered by CM. (Except the Product Specification which is under formal change control)

Reason: To document the completion of the Critical Design Review and the date it was accomplished. Tracking of progress is visible on the documents. Risk is minimized.

Just as the Product Specification can and should be released prior to the Preliminary Design Review, so should some of the drawings be prereleased prior to the Critical Design Review. After all, this process should be an evolution—not revolution. The long lead items should be prereleased to allow purchase of the pilot parts. The test specification may have to be prereleased to allow Test Engineering to proceed. Parts or assemblies used from existing designs would have been previously released. Evolutionary prerelease must be encouraged to avoid bunching the work and the resulting delays.

Product Pilot Phase

In the Pilot Phase, the Loader Company will include the following in the standard:

- The kind of tests that are required for the pilot unit(s).
- That informal change control will be with CM.
- Revision control will be numeric.
- The master drawings must now all be under CM's control.
- Formal release on an item by item basis will be encouraged.
- Engineering and field support will review the spares item list for release.
- A meeting of the Design Team and the top management to examine:
    1. The latest Product Specification.
    2. The Pilot Unit(s) and the test results.
    3. The latest costed BOM, pricing issues, etc.
- If management (and customer if applicable) approve, the remaining drawings and specifications must be alpha released.
- The Product Specification will be revised (to the next alpha revision), whether or not changes are made.

Progress from the Pilot Phase to the Production Phase is marked by three milestones: completion of the Qualification Test Review, all drawings alpha released, and the Product Specification revised (next alpha character). This constitutes passing of the Production Baseline.

Rule: The product must be approved and listed by any and all certifying agencies prior to formal (alpha) release. The end product document shall not be alpha released until such approval and listing has been obtained.

Reason: Product liability risk too high to do otherwise.

Rule: All critical components must be qualified (tested) before formal release. Design Engineering, Manufacturing, and Field Support must agree on which components are critical.

Reason: Assures the repeatable quality of the component and assures that there is an agreed-upon method of testing it.

Rule: No assembly may be formally released (alpha rev) until all its part drawings, assembly documents, specifications, and referenced documents have been formally released.

Reason: Minimize the risk. Keeps people from being misled by the revision status on the documents or in the MRP system.

The production of the product entails significant dollar expenditures. It should be done only if confidence in the design is high enough to formally release. The product cost is now very quantifiable. The BOM is in place and can be accurately costed. Notice that the product cost is a subject for constant review as the product design, the drawings, and the BOM evolve.

The budget authorization should also be a subject of constant review. This helps to assure development cost stays within goals. It also aids the evolutionary release progress by authorizing spending for portions of the next phase: long lead items, tooling, etc.

Product Production Phase

The drawings and specification masters are under CM control. The *letter* revision is used. Formal (but fast) change control will be used. If the Design Team has done its' job well, fewer changes will result. The Loader Company will now prosper from the profits on this product.

Product Phase-Out

Lastly, when the product is no longer to be produced, the Front End Loader Company will:

- Check the Used On for every item.
- Those items unique to the obsolete product, will be revised to indicate "Not used in current production" in the reason for change block and enter "OBS" in the revision block.

Several issues arise in this phase that are highly individual company-dependent:

- The definition of "obsolete," "superseded," "canceled," "redrawn," etc.
- What if an item is still on a spare item list but is not in production?
- What do applicable agency specifications require?
- What are the company support life requirements?
- What are the liability issues?

All of the related factors must be analyzed and definitions written accordingly. The significance of this "phase" is dependent upon the complexity of these and other issues. The action required is usually to make a document change (by the normal change process) in order to implement the necessary terminology into the database, on the face of the drawing, and / or in the revision block.

There is a key to making this "phase out" a practical day to day event. Look for obsolesence of each deleted part on each design change. If the part has no Used On, obsolete it as part of that change.

Management of the Release Process

Written approved standard(s) allow the company to proceed with the development in an orderly fashion. It is not a reason to expect every product to be done identically, however. The management can use the standard to manage by exception.

Example: Since the FEL-200 is a spin-off of the FEL-100, management may choose to bypass the Definition Phase by starting the project with an agreed-upon specification.

Example: The management may have high confidence in receiving
Underwriters Laboratory approval, and may therefore
decide to alpha release and to risk building deliverable
units expecting agency approval *prior* to shipment

Some companies have *many* exceptions. But this should not be a
reason to do without a standard. On the contrary, a standard will yield
understanding as to what is to occur if there are no management exceptions.
This gives management the normal condition against which to consider
exceptions. The standard, therefore, is the basis for "management by
exception."

Many companies may decide to proceed even if all the rules have
not been met. This is typically done after a Deviation is written and
approved. The Deviation spells out the exceptions that are allowed, the
person who will clear that item and their committed date for clearing.

A company without a standard will tend to have a totally different
method used on each product it develops. The confusion will tend to
lengthen the development process. It has been demonstrated that it is
better to have a standard and to be flexible about its application.

MRP Status Codes

Most MRP BOM systems have the ability to identify part numbers
with a "Status" code. This code is in the item master file (database). It will
typically print out on key reports, such as the Purchasing Decision Reports.

Different codes / acronyms are used in different systems. In one
case, the MRP system has three codes—NIS, PRE, and REL. Include in
the release standard a definition of each. The definition must be compatible
with the document release revision status. Example:

NIS = Part Number Assigned but not prereleased.

PRE = Numeric Revision, is prereleased.

REL = Alpha Revision, is released.

This allows the status of the part (in MRP) and the status of the
document (Rev) to be compatible. The coding in the database is for
everyone to see and use. It is another necessity to "bridging the gap."

Release Form

Some companies design a special form to accomplish the release
of a drawing, spec, etc. The information which must be captured for any

release is:

- Product and / or project number.
- Document or part number(s) released.
- Reason for release (Production Release, Phase out, etc.)
- Test record per the applicable baseline.
- Management meeting that gave authority to pass the baseline.
- Revision level (numeric or alpha)
- Approval(s).
- Dates of release.
- Number (control or form sequence number).

When parts are released, they may not have a "home," such as long lead item release prior to structuring. The formal Used On relationship will come when a parts list is released.

Almost every element above must already be on the design change form. Because of this overlap, the same form is often used for release and change. This issue is very much a matter of a personal preference. Thus, if your company has a separate form or uses the same form, and it works, don't change it.

If you prefer a separate form, layout the above information and you will have a sound release form. The release form is also a very good automation application. Put it on line for sign off and distribution.

Release Checklist

In order for any release to be accepted into CM, it should pass a check/reject point. The checklist will be different for each baseline. The list can be prepared from the baseline standard. Put the checklist into the Release Standard, and have it approved by the appropriate top management. This checklist should have a series of crisp 'yes' or 'no' questions. A partial checklist for formal release follows:

- Have all drawings been properly signed?
- Are all drawings in accordance with the applicable standard(s)?
- Are marked-up drawings (for "same as except" conditions) in accordance with the mark-up standard?

- Are all the documents to be released included or previously released?
- Have standard parts and assemblies been used where possible?
- Before an assembly is alpha released, have all its parts been formally released?
- Before the product is alpha released
    1. Has everything in the structure been alpha released?
    2. Has the management approved baseline requirements?
    3. Has applicable agency approval been obtained?
    4. Have all the document numbers assigned to the project been accounted for? (need not hold up product release)

Checklists are a summary of the requirements in the standards that you wish CM to look for.

Rule: Every company should have a set of agreed-upon release criteria that is put into a standard in the form of a checklist.

Reason: To attain a release by release-auditing of standard release requirements.

Rule: Before an item can be formally released, it must pass the checklist standard. If it fails any part of that checklist it cannot be released. CM assures this.

Reason: The agreed-upon requirements must be met.

Application of a well thought-out and agreed upon checklist will aid in management by exception.

Closing the Gap in Pilot

The Design Team has helped close the gap between Design Engineering and the rest of the Company. The tendency is to dissolve the team when the Pilot Production Phase starts. "We're done with that design, now lets move on to the next challenge." This is the worst possible thing that can happen. If fact, the Design Team should not only stay essentially intact during pilot, but:

Rule: The Design Team should move physically into the pilot production area. Perhaps not every design engineer but certainly the Project Engineer and all the non-engineering representatives should move lock, stock, and desk into the pilot area. This includes the CM representative if he or she is dedicated half time or better to the project. They should continue to meet regularly although less frequently.

Reason: The team spirit that has developed must be held together until the design is built and tested by production workers. Problems will arise and the communications are much faster and more accurate when these people are together.

If the Design Team has functioned well to this point, the volume of problems / changes required is relatively low. However, they will still occur. The design change process should be administered by CM during pilot. It should be informal (under numeric revision control). This might mean that only the Design Engineer and CM are required to sign the change. At the very most, <u>one</u> Manufacturing representative may be added to the sign-off.

When released to production, the Manufacturing Engineer should rotate into production. The team, although diminished in numbers, should move to the production area. This is critical to good communications and training of the new people involved. They will phase out of that product as the problems diminish.

Catch 22

As time progresses, the change control process begins. If the release <u>or</u> change processes are slow and cumbersome, the engineers will be reluctant to release the documents. They will tend to hold them and release them in bunches only when absolutely required. If this is done, there will be times when little is occurring and times when batches of documents are released together.

This batching slows the process. In turn, the engineers view this slow progress as reason to hold documents under their control as long as possible. If the change process is cumbersome, it amplifies the batch affect. It is therefore critical that CM design and implement fast release and change processes. Much more is said about the fast change process in Ch. 9.

The Release Process

As previously discussed, the release process must be evolutionary. It must be in parallel with the design and concurrent engineering team process. The document release process must handle a single drawing, assembly documentation, a group of parts, documents, or a combination of these.

The checklist will vary but the process can be the same for any phase. One systematic way of quickly releasing documents is needed. First, examine the tasks that need to be performed during this release system.

Release Process Tasks

For the Front End Loader Company, the release process will use the change form with the minimum release blocks completed. On this form (or on the documents to be released), will be indicators about the following activities:

Design Team Review Completed. The signature of the Design Engineer who created the document is in the title block. By policy, that engineer is required to sign after the team has reviewed the document. This gives an opportunity to incorporate ideas from the rest of the team.

New Drawing Sign-Off. The Manufacturing Engineer (and possibly the Field Engineer if the item is field replaceable) must also sign the document. Recall that their signatures may be in the title block or in the margin.

"Same As Except." The mark up of similar drawings will be accepted as "new" drawings. The mark up must be done with high discipline as described in the chapter on change control (Ch. 8). These drawings must be signed by the Design Engineer and ME (and the FE if the item is field replaceable).

Item / Unit Testing. An indication that the testing required by the applicable baseline has been satisfactorily completed. Typically the unit serial number(s) tested and a reference to the test report should appear on the form. The testing might be for a component, assembly or the entire product—whatever level is being released.

Initiation Of The Release Form. The Cognizant Engineer must initiate the form with the required information. This must be done neatly so that it does not have to be redone in CM. The Drafting Department or CM might be helping the engineer, but the responsibility remains with the

Cognizant Engineer. The Cognizant Engineer then puts the form and the documents to be released together and gives the package to CM.

CM Check. CM immediately reviews the package against the checklist. This is a "go" - "no go" point. If all items are acceptable, CM will proceed. If any item(s) are not acceptable, the specific requirements are noted and the package is rejected.

Rule: Once passing this check, the release will not be stopped, revised, put on hold, etc. The release has passed a point of no return.

Reason: Discourages frivolous release actions.

CM Accepts (Signs). If all items are checked and correct, the CM Technician immediately signs the release form (ECO), assigns it a control number (ECO number) and assigns the applicable revision number or letter. This is an indication that the release is technically acceptable. The date is noted on the release form.

Drafting Of "Same As Except." CM can make new drawings or add tabs to existing drawings from the mark-ups (same as except). With the release form as authority, they can enter the engineer's name as "creator," thus "signing" the drawings. CM is responsible for the exact translation of the mark-up.

Support Documents. The applicable support documents (catalog, maintenance manual) are created or expanded as a result of the release. They do not become part of the release package. When the support documents are complete, a release form copy is sent from Publications to CM. If they are to be microfilmed, then the notice of completion is sent after filming.

Input To MRP. All design item data and assembly data must be input to the database. The accuracy must be checked by comparing an output report to the input parts list. CM should do this for all design elements. They do not hold entry while waiting for manufacturing data entry or support data entry. Those activities occur as a result of the release.

Manufacturing Release. CM matches the MRP output parts list with the package. The release form and package are reproduced as minimally as possible and distributed. The date is recorded. The form can be liberally distributed but the documents should only need to be copied for manufacturing once. The copy would be divided among the ME, TE, Buyer, etc. If they need more copies they should go to the print room. This saves time, cost and trees.

Manufacturing Notification Of Release. Manufacturing was, of course, amply represented on the design team. The receipt of a copy of the release should therefore not be a surprise to them. The release form is their formal authority to use the items released for that phase. Their process documentation is *not* part of the release package. The manufacturing data is added to the MRP as a result of the release. A copy of the release form is returned to CM as an indication of completion of the manufacturing data entry.

Microfilm Complete. After all the items to be microfilmed, imaged, digitized or otherwise preserved are completed, the release form is returned to CM noted "Preservation Complete."

Close The Loop. The various functions noted above have notified CM of the completion of their tasks or of receipt of the package. As each notification is received, CM notes the date and, when all are received, CM closes the release.

The above list constitutes the elements of the release process. Those elements imply some procedural steps, but are not complete from a process standpoint. The temptation is strong to merely put this list into a written procedure (standard) and sit back and relax. After all, these are the tasks that need to be performed to release, aren't they?

Release Procedure / Flow Diagram

Number these activities one through fourteen. One could then boast that we have a procedure. Indeed we would. It would be a string of fourteen tasks in series and would probably be performed in that same sequence. Performed in serial fashion, it would be the longest possible path for release. It would be a series process.

This would not constitute an efficient system, however. To create an efficient system one question needs to be asked, "What is the arrangement of these tasks to produce the shortest possible path from start to finish?" Or stated another way, "What tasks can be done in parallel?"

To create a fast system, the relationship between each task must be carefully examined. What task(s) is required to be completed before this task can be completed? What other task is dependent upon completion of this task? For example:

- The team must review the new documents before they are signed.
- Documents must be signed before the engineer signs the release ECO.

- The documents must be with the release ECO to pass the checklist.

Add "responsibility" to each task and put circles around each activity / responsibility. The result is the start of a flow diagram. See Figure 36.

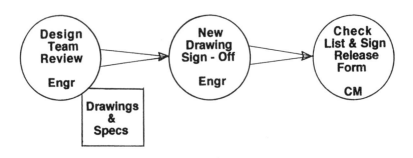

Figure 36. Starting a Flow Diagram.

Notice that responsibility is always singular. The Cognizant Engineer can't do the team review, but he or she is <u>responsible</u> to assure that it occurs. CM might be chartered to call the team meetings, to keep action items, etc., but this doesn't take away the responsibility of the Cognizant Engineer.

Next, take every task involved and carefully examine each relationship. This *systematic* approach will put tasks together into a process. It is *a picture worth a thousand words.* See Figure 37

If the design team is working, the only functions that sign the release document are Design Engineering and CM. Manufacturing and Field Support (if affected) had one representative sign the drawing or marked-up drawing.

After the "same as except" mark-ups are made into new masters, only CM signed them. Many companies use this approach. The responsibility for clear and correct mark-up is the engineers. The responsibility of correct incorporation of the mark-up into the master belongs to Configuration Management.

The point of origination of the release form is noted. To clarify, a few notes may be added. Too many notes, however, is an indication that

standards are needed. The titles of the task are traceable to the task list.
We could have numbered the tasks and shown the numbers on the flow
diagram.

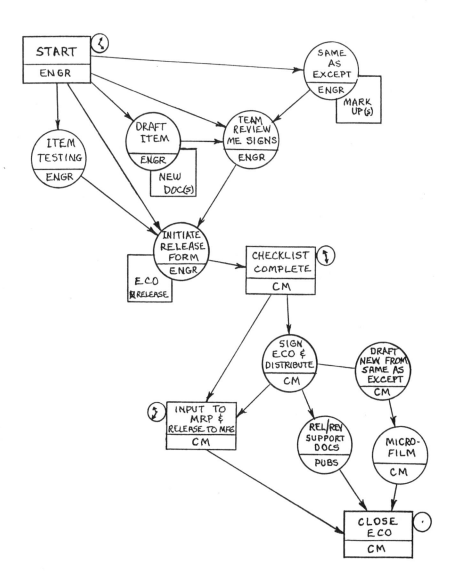

Figure 37. Release process Flow Diagram.

Rule: Do *not* write procedures to describe a system. Make a flow diagram and put the flow diagram and task list into a standard.

Reason: Although it can be done, the description of relationships is difficult and confusing when in procedural form. Parallel relationships are particularly hard to describe. The picture is also a better training tool.

This is now a release *process.* All of the required tasks are in their proper relationship and documented into a standard.

Measure The Process Time

Measurement, in and of itself, tends to improve performance. Don't try to measure every point in the process. This is a common mistake. It yields so much data that it is difficult to pick out what is important.

Rule: Measure the Release Process time in meaningful pieces, and report the results to the top management.

Reason: The project goal was to beat the competition to the market. Tracking release time will allow future projects to learn even better ways to handle the release. This will yield a constant improvement program.

The key points in this system are flagged with a small "clock." There are four clocks dividing the process into three parts. Each measured point in the process needs to be described in the task list or in the standard. The above task list described the "Checklist Complete," "Release To Manufacturing," and "Close;" each is a major process milestone. These are three of the four points to measure. The fourth is the "start" point. The "start" milestone is an arbitrary date. It could be the first date that the release was discussed at a team meeting. Probably the best choice is the program start date. Some companies use the first team meeting date. Consistency from program to program is the significant part of this choice.

Visibility

Measurement of the Release process time will be most effective if the results are made very visible. All the dates can be kept in logs. A more visible method is to log all the dates on each release form. Each week or month a chart or graph can be prepared to show project management and top management how long the major portions take.

For example:

March Releases - in Work Days

Project	Start to Checklist	Checklist Release to Mfg	Mfg Release to Close
FEL-100	28	3	4
FEL-200	39	2	4

In time, comparisons can be made against historical averages for that type of product. Benchmark the performance with other companies in your kind of business. Goals can be set. For example, *one day* is usually a realistic goal from Checklist to Release to Manufacturing, if the MRP system allows on line ("real time") up-date. If the MRP only allows over night update, two days is typically a realistic goal.

Post the results and goals in prominent locations. Send them to the top management. Review them with your people. Make CM the source of reliable release time reporting.

This writer is not alone in believing that the process time is very important. R. D. Garwood stated in a white paper, *"The single Most Important Factor In Determining a Products Profitability is Time To Market!"* The fast release process is such an important company strategy that:

Golden Rule: The Time To Release Is Critical To Profitability.

7

The Need to Change

If the Design Team functions properly, the number of design changes required should decrease. It is, however, unrealistic to believe that the need to change can be eliminated. Humans do not do everything right the first time. And, we engineers are human. Besides, what is thought to be "right" when the design was released, can change as well. Compression of the new product design and release "window" also results in changes. If a mind-set of *constant improvement* is taught and followed, changes will result. This is not to encourage changes solely to exceed the Product Specification without a plan. It is to encourage changes which are cost reductions or to meet the specification, including safety standards and failure rate specifications.

Some needs are identified by customers when using the product. Some needs are recognized by the Field Engineer when maintaining the product. Some are identified by the production people when assembling the product. Some while testing the product.

The question is *not* whether or not changes will become necessary, but rather, *how quickly do we recognize the need to change, and respond to that need.*

Field Failures

Listen to your customers. React to their questions, complaints, reports, feelings, and suggestions. *Every* communication from a customer should be logged and followed to conclusion. Every communication should

152

be divided into its parts and every part followed to a conclusion (closed loop). Every portion of a customer communication that pertains to the product, should be sent to the Project Engineer for evaluation. Every customer letter should be copied for each engineer who might be affected. The management must <u>train</u> people to do this, <u>demand</u> that it be done, and *do it themselves.*

Rule: Have a simplistic form that captures the date, customer name, persons name and comment about any design or function related issue. Positive comment, negative comment or questions must be fed back to the cognizant engineer. Require its use.

Reason: Doing so will allow a competitive edge. It is too easy for a sales person, field person, or manager to "write off" a problem because it is the first time *they* have heard about it.

By these methods, the information indicating potential problems are in the hands of the person *responsible* to fix them. Let the Project Engineer respond to the customer and copy the sales person or who ever received the communication. In this manner, and only in this manner, will the engineers be able to make the quantitative and qualitative judgments which are his or hers to make.

Larger companies may have a Field Service organization that takes all customer problems. This works very effectively when they are well trained. They respond to problems which they are confident about, and refer others to the Project Engineer or Cognizant Engineer.

Keep track of the elapsed time from receipt to response. This is probably a Field Service or QA function, not CM. Report the turn-around time to top management.

Keep track of the data in a systematic way and also send the data / reports to the Project Engineer and Design Management. Do not let the report be the first time the engineer hears about a problem, however. No matter how meaningful and timely the failure reports are, they do not have the impact that one-at-a-time communications do.

Reliability And Other Test Data

This data is normally fed back to the responsible engineers in a report form. This is satisfactory providing the report is timely. Again a response to each item should be expected on a timely basis. CM doesn't normally take part in this process either.

Production Problems

When the machinist or assembly operator believe that they have a design problem or wish to request a change, there needs to be a simple method of communicating to the Cognizant Engineer. This could be a simple form to fill out. This form is most often called a Request For Change. If your company doesn't like forms, the telephone number of the Cognizant Engineer on a list will suffice. The change form should not be used for reasons that will be discussed.

Rule: All the production people should be given a brief training session by CM or their own management as to the method for identifying problems / requesting changes.

Reason: This helps to assure feedback from an important source of problems in the quickest fashion.

Have CM train the production management and they, in turn, train their people. Coordinate the training with the Manufacturing Engineering Department so that distinctions can be made between design and process documentation / changes. The information required on the request for change should be limited. Keep it simple. Prepare a form and form instruction that indicates which blocks *must* be completed by the requester.

Request For Change

Getting feedback to the designer from anyone inside the company can be done with a very simple form (and the associated training). The information required by the Cognizant Engineer is:

- Originator's name and phone number
- Origination date and date forwarded
- Description of the problem / justification for changing / reason for change
- Description of fix (if known)
- Document / Part Number(s) affected
- Control number
- Used On / Product(s) affected
- Cognizant Engineer's decision: accept / reject
- Reason for rejection

The form is therefore very simple. See Figure 38.

Engineering Change Request	EC³ Corp	ECR #
REASON FOR CHANGE / DESCRIPTION OF PROBLEM		

DOCUMENT # / ITEM # / PRODUCT # (AS KNOWN)

PROPOSED SOLUTION (IF KNOWN) (ATTACH MARK UPS IF POSSIBLE)

REQUESTERS NAME	PHONE NO
REASON FOR ACCEPTANCE / REJECTION	

ENGINEER SIGN	PHONE #	DATE	PG of PGS
CM DATE RECEIVED	CM TECHNICIAN		DATE TO ENGR
DATE RECEIVED FROM ENGR	DATE BACK TO REQUESTER		

CM # 001

Figure 38. Request Form.

Avoid Temptation

Avoid the temptation to add more information than is shown. The more information added, the higher the likelihood that you are trying to "preprocess" the actual change. This is a mistake that many companies make. They add disposition of materials, effectivity, approvals, etc., etc. There seems to be an irresistible urge to start processing the change before the Cognizant Engineer has even heard about the problem.

One large computer company had a 120-day process time. Upon examination it was obvious that the same information was on the request form as was on the change form. In fact, the request was going through a process that was very similar to the change. The information and decisions made during the request process were near identical. The difference was that the request cycle was on the basis of "what if we made this change," while the change process was on the basis of "we will make this change." The result was that all the information and decisions made during request had to be reviewed during the change process. Many times the information changed because of the elapsed time between the request and the change. The cognizant engineer was also in the process. It was his / her decision to accept the request, reject it, or recognize the problem while designing a different fix. Examination showed that the first pass (during request) was essentially wasted. They took forty-two days out of the process by "boiling down" the information required at request.

Rule: Do not try to "preprocess" a request as a "what if we change."

Reason: It will be a waste of time and energy because even if the design remains as requested, the time lapse will require review of all prior work. The Cognizant Engineer is also likely to design a different fix.

Rule: The request for change should contain only enough information to allow the Cognizant Engineer to make a decision as to whether or not there is a problem that needs fixing.

Reason: The Cognizant Engineer needs to recognize the problem and determine what is the best fix prior to processing the change.

Realize that we are dealing with the *design* of the product. There-
fore, there is no reason for the Production Supervisor, Manufacturing
Engineer, Production Engineer, Industrial Engineer, or anyone else (except
CM) to get between the requester and the Cognizant Engineer. These
people can submit a request of their own if they wish. They should not edit,
modify or change the request. Above all they should not delay the request.
The easiest way of assuring this is not to allow them in the request process.
Most of these people are on, or are represented on, the design team. The
single exception is to have the CM organization log each request to assure
timely response.

A good way of designing this process is with a multiple copy form
(snap set). The requester can keep a copy while another copy is returned
with the Engineer's decision as to change or not to change (request
rejected).

The Request Flow

Assuming that the CM Department is in the flow, the flow diagram
for change requests would appear as shown in Figure 39.

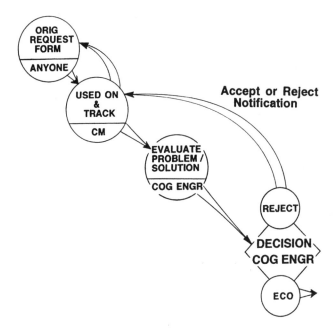

Figure 39. Request process flow.

The CM Department is also in the flow to add the "Used On." This is done so that the Cognizant Engineer knows all the applications affected. They must also assure a timely response—either positive or negative—to the requester. Does the responsible engineer accept the problem as a legitimate one, or not?

Configuration Management should also measure the throughput time and report on the results. Again the average throughput time should be reported to the top management in engineering and manufacturing. The management should set a goal for the average throughput time expected. Ten work days, for example, might allow ample time to process the paper through CM and for the design Engineer to accept or reject the problem. This might allow two days to process the paper (one on either "end") and eight days for the Engineer to analyze the problem.

Remember, this process is not closed until the "accept" or "reject" is returned to the requester. This point is also the start of the change process covered in chapters 8 and 9.

Costing a Change

Pressure to change comes from many directions. Most needs are legitimate. Sorting out which needs are legitimate and which aren't is the challenge. The costing of changes is the missing element.

Most companies do not cost the change before it is released. It is often said that "we cost our changes and the average change costs $725." What was done was to add up the budget for the Configuration Management functions and divide that number by the number of changes in the same period. The result is *not* the cost of the change—it is the administrative cost *per* change. This is not a bad number to have, however. If you network with other similar companies and compare functions and cost per change. This is a good number to use for the cost of "records only" changes. The cost of a product change is usually more significant than just CM costs, however.

Design and Development Cost

Another significant cost is the time to analyze, design, model, test, and communicate the design change. This is a cost that the engineer usually evaluates before launching any significant change. This is crucial to estimate when a change is intended to reduce manufacturing or field service costs.

A benefit of Concurrent Engineering / Design Teams is that the cost estimation can take place in well-led teams. The Industrial Engineer can estimate the design, manufacturing and field related costs *even before* extensive development time is invested. Such "Value Engineering" analysis is an invaluable cost-avoidance measure. It might be done before the request for change is accepted or rejected. The cost might be "fairly obvious" or "not an issue." The decision would be made by the team leader. The IE would be estimating the effectivity of the change (by consultation), the disposition of the old design parts, etc. in order to prepare a cost estimate.

The design and development costs must be weighed against the product, manufacturing and field related costs.

Manufacturing and Field Costs

Generally, the most significant (and most ignored) of all change costs is the manufacturing and field support related costs. These costs are not necessarily apparent to the engineer making the change. The affect of the change on the vendor, fixtures, test equipment, etc., are costs that one could expect the Cognizant Engineer to analyze and estimate. However, this will probably take a "back seat" and or not get done in a quantitative manner. You can also call in the Accounting Department and expect them to estimate the change cost. Better to place the responsibility where most of the cost is—in Manufacturing.

Rule: Estimation of change cost should be done by Manufac-
            turing.

Reason: Most of the cost elements are likely to be Manufacturing
            cost. They also have more reason to do the task quickly
            since they have the most scrap, rework, etc. at risk.

Costing changes is a complex task. This probably explains why the vast majority of companies do not do a quantitative estimate. Lets look at this complex picture by reviewing a cost form.

Change Cost Form

Figure 40 shows a form for calculating the total first year manufacturing cost of a change.

| ECO COST ESTIMATE | ESTIMATOR | DATE | DESCRIPTION OF CHANGE | COST REV | ECO # |

UNIT COST

OLD PN	STD #	QTY PER UNIT	$ PER UNIT (AxB)	SCRAP #/ITEM	REWORK #/ITEM	NEW PN	STD #	QTY PER UNIT	$ PER UNIT	ExF	QTY IN FIELD KIT	FIELD KIT-#	VENDOR TOOL	COMPANY TOOL	TOTAL #
	A	B	C	D			E	F			G	H	I	J	

OLD PART # = ___ +/- NEW PART # ___ = MATERIAL DIFF/UNIT # ... K

DIRECT ASSEMBLY LABOR HRS DIFF ___ x #/HR ___ x BURDEN FACTOR ___ = ASSEM #/UNIT # ... L

DIRECT TEST LABOR HRS DIFF ___ x #/HR ___ x BURDEN FACTOR ___ = TEST #/UNIT # ... M

PRODUCT UNIT COST/(SAVINGS) K + L + M

UNIT $/YR

ANNUAL SCHEDULE QUANTITY x QTY

ANNUAL PRODUCT UNIT COST/(SAVINGS) = #

IMPLEMENTATION COST

PLANNED EFFECTIVE WEEK: IMPLEMENTATION COST = "ONE TIME" OR "START UP"

VENDOR   Dx REWORK QTY + I + PREMIUMS + CANCELLATION = #

MFG   Dx REWORK QTY + J + TEST EQUIPMENT = #

MATERIALS: Cx SCRAP QTY + DOCUMENTATION + INSPECTION EQUIPMENT = #

FIELD: (H + KIT LABOR x KIT QTY) + RETURNS REWORK/(CREDIT) + CRIB REWORK/SCRAP = #

| PG OF PGS | APPROVALS FOR CHARGE-BACK | FIRST YEAR TOTAL = # |

FORM # CM002

Figure 40. Change Cost form.

This form does not estimate the design and development cost. It does not estimate the CM department cost. It does not include the process sheet change cost. Those costs are included only as a result of using burden (overhead) factors. An "activity based" cost form would not use burden factors and would include these costs. With this exception, the form precisely quantifies the total cost of the change for the first year. Here is how it works:

1. The old (deleted) item cost is calculated in the upper left corner. The old parts are listed. The standard cost "A" and the quantity per unit "B" are multiplied together and totaled.

2. The new item cost is similarly calculated in the upper right of the form.

3. The difference between the old and new item cost is put into block "K."

4. The scrap "C," rework "D," as well as "G," "H," "I," and "J" are calculated and entered for later use.

5. The direct assembly labor difference (between old and new designs) is calculated as shown and placed in block "L."

6. The direct test labor difference is calculated and entered into block "M."

7. The product unit cost or savings is the total of K, L and M.

8. Multiply the unit cost times the next year's schedule quantity to attain the annual product unit cost or savings.

9. Calculate the vendor-related "one time" cost by using the D and I costs from above that are for vendor parts. Add the vendor premiums and/or cancellation charges.

10. Calculate the manufacturing "one time" cost by using D and J costs from the items above that are "Make" items. Add cost for modifying or adding test equipment.

11. Calculate the "one time" materials cost by using C from above times the scrap quantity. Add the cost of adding or modifying inspection equipment.

12. Add up field related "one time" costs.

13. The total of the annual product unit cost (savings) and the "one time" costs yields the *First year total* cost of change.

Keep in mind that all Accounting Departments do not necessarily include the same elements into "direct" or "burden" categories. The Industrial Engineer assigned to do the costing of changes needs to examine and revise this form with Cost Accounting.

Cost Policy

Many issues arise when discussing change costs. Shall we cost all or only some changes? What costs are to be included? Will costs that are normally part of overhead be included? Who will calculate the costs? Who will furnish labor and overhead rates? Who will approve the expenditure? Should product unit costs be annualized? The fact that there are so many perplexing questions probably deters estimation of costs. However, it is imperative that all the associated questions be answered.

Rule: A standard or policy is required to determine the company's attitude toward change costs.

Reason: Avoids creeping elegance. Tends to move engineers from mature products to new products earlier. Failing to estimate costs is probably *the single most significant CM-related reason for erosion of profit margins.*

Which Changes To Cost

Certainly class III (document only changes) changes would not require a cost estimate. As discussed earlier, their cost can be averaged by adding appropriate budgets, and / or parts of budgets, and dividing by the number of changes in the same period.

Class II (interchangeable) changes might be ruled out also. Perhaps a better way to handle class II is to have an option available to the team to request a cost estimate on an exception basis. Thus, if they feel that the class II change merits, the estimate would be done. Another method used is to make the CM Manager or the team leader the only person who can request an estimate on a class II. There are two categories of interchangeable changes that should be costed.

Guideline: Cost any class II change that is "to exceed specifications" or is said to be a "cost reduction." Designate a single party to determine if any other class II changes should be costed.

Some companies say that all cost reductions should be estimated. A standard policy is then set for the "payback period." Thus if the savings pays back the cost in, say, one year (or whatever the cost policy states) the change would be released. This is another way to prevent "creeping elegance."

Some companies consider any change required to meet specifications or safety standards as changes that "must be done" and therefore do not need to be costed. Some say that just because a change is not interchangeable, isn't enough reason to cost it. Since the design fix chosen *may not be the only method* to fix the problem:

Guideline: Cost all class I (interchangeable) changes regardless of
        the reason for change.

Typically, class I changes are the minority of changes but have the greatest impact. This is a fairly easy proposition to verify. Take a sample of the changes from your recent history and get the IE to cost each change in the sample. This will help you set your companies cost policy.

Dollar Approvals

The other part of your cost policy is to determine who is authorized to approve the cost. Many Accounting departments already have a "delegation of authority." This may be all that is needed. Often that existing policy can be used for design changes. If there is not existing policy, set a policy for the level of approval such as pictured in Figure 41.

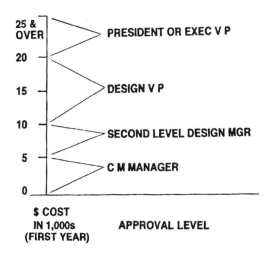

Figure 41. Change Approval based on cost.

64   Engineering Documentation Control

Charge Back Of Costs

The one-time costs resulting from a design change can be charged back to the "benefiting" or "causing" department. A few companies choose to do this under the assumption that the changes may be more carefully considered if this is done. The most frequent use of this technique is for the so called "mandatory" change. This generally means that the customer or Design Engineering dictates the effectivity of the change. Some companies then charge the cost back to Design Engineering. Limited experience with charge back indicates no conclusive evidence as to its resulting in lower cost per change or reduced volume of changes. Limited experience with charge back would indicate:

Guidelines:

- Cost charge back should be done per the numbers on the design change cost estimate. This can assure better estimates. It also eliminates the need to reestimate or gather actual costs.

- Charge back of one time costs is fairly easily accomplished.

- Charge back of product unit cost differentials is very impractical to do.

- Manufacturing should absorb the one time costs associated with any change whose purpose is to reduce manufacturing cost.

- Field Service should be charged with the one time costs associated with any change whose purpose is to reduce maintenance cost.

- Engineering should be charged with all other one time costs. This should encourage improved "up front" design (as much as time allows).

Dollars Without Delay

It is often asked, "But won't estimating the cost hold up the process?" Of course it can, but it need not.

Rule: The change process must not be delayed by estimating and approving the change costs.

Reason: It would be counter-productive to hold up the process and thus create more "bad" parts.

This can be achieved by following five steps:

1. The company policy must be clear and approved at a high enough level to assure "agreement." (The changes to be costed, the form to be used, the cost elements to be included, etc.)

2. The person responsible for the change estimating must be identified.

3. Limit the changes for which costs will be estimated.

4. The estimating process must start with the Design Team discussion of the change.

5. Approval based on the cost must be obtained by CM before release to manufacturing.

More about how the costing ties into the total change process later. Costing of changes must be included in CM strategy. Without a policy in this critical area, a company is open to "creeping elegance." The need to change must be factored by the cost of change in order to avoid profit erosion. Thus:

Need To Change + Cost of the Change = Continued Product Profitability

8

Change Control

Change control is generally thought to be the beginning, middle and the end of Engineering Documentation Control / Configuration Management. Of course it is not the whole subject, but it is the single most important process in the entire system.

The mere thought of change strikes fear in the hearts of engineers, managers, and other manufacturing people. The change process is usually undocumented, slow, confusing, variable, and the source of considerable finger pointing. In most companies, it grew by chance as the company grew. Most companies need a considerable amount of analysis and redesign of the process.

To analyze the change process properly, it is necessary to examine all its facets, one at a time. First of all, what is a change?

Definition: A modification which affects only the documentation *or* a modification to a product(s) which is necessary to make that product:

- Meet the product specification
- Meet the safety standards or specifications
- Manufactured at a reduced cost
- Maintained at a reduced cost
- Exceed its product specification

Notice the specific inclusion of safety requirements. This is a necessity for product liability and for keeping the customer first.

Rule: Safety specifications should be included or referenced in the product specification. Official company standards might constitute the safety specification. In this case, the standard should be referenced in the product spec.

Reason: Safety requirements are a critical part of the design criteria and must be written for all to see.

Why Change?

The last category—change exceeds (over and above) specification—is one area where changes can be avoided. Unless your company has a plan with a goal of purposely making such improvements, this type of change isn't necessary. They shouldn't be done! Call this category "Creeping Elegance!"

Rule: Changes *solely* to exceed product specification should not be done.

Reason: They erode profit margins.

This assumes that the product specifications are well thought out and complete. It assumes that MTBF (Mean Time Between Failure) and MTTR (Mean Time To Repair) requirements are in the spec. This is the first place to look if you feel you have too many design changes. Chances are high that there are engineers assigned to mature products who feel its their duty to improve the product. Reassign them to newer products.

Another area for potential reduction in changes is the "cost reduction." The change must be costed. The cost of making the change must be compared to the savings. Let's say that manufacturing can save $0.20 per unit with a change. Sounds OK, but what will the one time cost to make the change be? And how many units do we make a year? How long will it take us to pay back the one time costs? Let's say we make 1000 units per year. That is a yearly savings of $200. Still sounds OK. But what if the one time cost of making that change will be $1500. A payback in seven and a half years! Hardly worth the investment! What would the relationship need to be for your company before it would be worthwhile?

Rule: Each company needs to develop its unique rules for cost reduction payback expected. Write it into your policy.

Reason: Avoid cost reductions that aren't fiscally viable.

The payback policy period should vary depending upon the expected life of the product. The shorter the expected life, the shorter the payback period. Company policy in certain computer products expects a payback of six months. Certain machine tools have a policy period of six years.

The question needs to be asked, "Why is the change needed?" Ask that question on the ECO (Engineering Change Order) form instead of asking for the "reason" for change. Ask the engineer to check one or more items (from the definition of change) as follows:

- Drawing-only change
- Meet the product specification
- Meet the safety standards or specifications
- Reduce manufacturing cost
- Reduced maintenance cost
- Exceed product specification

Checking one or more of the above, gives definite indicators for further treatment.

Deviations, Waivers, Off Specs, Etc.

Before discussing the correct method to use to make a change to the product or its documentation, there is a need to understand what methods should *not* be used to make a change.

Rule: A Deviation should *not* be used to change the design or its documentation.

Reason: A Deviation is a temporary departure from design document requirements. After a specific timeframe or a specific number of items, the intent is to return to the specified design. One fast and accurate method of changing the design is all that is needed. It's not a Deviation.

Rule: The CM Manager should sign all Deviations when they are being used to make design changes.

Reason: To make sure that they are not used to change the design.

Deviations must not be allowed to continue beyond the agreed upon number of units or timeframe. The number of units or timeframe should be specified in the deviation. It is most important that the root-cause problem is fixed. Thus:

Rule: A specific individual must be designated to "clear" the Deviation. This is the person who is closest to having the total responsibility for the actions which must be taken to assure that no more units will have the problem.

Reason: The alternative is to write another Deviation because the problem continued or occurred again, and again, and again.

If Deviations are written and approved over and over for the same dimension or specification, then the requirement should be reviewed for possible design change. A sample Deviation form is shown in Figure 42.

DEVIATION AUTHORIZATION EC³ Corp	DA #
Reason For Deviation	
Specific Quantity of Items or Serial Numbers Affected	
Description of the Deviation (Be Specific - PNs, Document Numbers, Attach Marked Prints, etc.)	
Name of Person and Organization Responsible for Clearing DA	

Expected Clearing Date	ECO Required ? Yes No
Renewed DA ? Yes No	Previous DA #
Quality Assurance Date	Cognizant Engineer Date
Manufacturing Engineer Date	C M Date

Form # CM 003

Figure 42. Deviation Authorization form.

Another name used for a Deviation is "Off Spec." The same rules should apply to an Off-Spec as to a Deviation.

Some companies use Waivers as well as Deviations. The Waiver may be used as a "before-the-fact deviation." That is, the vendor sees a problem producing the part to the drawing. The vendor may request a Waiver. The same rules should apply to the Waiver—it should not be a method for changing the design or its documentation. The Waiver may, of course, trigger a design change. Many companies reverse the roles of the deviation and wavier as described above

Urgency

Often companies invent a "quick change," "floor change," "temporary change," "emergency change," "red-line change," etc. This is often done in addition to the normal ECO form/process.

Rule: A company should have **one** fast, accurate and well understood method of changing the design and its documentation.

Reason: One method is the lowest cost, least confusing and the simplest to use, operate, maintain, etc.

Oliver Wright states in his book *MRP II* that *"When one system doesn't work, companies develop several other systems to try to do the same job."* My experience shows that it is not unusual to find two, three, or four ways of making a design change at many companies.

The existence of two or more systems is a symptom of a problem—the "normal" system is probably too slow. Somewhere along the line this was recognized, but the solution was to create another process instead of making the "normal" way fast and accurate.

All companies, should develop one fast and accurate ECO (Engineering Change Order) form and process. There should be only two kinds of ECOs.

Rule: Two kinds of ECOs will be processed by our fast, accurate system. One is *Fast* and the other is *Hand-Carried.*

Reason: Some changes are more urgent than others.

It is imperative that the change order precedes the hardware change. To prevent getting the cart (hardware) before the horse (change document), the change process must be fast. As you will see later, it is very reasonable to expect a fast system to process changes through CM in *five work days average time.* The "hand-carry" through the same process should happen in *one half day.*

Rule: The "hand-carrying" will *not* be done by CM. It will be done by the person who says that this change is so important that it must be hand carried.

Reason: Avoids having most changes called "hand-carries." If someone else has to do the extra work, it is easy to overstate the urgency.

When the hand-carry ability is coupled with a normally fast system, the number of changes that are hand carried are few indeed. Experience shows that less than 5% will be deemed so important as to require hand-carry treatment. If a company has a second and / or third shift, it will often be necessary to have a "design" person on that shift. That person must have the authority and knowledge to hand-carry a change.

Having these two kinds of changes also eliminates the need for classifying changes as to their urgency. In one situation, an electronic company determined whether each change was Routine, Urgent, or Emergency. I asked if the throughput time was measured. The answer was "No!" They started measuring the elapsed time. They measured time through CM (*from* engineer complete *to* release to manufacturing). What they found was:

Urgency	Work Days Average
Routine	38
Urgent	76
Emergency	103

Yes, you read it right! The emergency changes took almost three times as long as the routines. There were many problems with the process, one of which was to take more time to debate about the urgency classification than it should have taken to process the change.

Rule: Do not classify changes by urgency. (Except "Hand Carry")

Reason: It takes more time than it's worth. All changes should be important and all should be processed quickly and accurately.

It is not uncommon to find urgency classifications such as "emergency," "line down," "site down," "routine," "normal," etc. Seldom are process differences apparent, however. Use of the word *mandatory* is common. Does that mean that other changes are not mandatory? With urgency classes of *normally fast* and *hand-carried,* the process will be the same, but the hand-carried change will be specially treated. The people in the process will have standing instructions to drop what they are doing and to process the hand-carry first.

Class

Companies often classify changes based on the interchangeability definitions.

Class I   =   Non-interchangeable changes

Class II   =   Interchangeable

Class III =   No affect on the parts (Records Only)

This is done for the ease of expression and to skip steps in the change process based on class. It is easier to say Class I than it is to say "Non-interchangeable." This class also ties to the change of part number (class I) or revision level (class II).

Rule: No criteria, other than interchangeability, should be used to classify changes.

Reason: No other criteria has the significance of interchangeability. Other classifications are likely to be counter-productive.

Steps in the process can be skipped. For example: A class III (Records Only) change doesn't require more than the engineer and CM signatures. There is no need to obtain other signatures, nor does it require look up of the "used on."

As discussed, the cost treatment might be different between the classes. Other examples will be apparent later.

What Makes Up A Change

The question is often asked, "How many problems can I fix with one ECO?" The answer is "ONE."

Rule: One problem, one fix, one ECO.

Reason: It is easier to understand the problem and the fix when they are "stand alone." More importantly, each fix tends to have a most logical/economical point of incorporation. Two or more problem/fixes in the same change would cause "splitting" the effectivity or compromise the effectivity of one or both changes.

Exceptions:

1. If the conditions merit a "short term" and a "long term" fix, and it is not economical to wait for the long term fix, two ECOs are acceptable.
2. Several class III changes to the same document.
3. Several class II changes to the same item providing they can be economically effective at the same date.

Some companies make one change to one document with one ECO. Thus, when one problem results in a change to more than one document, they need multiple ECOs to document that change. The usual practice is to cross reference the ECOs to each other. The "rub" comes when the change must be talked about as a whole (say in a parts catalog). Which ECO number is used to refer to that change? Will a different number or all of them be used on a traceability report? This is a method that is used successfully. Since it is cumbersome, better to use the one problem, one fix, one ECO rule.

Software Changes

At first glance, the software "Release" would seem to be a batching of changes to the code. This is true at most companies. Because of the intricate inter-relationship between many software code changes, they are typically tested as a group (Software Release). The release is then made by an ECO. This allows the company to limit the media distributions to customers, dealers, Manufacturing, etc.

Often companies devise a unique form for making software changes. Careful preparation of the form and form instruction will allow the same form to make software changes, firmware changes and hardware changes. The important aspect is that a minimum level of control is present, not what the form is called or if a different form is used.

All the same principles that are required for hardware or specification changes apply to software and firmware changes. The CM organization should control the revision levels and maintain a file representing the latest code, as well as down-level code files. Again, stand-alone ECOs can be a totally acceptable substitute for keeping down-level files. A separate software ECO should be written for each code change, then a "release ECO" written to batch those code changes that have been tested together.

What Goes In The ECO Package

What does or doesn't go into the ECO package is a critical decision. The more documents required to be in the package, the longer the process time. The required content of the ECO package is simply stated.

Definition: The ECO package must contain all the documentation required to define the change to the design documents which represent the item(s) being changed.

Rule: Only those pages of the design documents which are affected need be included. Manufacturing and support documents will not be included.

Reason: The unchanged pages are costly to include and inclusion lengthens the process time. Inclusion of manufacturing and support documents will delay the process unnecessarily.

A careful examination of the distribution of the package is also required. Many times, a copy of the ECO form itself is an adequate substitute for the entire package.

The combined affect of these savings methods can be substantial. One large electronics company cut the ECO package size and costs as shown in Figure 43.

Old System		New System
27	Pages per ECO	17
x40	Copies per ECO	x25
1080	Total sheets per ECO	425
x90	ECOs per month	x90
97,200	Sheets per month	38,250
1,166,400	Sheets per year	459,000
	Reduction in sheets per year = 707,400 @ $ 0.10 per sheet	
	Savings per year	$70,740

Figure 43. Copy cost savings.

This savings only reflects the paper and reproduction costs.   The handling, reading, filing, etc. probably tripled that figure.

The package must, of course, include all new design documents required to define the change. It must also include precise indications of the changes required to existing Design Documents.

The manufacturing and support documents will change as a result of the design change. They will be addressed in the implementation phase of the change.

Depiction of Adds and Deletes

Two methods are generally used in a change order to depict the change. The most prevalent method is the use of "From-To" drafting. This is called by many names—"Was-Now," "Was-Is," etc. The essence of this method is to describe all the changes in terms of what is the current configuration is and what the new configuration will be. In this method the steps are usually as follows:

1. The engineer marks up a set of documents to depict the change. Messy mark-ups are done without a standard.

2. The CM person studies the mark-ups, goes to see or calls the engineer as required to interpret the mark-ups. This may require several iterations since the engineer is not always available.

3. The CM person "drafts" neat and legible "From (old) - To (new)" descriptions.

4. CM has the engineer review and/or sign the "From - To" drafting.

5. When the ECO is approved, the "From-To" is used to update the master documents.

Did you ever wonder what Lincoln's Gettysburg Address would have been like if someone else had to interpret those notes on the back of an envelope? What happens if CM assumes they understand the mark-ups? Errors result! The CM person makes some assumptions about the mark-ups or the engineer doesn't review the "From-To" closely. This method induces many errors. The engineer also is given another opportunity to change his mind. Or the engineer will submit the change before completing the testing. The result—change(s) to the change.

The other method employed is to use the mark-ups *directly* in the ECO package. The process now looks like this:

1. The Engineer neatly marks up the documents per the company standard.

2. Eliminated

3. Eliminated

4. Eliminated

5. The Marked Documents are used by the CM person to update the master documents.

One drawback to the use of marked documents is that some are larger than "A" size sheets. Some companies cannot reproduce larger prints. The solution to this problem is to cut and paste the mark-up in CM to reduce it to "A" size. This can be done with most changes. Study a sampling of your past changes. The result is usually such that:

Rule: Use of marked documents is almost always faster, lower cost and more accurate than use of "From - To" descriptions.

Reason: The fewer steps in a process, the less opportunity for error, the fewer process minutes required, and the least lapsed time is used.

The key here is to develop a standard for mark-up and enforce its use. To use the technique on parts lists, the parts list must be double-spaced. If CAD or MRP system is your official parts list, it might have to be reprogrammed to be double-spaced. The double-space option can be programmed to be "on demand," thus adding paper to the process only when a copy for mark-up is to be produced.

This method also requires the master documents to be very high quality—capable of two or three iterations of reproduction and still be highly readable. Thus:

First generation: The engineer asks for a "latest revision mark-up quality print"

Second generation: The marked prints are reproduced as part of the ECO.

Third generation: The ECO is microfilmed (if applicable)

It might be that Drafting, CM or a technician helps the engineer "up front" in the process. In that case, they would probably do the mark-up for the engineer. In any case, the mark-up standard is a key. What should the standard say?

Mark-Up Standard

The company standard for mark up of design documents would include requirements as follows:

- The CM Department must maintain document masters of quality to allow two (or three) generations of highly readable reproduction.
- Requires the use of mark-ups by all engineers unless the change can be completely described in the space allowed on the ECO form.
- Mark-up shall be done in red pen. Specify size and type of pen if required.
- Neatly hand letter mark-ups in a script slightly different than the original. CAD overlays are allowable.
- Circle (or underline) deletes—do not obliterate.
- Write adds along side or immediately below the original.

Figure 44 shows a method for marking up a parts list. Note that the deleted item is underlined, not obliterated. The added item is written in immediately below the delete. Also notice that the item now changing was changed previously. ECO 2204 made the previous change. The current mark-up will now result in the CM function adding the ECO and effectivity week for this change (WK 50 ECO 2844).

Figure 45 depicts one method for marking up a pictorial drawing. The delete is circled and the add is written in below the delete. Other conventions may work as well. The critical thing is to specify a simplistic method that is best for your company.

Similar conventions can and should be developed for specifications and other textural documents. Most word processing systems have methods for distinguishing deletes and adds. In the simplest form, *italics* can be used to show additions and underlining to show deletions. Some systems display a marginal line to show the new text.

Same As Except

When a new item is required by a design change, the new specification, drawing, parts list, etc. must be included in the ECO package. If the new item is nearly the same as an existing item, the "same as except - marked print" technique may be used. This means that the Cognizant

3-02-95	REV C	ASSEMBLY PARTS LIST					223456-01
FRONT END LOADER - FEL-100			PG 1 OF 1			AUTHOR FBW	
FIND #	DESCRIPTION		PART NUMBER	QTY	U/M	IN/OUT DATE	ECO #
1	Motor Mount						
2	Tire, Large						
3	Frame						
4	Tire, Small						
5	Bucket, 4 Yard		523456-01	1	e a	wk 42	2204
5	Bucket, 4 Yard		523456-03	1	e a	wk 43	2204
6	Bucket Arm		523456-04			wk 50	2844
7	PCB Elect Ign						
8	Nameplate						

Figure 44. Marked-up Parts List.

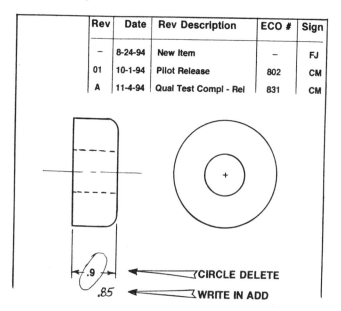

Rev	Date	Rev Description	ECO #	Sign
–	8-24-94	New Item	–	FJ
01	10-1-94	Pilot Release	802	CM
A	11-4-94	Qual Test Compl - Rel	831	CM

CIRCLE DELETE
WRITE IN ADD

BOTH IN RED PEN

Figure 45. Mark-up of a pictorial.

Engineer need not have a new drawing prepared to accompany the change. Rather, a mark-up of the similar-item drawing can be made. The red-marked document will be used to incorporate the change into a new master and assign it the next available part number.

The time that Drafting or CAD departments spend incorporating changes and doing "same as except" can be quantified. The resulting number of people should be shifted to the CM organization.

Revision Drafting and Daisy Chaining

Incorporation or revision drafting does all changes to masters (CAD included) and creates new masters from "same as except" mark-ups. This function is a critical part of the CM responsibilities. It needs to be part of the CM organization. The reasons that it should be part of the Configuration Management organization are:

1. The responsiveness or "sense of urgency" is not typically present when the function is part of a drafting or design group that also works on new products. The new product documentation will typically take precedence. A slower change process results.

2. The CM organization is much more likely to update the master documents on a change-by-change basis instead of "queuing" several changes before the master is updated.

When changes are allowed to queue, negative things happen. First of all, the latest revision print is not available to those who need it. If one asks for a print, they must be given the last update of the master and all the "attached" changes. This is an insensitive attitude toward the CM customer. The buyer and vendor are burdened with the problem. Then, the latest print is not available to mark up for the next change.

The issue of "urgency" is raised. The resulting time spent to prioritize the Incorporation Drafting effort can exceed the time to incorporate the change into the masters. Changes are sometimes revised only to change the assigned revision levels.

Since several documents may be affected by one change or several changes affect the same document, the resulting entanglement creates a significant amount of debate and *make-work.* It occurs so frequently in American industry that it is given a name, *daisy chaining!* The term tends to mean different things to different companies, but it is usually a direct outgrowth of queuing changes to documents.

Queuing Changes

Interchangeable changes to a single part or document may be queued and made as a group. This is typically done by making some judgment as to the criticality of the change. The responsible engineer should do the queuing so that CM gets into the habit of processing all changes immediately upon receipt. This includes revising the master drawing. Doing this means that the revision level increases with each change. This also places the responsibility for determining what is or isn't critical where it belongs—with the Cognizant Engineer.

ADCN

The Advanced Document Change Notice (ADCN) is an often used method to make changes without revising the master documents. A limit of the number of ADCNs that can be "accumulated" against any single document is set. The DoD sanctions this method. A copy of the ADCN is placed with or noted on the master. If someone asks for a print, they are given the print plus the accumulated ADCNs.

The affect of the practice is negative. It precludes the use of marked prints for changes since one cannot obtain the latest revision print to mark up. It places a burden on the CM customer to "integrate" the changes before use of the drawing. It tends to force the changes accumulated to be made effective together—usually when the master is updated. In the meantime is production building parts that will need to be scrapped or reworked? It costs time to copy and attach the ACDN to the print master. All these negatives and what positive? The time to incorporate each change is the same. It saves pulling and refiling the master drawing!

There is nothing "advanced" about the practice. It makes the CM customer suffer for very little, if any, savings. The practice should be abandoned in favor of a fast change process wherein the master is updated with each change—and promptly.

Who Signs

The most debated issue in the change control system is the signature requirements. Everyone wants to sign. As a famous old comedian used to say, "Everybody wants to get into the act!" This is one of the most significant contributors to long throughput time. The number of signatures must be minimized. First of all, the minimum signatures and the signers responsibilities:

- Cognizant Engineer signs: new design docs
  (responsible for the design)   marked-up docs
                                                     ECO

- CM signs: ECO
  (responsible for the BOM & ECO system)

- Manufacturing Engineering signs: new design docs
  (responsible for manufacturing process)   marked up docs

- Manufacturing Production Control   ECO
  (responsible for implementation and effectivity)

If a change is a class III (records only) then no manufacturing signatures are required—only notification. If the change is occurring during the Pilot Phase, many companies have an "informal" change which does not require Manufacturing signatures. A compromise position is to require only Manufacturing Engineering signature on the pilot phase change. This is done on the basis that the changes will affect all the pilot units and therefore there is no "effectivity setting" to be done.

Notice that the technical people are signing the design documents. The Manufacturing Engineer does not need to sign the ECO. The ME should have signed the design drawings and the marked drawings "up front" in the design phase of the process.

Three people (total) need to sign the ECO form: the Cognizant Engineer, CM, and the manufacturing representative who is setting the effectivity. This same representative should be responsible for implementation of the change. The person manufacturing assigns to sign the ECO should set the effectivity after consultation with and analysis by all other manufacturing people affected. Some companies have an implementation team for some or all changes. Having one person responsible for coordinating the implementation may make better sense.

If the product is repaired in the field by company personnel, and if the ECO indicates that action will be required by the Field Support people, then add:

- Field Support signs: ECO
  (responsible for implementing in the field or on repair)

Any change which affects the spare parts list might be signed by Field Support. If the decision as to which ECOs will be incorporated in the field or on repair is made on the ECO, the field person should sign the ECO.

If any of your customers have change approval authority, then add:

- Customer signs: ECP / ECN

The term ECP (Engineering Change Proposal) is most generally used when the customer has approval authority. The term ECN (Engineering Change Notice) is most used when the customer has review authority.

Rule: No other signatures than shown above are needed for accurate processing.

Reason: More signatures will slow the process and compromise the accuracy.

Where is QA? you ask. Quality Assurance should monitor the process, sit in the design team meetings, and audit the processes. Signing one hundred percent of the changes is like trying to inspect quality into the parts by inspecting all the parts in a lot.

Where is Sales, Marketing, etc.? How about other manufacturing or field departments? They should receive a copy of the ECO cover sheet at standard distribution points. They can come to CM or Production Control to look at the entire change if necessary. They can all take exception to any change by use of the chain of command. This is "process management by exception."

The responsibilities of each person/function in the process must be crystal clear. This is where the standards again come into play. The Policy, Procedure (Flow Diagram), standards, form, and form instructions are critical to this clarity. They must state each person's responsibility very clearly. Those not signing should receive an ECO cover sheet. They should have the responsibility to contact their representative if necessary. The resulting responsibility "wheel" looks like Figure 46.

There are many functions potentially affected by the change. It is totally impractical to have them all signing. It is equally impractical to expect CM to coordinate all those signatures. Thus, make a signature "wheel" for your company or division and limit the people directly in the act.

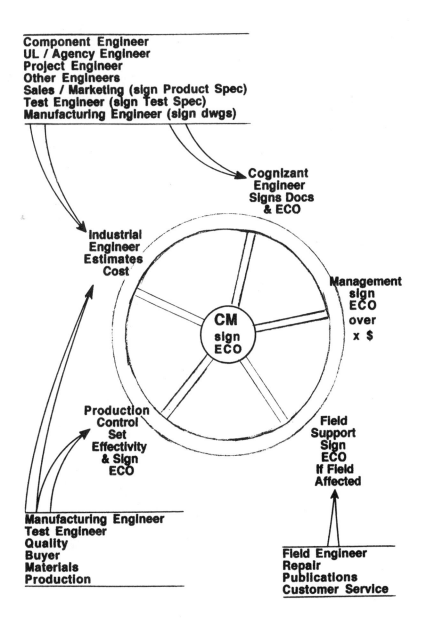

Figure 46. Signature / Responsibility "Wheel."

Mark-Ups in Production

Take care that the mark-ups do not get to the production floor. Most auditors are very concerned if they see marked prints on the production floor. Once marked prints are allowed to be on the floor, what stops any person from changing the design by merely marking up a print? Again the Manufacturing Engineer and the process/routing is the key. As previously discussed, the ME should use the ECO and its mark ups to revise the manufacturing process. This keeps the prints and the mark-ups off the floor. See Figure 47.

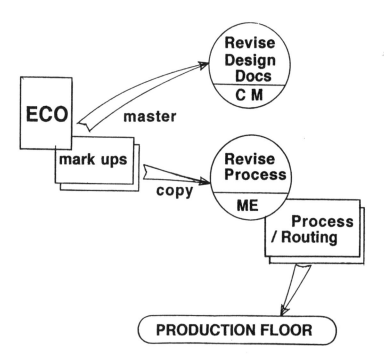

Figure 47. Control of Mark-Ups.

Customer Review and Approval

In the vast majority of product purchases, the customer has no review or approval right whatsoever. It is expected that good interchangeability rules will be followed. The product specification and warranty are the buyers' expectation. If the product doesn't perform as promised, then the problem must be fixed. It is not expected (nor desirable) that change review or approval occur. It is certainly not cost-effective for the company or its customer to go through paper routing processes. This is why the Product Specification, Test Specification, and Specification Control Drawings (for the Vendor) become so important in Configuration Management.

Rule: Do not give customers change review or approval authority.

Rule: If negotiations make it necessary, give the customer review authority.

Rule: If necessary, give review or approval authority only on the following basis:
  - Written contract agreement.
  - Class I changes only
  - Increase the price for the paper processing
  - Reserve the right to increase the product cost if the customer requests changes or if approval delays cause costs to increase.

Rule: Give approval authority only if the customer agrees to be bound by a specific approval time.

Reason: To keep the product cost down and to compete in the world market.

The customer approval, if absolutely necessary, should be subject to a contractual clause, such as: *"If approval/disapproval is not received within 10 working days, the change shall be approved by default"*

Companies have obtained contracts with this default clause because it is good business for both parties. Most customers know that the longer the wait, the higher your costs go. The higher your costs, the higher their price. About ten to fifteen percent of the companies in our university seminars are currently contracting in this fashion.

There are those that say ten days is not enough time. In most businesses there is seldom a design change that cannot be analyzed by a competent engineer in less than four working hours!

Working the customer contract requires a fair amount of work on the part of the CM Manager or Engineering Services Director. The work done in the contract phase will be more than returned in the execution of the contract, however. The Contract Administration people won't be anxious to change the contracting policies. They will also typically agree when they realize the benefits. The customers' representatives at contract time are also aware of the need for speed because they want the product sooner, not later.

Effectivity

There are essentially four forces at work to impact the optimum point to incorporate the change (effectivity) in the product.

T_1 = *When does the customer want it?* If the customer requested or requires the change, they may desire to see the change quickly. If the customer is paying for the change or added feature, they may wish to "cut it in" at the lowest cost point.

T_2 = *When does the design engineer want it?* The responsible engineer will often have an opinion as to when the change should be effective.

T_3 = *When does minimum cost require it?* The estimation or calculation of the associated costs will tend to point to a time in the future.

T_4 = *When are parts or tools available?* The longest lead-time part or tool will be a major factor in the incorporation time for the change. This point in time may be different than any of the above!

Lets take an example from the Front End Loader Company:

Example: The customers are having a problem with the steering wheel cracking. They want the problem fixed yesterday.

The responsible engineer has a fix for the problem: a new resin to mold the steering wheel. No change in the mold is necessary. There is no difference in the material cost from old to new resin. The engineer wants the change this week.

Material Control says we have enough of the current resin to last five weeks. The old resin is a special blend that cannot be returned. Both old and new resin will cost about $3,000 per day at current production rates.

Purchasing says that without a special expediting charge, they cannot get the new resin for three weeks.

When should this change be made effective? Effective week: 1, 2, 3, 4, or 5?

Discussion: The example is one used in the University Engineering Documentation Control seminars. Answers range from week one to week five. Considerable debate results. The situation is not unlike many debates witnessed in CCB (Change Control Board) meetings.

Which week you chose depends upon what *assumption* you made about the severity of the problem. We know that more than one customer had the steering wheel crack. We do <u>not</u> know:

- How many steering wheels cracked?
- How many customers have experienced the problem?
- What werre the ages of the wheels that cracked?
- What is the total field population of identical steering wheels?
- Does the crack present any current or future safety problem?
- Has the engineer, field support and management made a decision to retrofit the field?

Our ECO form instructions for the engineer should require quantitative information about the problem. In this case, we should expect the engineer to pass along at least the number of units that have failed, the total number of units in the field, and probably the estimated Mean Time Between Failure (MTBF). It is also critical to know if there is an operator safety issue involved. Our ECO form should indicate whether or not the engineer is expecting the field units to be changed. The effectivity decision would be much easier to make given this information.

Rule: Assure that all pertinent and quantitative information about the problem is included in the ECO package.

Reason: Intelligent decisions about the proper effective point cannot be made without them.

What will happen in this example if all the facts are known? Examine the effective point issue given all the facts:

Conclusion: (Assuming no real safety issue is present)

- If the failure rate is low and no field retrofit is planned, week five would seem like the logical effectivity. This minimizes cost.

188 Engineering Documentation Control

- If the failure rate is high but no field retrofit is planned, week one might be the optimum effectivity. This maximizes cost but keeps field failures as low as possible. It puts as few potentially bad units into the field as practical. This puts the customer first.

- If the failure rate is high and field retrofit is planned (say on a failed unit basis), then minimizing manufacturing cost at week five might be the optimum point. The cost of retrofit in the field must be compared to the manufacturing cost, however.

Conclusion: (Assuming safety is a real issue)

- The change should be effective in week one. Field retrofit should be part of the plan.

It is natural to have engineering want to see the problem fixed as soon as possible. It is natural for manufacturing to want to minimize the cost. One of the ways to close this gap is to charge the cost back to Engineering. The CM organization must bridge this gap.

Charge-back of costs (price change) to the customer is also a real possibility. When the change is required by the customer and it is not required to meet specifications, the customer should pay for the change. It is surprising how many changes are made because the customer required it, but the change process doesn't allow for an increase of price. Most companies need to develop a policy for charge-back to the customer. It is too often left on a random basis.

Effectivity Responsibility

The customer's requirements and wishes are important and must be stated on the ECO. The Engineer's wishes and quantitative information are important and should be stated on the ECO. It is important to know if the change is required to meet specifications, etc. Input from other people is important.

Rule: The final responsibility for determining the effective point of the change should lie with manufacturing. If customers are dictating the effective point, that information must be stated on the ECO and manufacturing must comply with the customer dictates.

Reason: Most changes are "driven" by material or other manufacturing factors and this is a very dynamic picture.

Sample your changes and see if this typical condition isn't true for your changes. If it isn't true for you, then figure out what is "driving" the effective point and place the responsibility accordingly. If you fit the norm, place the responsibility in manufacturing, probably in Production Control. In many manufacturing companies, the material cost is two thirds or more of the product cost.

Rule: Production Control will be responsible for setting the effectivity plan, tracking that plan, revising it as conditions change, and capturing the actual effectivity after implementation.

Reason: In most companies, the Production Control function is in the best position to analyze all the factors (most of which are material-related) on a continuing basis.

The current stock, in process, on order, in MRB (Material Review Board), etc., must all be considered. The lead time, cancellation charges, schedule changes, etc., are all part of many change effectivity decisions.

There are companies which do not fit this "norm." Casting or molding companies might have the mold revision time as the typical "driver" of the effectivity. In this situation, the mold design or build group might be the best place to set effectivity.

The same department should be responsible for coordination of the implementation of the change. Regardless of who it is, a single function must be responsible for both the effectivity and implementation coordination tasks.

The Effectivity Pipeline

Most changes are not dictates from the customer or real safety issues. However, the engineer still wishes to indicate when he or she thinks the change should be "cut in." A very good method for this communication, that is applicable to almost every company, is the use of the Effectivity Pipeline on the ECO form. A "check" on the pipeline would indicate that the change would be cut in *at that point and in all earlier units / points in the pipeline.* An example for the Front End Loader Company would look like this:

X - Next customer order

X - Next Purchase Order

X - At The Vendor

X - In The Warehouse

$$PC \checkmark \qquad X - \text{In Assembly}$$
$$E \checkmark \qquad X - \text{In Test}$$
$$X - \text{In Run In}$$
$$X - \text{In Finished Good Stock}$$
$$X - \text{In the Field}$$

In this case the engineer put an "E" at the point expected that the change should be cut in. The further down the pipeline, the higher the implication of urgency. Some companies try to get at this issue by classifying changes as mandatory, routine, etc. Examination of the pipeline method of communication will show it to be much more precise. Production Control has indicated the point of effectivity chosen with a "PC." This gives a running record as to differences between the engineer's expectation and PC's plan. The engineer should be on the ECO cover sheet distribution and can take exception (if necessary) to what manufacturing is planning. CM should resolve any such issues raised by the engineer.

Since the impact of the change increases significantly as you go further down the pipeline, it is important that you develop rules for your company regarding the level of management that can approve a changes to be cut in to field units, finished goods stock, etc. If you calculate the cost impact, and sign off accordingly, this concern is covered.

The pipeline information is, of course, somewhat meaningless without the effective date plan and the disposition of old-design parts.

Dispositioning

The engineer also needs to indicate what he / she wants to happen to the old-design parts. The typical way of doing this is to indicate for each old-design part:

  ▪ Scrap   ▪ Rework   ▪ Use as is   ▪ Return To Vendor

At many companies, the engineer is not in the proper position to decide whether or not to rework. This decision is probably better left to manufacturing based upon the economics of rework and how urgently the part is needed.

Rule: Have the engineer indicate whether or not the parts are *reworkable.* Let manufacturing determine whether or not to rework.

Reason: The resulting costs will probably reside in manufacturing and they would be in a better position to determine the economics of rework.

Thus the indication on the ECO form should be:

- Scrap   - Reworkable   - Use as is   - Return to Vendor
- Manufacturing To Rework: ___Yes   ___No

The Manufacturing Engineer or Industrial Engineer would inform Production Control as to whether or not it is economical to rework.

The same person who is responsible for setting the effectivity should be responsible for determining how to dispose of the old-design parts. Some companies indicate the quantities to be scrapped, reworked, etc., on the ECO form. Most companies find that information to be too dynamic to be entered on the ECO form.

Each old-design part must be dealt with on the ECO form. Companies that do not make a conscious decision on each old-design part, are unconsciously increasing their excess and obsolete part inventory. It is therefore, critical that the disposition plan be shown on the ECO form.

Effectivity Planning and Communication

Plan the effectivity of all product changes (class I or II) by date. The planned date should be entered on the ECO form when it is first processed. Subsequent changes to the plan (as conditions change) should also be placed on the ECO form. If a specific effectivity is required by the customer (and properly negotiated) then this effectivity should be specified by engineering on the ECO.

In order to establish which units have the change (Traceability or "Status Accounting"), the change must be tracked to implementation in the product.

Rule: When the change has been implemented, Production
        Control will notify CM of the actual effectivity.

Reason: CM must know when all product changes are effective
          and must notify all others who need to know.

The best way for this communication to take place is probably by copy of the ECO cover sheet. The effectivity needs to be precise on class I changes but can be approximate on class II changes:

- Class I (not interchangeable) must be traced to serial number, lot number, or other "Mod" identifier which is "unit exclusive." That is, one must be able to look at a unit and see from its serial number, lot number, or code whether or not the change is present.

- Class II (interchangeable) need only be traced to the date implemented on the production floor or at the vendor. Should it become necessary in the future to more closely identify which changes do or do not have the change, this can be done with this date.

The cost of tracking each change to every specific unit is expensive. In most companies, the majority of changes are class II. Often 80% to 95% are class II. By exactly tracing class I and approximately tracing class II, the wheat is sorted from the chaff and the cost of tracking is minimized.

The date that every unit ships, regardless of its change content, needs to be known in most companies.

Rule: The date that each serial number (or other Code) is shipped needs to be known for warranty purposes. Manufacturing is responsible for capturing this data and making it available to all who need to know.

Reason: The company needs to know the earliest date the warranty could start.

Knowing the class II effective date and the date each unit was shipped allows traceability to approximate serial number should it become necessary. Since class II changes are interchangeable, this will seldom be necessary.

Typically the Shipping Department would be responsible for capturing the date each unit is shipped. They would make a list (or input to the database) of the date each serial number (or code) shipped.

Effectivity and the Parts List

If you have an MRP system, the BOM module probably has fields for effectivity of parts list changes. These changes may be of a class I or class II nature. The typical Engineering Parts List looks just like the one for the FEL-100 in Chapter 2, Figure 9.

Remember the "IN" and "OUT" date columns? These would typically be used for the date of effectivity. Most MRP systems are programmed for this to be the *material issue date.* Thus the old-design part would cease to be issued on the effective date and the new-design part would begin to be issued on that date. The ECO number which made the change should be shown as a reference (common traceability thread). The original release date of the item also shows in some systems. Thus, a look of these columns in week 48 might indicate:

FN	Description	Part Number	Qty	UM	In Date	Out Date	ECO #
4	Tire, Small	42345602	2	ea	wk12	wk43	256
4	Tire, Small	42345604	2	ea	wk43	wk51	281
4	Tire, Small	42345605	2	ea	wk51		

The original tire called out in this parts list was the -02 part number. It was initially released on week 12. ECO # 256 made a change to delete the -02 in favor of the -04 part number. That change was actually effective on week 43. The next change is designed / planned (remember we are in week 48) to be effective in week 51. That change is being made by ECO # 281. It will change the small tire to the -05 part number.

The BOM / Parts List thus becomes key in knowing the "as designed" (or "as planned") configuration as well as the "as built" configuration. If your company doesn't have an MRP/BOM system, then another method needs to be devised to track the design / plan, and actual effectivity of all parts list changes. Use of the marked parts list in the ECO is a good way of doing this.

Effectivity / Make-to-Order

In make-to-order environments, the most-used method of setting effectivity is by order. That is, a decision is made to have any given order with or with out the change. This typically works fairly well. The MRP system must be able to "attach" a BOM to a specific order. An order-related BOM capability is a necessity if that method is used. If the MRP system has "lot number control," the timing of the lot (and all the related parts) can be managed.

Use of this method doesn't take one important condition into account, however. The material on hand and / or on order doesn't always match the order quantity. For a variety of reasons, the material status reality may call for an effectivity <u>within</u> an order. Make-to-order companies need to address this issue during their change process planning.

Sequencing Changes

The question always arises, "Does the order in which changes are incorporated have to match the order of revision level change of the document? The answer is, quite simply, no! This answer, of course, presumes that good interchangeability rules have been followed and that all revision level changes represent interchangeable changes.

For example, the changes to the loader bucket (52345601) might be done as follows:

ECO #	Revision	Description	Effectivity
228	A	Release for Production	Not Applicable
220	B	Side Plates Thicker	Week 27
301	C	Cleaning Spec Change	Week 12
280	D	Tooth Profile CNC Change	Week 20

Notice that the ECO number order also bears no significance to the order that the changes are to be made effective. Nor is the order in which the drawing is revised in the same order as the changes will be effective. The fact that this condition sometimes occurs is further reason for saying that the revision level refers to the document—not the parts. It is also further reason for not marking parts with the revision level.

Rule: The order in which the Engineer thinks up the changes, the order in which the changes are incorporated into the master drawings, and the order the changes are made effective, need not be the same.

Reason: Attempting to make them the same creates unnecessary constraints on the process and the documentation.

This condition is managed successfully in a vast majority of those companies who follow good interchangeability/part number changing rules. The order of incorporation is managed by the ECO, not by drawing revision level. The production process sheets, the vendor/purchase orders, etc., all "speak to" ECO effectivity. All drawing changes are separable by examining the revision block of the drawing and the ECO. They are therefore separable in time.

Tracking The Change

Production Control must monitor the schedule, availability of the -05 tire as well as the stock status of the -04 tire. They must be aware of the customer's wishes as expressed on the ECO. If the plan date must change, they will notify CM who, in turn, will change the week 51 date to the latest plan.

CM should also make sure that the date change isn't violating the intent of the change. When the change actually becomes effective, PC will transmit the actual date to CM. This is the "as built" or "as shipped" configuration.

Production Control must also follow class II changes which do not affect the parts list. The date to be used must be defined. The definition of the date might vary depending upon whether the change affects a vendor, the fabrication department or the assembly department. The actual date of effectivity must be returned by Production Control to Configuration Management. CM would enter this date on the ECO and redistribute it.

Production Control must also follow Class I changes through production until the actual Serial Number(s) affected are known. Depending upon where the serials are assigned, manufacturing may have to attach tags to the changed units (identified by the ECO number) in order to trace to the units which have the Class I change. This would be done until manufacturing was confident that all the old-design units have been "flushed" from the floor.

Another method used is to change the product date code on the day that the change is actually effective. Another is to affix a "Mod Letter." These "Mod Letters" are assigned to Class I changes. The convention may be to add the letter when the change is present or to "scratch" the letter from a preprinted label.

The tracking method used is not important providing it works for your company. All methods have issues, pros and cons, associated with them. The method chosen needs to be carefully thought out and documented in a company standard. CM and Quality Assurance must monitor this process to make sure that it works—*all* the time.

Status Accounting (Traceability)

Simply put, "Status Accounting" is knowing what is in the product. During design and production, we discussed how the "as designed" and "as built" configurations can be determined. Given an ECO number, it was tracked to the date or serial effectivity.

Usually people have "problems," however, not "ECO numbers." Thus, the need arises at most companies to have access to this data by other than the ECO number. Given an assembly part number, or product SN, or date code, or mod code, or date of manufacture, or a failure symptom, how do I know what is in the product? The reports generated to fulfill this need are called Configuration Traceability Reports.

The most common configuration traceability report is the Illustrated Parts Catalog (IPC). In this publication, the parts and assemblies which are spared/field replaceable have been pictorialized and listed. All changes to those field replaceable items' part numbers are shown by part number with the corresponding effectivity. Thus the data is retrievable from the standpoint of a "person with a problem" using the IPC.

Over time, the maintenance manuals also become a configuration traceability report based on failure mode. Many times, companies develop special "traceability" reports for special purposes. These reports are far too numerous and unique to discuss here. There are, however, four significant questions that need to be asked before such a report is devised:

1. Is this report needed because the Illustrated Parts Catalog or Maintenance Manual is not timely or up to date?

2. What changes will be included in the report? Class I, Class II, all part number changes?

3. Will the report be done for the product "as shipped" or will field change incorporations be fed back and included?

4. If field changes are not to be included, will there be another report that tracks changes made to field units?

Thus, *Status Accounting* is simply defined as: *Knowing what is in and planned to be in each product by ECO Number, date, Serial Number, lot number, "mod," or other code to the extent necessary for your kind of business and your kind of product.*

Change Modeling and Testing

Most companies produce a prototype model(s) of every new product. Many *pilot-produce* several units of each new product. When it comes to design changes, however, this practice is often not required or assumed to be part of the design task. As a result, many changes get modeled and tested for the first time on the production floor. The results are often disastrous. Almost every company has horror stories to tell about such changes.

Certainly class I changes should be modeled and tested. Perhaps class II changes at some companies should also be tried out in the lab. Each company needs to address their policy in this critical area. Some companies aren't even clear about modeling before release of new product options and features.

If practical, a production unit should be used to model and test changes. This will avoid problems resulting from differences between engineering's lab unit and the latest production unit.

The pertinent questions about the tryout of the change should be asked on the ECO form. What serial number was modeled? What date was it tested? What was the report number or page in the engineers note book where the results were recorded? Who performed the test?

This information should be required on the ECO form prior to technical release of the change to CM. That is, prior to the "engineer complete" point in the change process, the testing required must be completed. This places the responsibility where it belongs ,and the process time where it belongs—in the design phase.

A concern always exists that the change time will merely shift from the CM and implementation phases back to the design phase, that the total change process time will stay the same or go up. The only measured process changes of this sort, that this writer has witnessed, showed improvement all around. The parts and the whole of the process time decreased when modeling and testing requirements were inserted into the design phase.

Change Impacts

Most change forms ask the engineer to state whether or not the change will impact certain areas of the company. Does the change impact publications? Tooling? Test Equipment? Software? UL approvals? Will the field be retrofitted? Etc. This is all worthy information to know. It is, however, somewhat unfair to expect the Cognizant Engineer to know the correct answer to all the questions for every change.

Who should better know whether or not publications are affected than the Publications Department? The software than the Software Engineering Department? Tooling than the Manufacturing Engineering Department?

It probably helps to ask the engineer to give an opinion as to the impact of the change. The engineer may consider the change more carefully realizing the total areas affected. But what if the engineer is wrong?

Specify, in a standard, which department is responsible for reviewing and changing (if necessary) the engineers' initial thought. That department must feed changes back to CM so that the cover sheet can be changed.

Cover Sheet Revisions

The cover sheet, by standard, will change due to changes in the effectivity planning and due to corrections in the change impact. Such changes need to be tracked in some manner. A cover sheet revision date is necessary. The choice of a date as opposed to a number or letter is to avoid confusion with the drawing revision.

Notice that this is not intended to allow changes in the technical design of the change to the product. "Changes to the change" are, as you will see later, to be outlawed.

Change Forms

The Engineering Release and Request for Change forms have already been shown and discussed in their respective chapters. There is also a need for an Engineering Change Order (ECO) form. This can be a third form or it can be combined with the release form. If it is combined, then a separate form instruction is needed for each use.

As previously discussed, combinating the request form with the change form can contribute to a compulsion to process a request as if it were a change. For that reason, keep them separate. Combining the release and change forms, however, seems logical. This is because many of the "questions" asked for each form are common. It is also logical to combine them because many changes include the release of a new item/document.

The form designed for the Front End Loader Company is two-purpose and looks like Figure 48.

Notice that this ECO form has all the blocks necessary to make it applicable as a release form as well as a change form. All of the features discussed under change control are present. A release or change involving more than five line-items would require a continuation sheet. Such a continuation sheet would have the same headings as the "documents affected" section of this form.

Form Instruction - ECO

The next step is to develop a form instruction for the change ECO. Start the form instruction by putting Find Numbers (FN) on a blank form such as Figure 49.

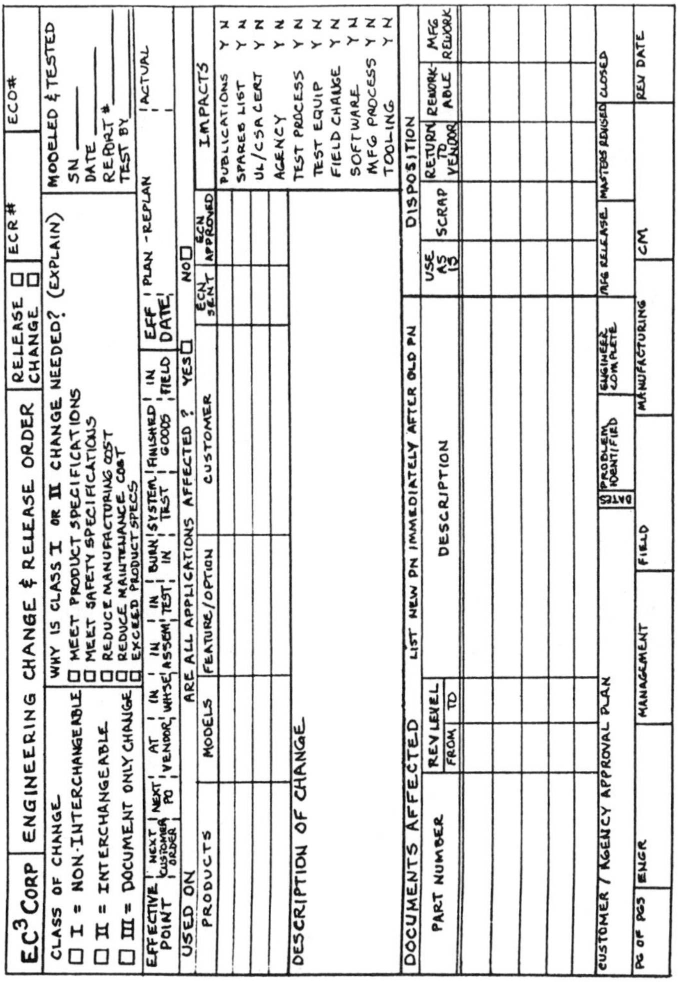

Figure 48. Change Form.

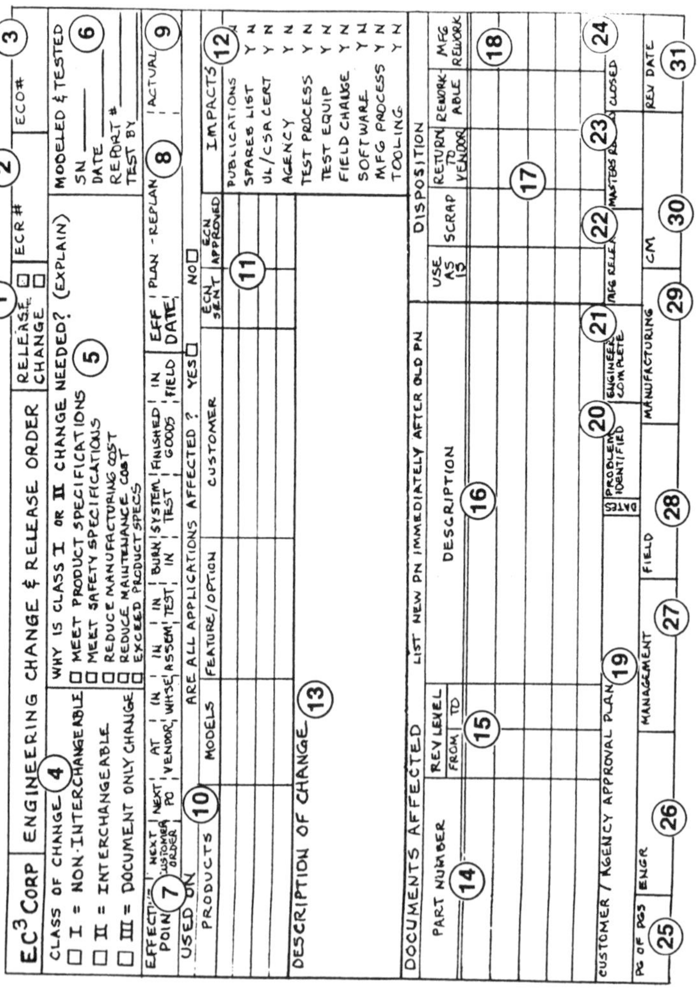

Figure 49. Change Form instruction.

The Front End Loader company's form instruction would look like the following (with *Comment* added to clarify):

PURPOSE
To define the information required to successfully complete the ECO cover sheet. To define the functional group responsible for completion of each block on the form.

Comment: The form instruction is not intended to show the sequence of process steps although some reference will be made to the sequencing. It is listed in "playscript" sequence.

OVERVIEW

- The form is designed to accommodate the "One problem, One fix, One ECO" policy.

- All engineering changes must have an ECO form as the cover sheet.

- This form must be completed using a black pen (or automated on line).

- It must be accompanied by the applicable marked prints, specifications, new drawings, "make-from drawings," etc., which completely define the change to the design of the product and its design documentation.

- CM may cut and paste marked prints to smaller than actual size as long as the Part Number and current revision are identified.

- The change may be described with "From-To" detailed descriptions if that can be completely done in the Description Of Change field of the form. If not, then the marked-up print technique must be used.

- Find Numbers (FN) may not be shown in the sequence completed. For proper sequencing, see the Flow Diagram.

- Other people may help the Cognizant Engineer complete the form but the responsibility for the accuracy of those blocks called "engineer" remains with the Cognizant Engineer.

INSTRUCTION

FN	Responsibility	Instruction
1.	Engineer	Check "Change Order" block.

2.	Engineer	Enter the ECR number if applicable. If the change was not initiated by an ECR, and a number is desired for tracking, see CM for an ECR number.
4	Engineer	Check proper Class of change. See Interchangeability Standard.
5	Engineer	Justify the need to change. Check the applicable block(s). Quantify the failures, failure modes, units in the field, MTBF, etc. Be specific.
6	Engineer	Required on all changes that are Class I hardware changes, all software changes and firmware changes. Enter the Serial Number(s) tested, the date the test was completed, the report number, and the name of the person who conducted the test.

Comment: A standard is needed to define when modeling / testing is required.

7	Engineer	Put an "E" on the effectivity pipeline at the point where you believe the change should be cut in.
8	Engineer	Complete only if there is a known customer requirement for the effectivity.
10	Engineer	Show the Used-On product(s), model(s), feature(s) / option(s), customer(s), as applicable. Indicate whether the change affects all applications: Yes or No. If a Used-On is lengthy and a print out is available, enter: "see attached."

Comment: If the change doesn't affect all applications then it must be *rejected* since the interchangeability must be true in all applications.

Comment: CM people are available to the engineer to look up and post the Used-On information. The engineer is *responsible* for this whether doing it personally or having CM do it.

Comment: Customers not required if no customer notification or approval is required. The "customer" is not typically part of an MRP Used-On. Must be separately maintained by working with Sales.

11.   Engineer   The date the Engineering Change Notice was sent to the customer and whether or not it has been reviewed / approved / time lapsed. (enter: Yes, No, or Time-Lapsed)

12.   Engineer   Give your best judgment as to whether you believe any of the listed items are impacted by the change. Y = Yes N = No

This is only asked as an aid to the various departments. Your opinion doesn't affect the various departments' responsibility to make this judgment for themselves.

13.   Engineer   Describe the change by listing the old condition as "was" and the new condition as "now." If the change cannot be totally described in the space provided, attach marked up documents in accordance with the mark-up standard. If mark-ups are attached, describe the change crisply in the space provided.

14.   Engineer   Enter all old / new part number relationships - old first, new next. When part numbers are not changing, enter the part number(s) of the items / documents affected.

17.   Engineer   Enter the disposition of old-design parts. Use a check (✓) in the correct block.

Comment: This entry, along with 7 above, constitute the engineer's effectivity "requirements."

19.   Engineer   State the Agency(s) (UL, CSA, VDE, etc.) for which approval has been obtained. If any customers or agencies are required to approve but have not, state the plan to obtain same, including a date the approval is expected.

20.   Engineer   Enter the date you first recognized the problem / need to change. If there was a corresponding Change Request, this would be the date it was accepted.

26. Engineer   Sign to indicate that you have reviewed the change with all other engineers who are affected and have obtained the ME signature on t h e drawings or mark-ups attached.

Comment: It is at this point that our flow diagram will require the package to go to CM and a checklist to be completed by CM. The CM Technician will:

  - Check the change against the latest Used-On report and the checklist.
  - If the ECO meets all the criteria on the checklist proceed to the next step.
  - If not, check the items not conforming and hand carry the ECO (with checklist noted to indicate non-conforming items) to the Engineer.

3. CM Tech   Assign the next ECO number form the log.

21. CM Tech   Enter the date that the Engineer delivered the change package.
Check time to be charged to CM for changes that pass the check.

15. CM Tech   Assign the last and the next revision letter or number to each revised document.

16. CM Tech   Enter a brief description of each item from the attached documents.

25. CM Tech   Enter "page of pages" on every page in the package. The ECO is always page one.

Comment: At this point, CM distributes the ECO and attachments per the standard distribution list. Remember: the ECO cover sheet is distributed to all who need to know, while the attachments are distributed only to key functions / locations.

7. Production   Enter "PC" at the point in the pipeline where it
Control   is intended to "cut in" the change.

8. Production   The effectivity planned date (class I & II).
Control   Class III enter "NA..

18. Production Control — Note the manufacturing rework plan by entering

NA - Not Applicable

Yes - Item will be reworked

No - Item will not be reworked

Vendor - Rework will be done at the vendor

Comment: An alternative would be to enter the quantity of items to be reworked, scrapped, etc. This could be effective in some companies while others would find quantity information too volatile.

29. Production Control — Sign and send a copy of the cover sheet to CM.

28. Field Support — Sign those ECOs which are noted to be effective "In Field."

Comment: When required, the Industrial Engineer must have completed the cost sheet and given it to CM by this time. See Flow Diagram.

27. CM Tech — Obtain management approval as required by the company standard for cost / approval level.

22. CM Tech — Input the change to the MRP system. Check the output. When correct, enter the Date of Manufacturing Release. Distribute the cover sheet.

Comment: Input to the MRP (manufacturing release) will not be held until the master documents are revised. Completion of the Incorporation Drafting effort will not be held until the MRP is updated. Both steps will be done in parallel. The CM phase will not be completed until both are done. CM process time will be completed whenever the later is completed.

23. CM Tech — Enter the actual date that all affected master documents / CAD were revised and distributed as needed.

9. Production Control — The actual effectivity of the change: a Date for class II changes, a Serial Number for class I changes. Send a copy of the cover sheet to CM.

24.   CM Tech   The date the actual effectivity was received from PC and all other activities are confirmed which are necessary to "close" the change.

Comment: There are several tasks that must be completed before this date is entered. Those tasks will be noted when the process is flow-diagramed.

30.   CM Tech   Sign and redistribute the cover sheet to all who need to know the actual effectivity.

31.   CM Tech   Enter the current date whenever the cover sheet is revised. Redistribute as necessary.

Notice that the form is complementary to the "closed loop process." That is, the feedback to CM of the actual effectivity (and other activities) and the distribution of that actual effectivity is closing the loop with all who need to know.

It is useful to have a colored blow-up of the form instruction for training purposes. The colors would correspond to the functions responsible for completing the block(s).

Recall that the form can be changed only for specified reasons. Changing of the effectivity plan is the principal reason. Changes to the cover sheet generally are allowed. Changes of the design of the change are not allowed. The process will be designed to be a "one way street"after the engineer and the checklist are complete.

The engineer must have the design of the change technically complete when turned over to CM. The completion of a check list will verify that it is complete. Having the process be an irreversible one prevents false starts, prevents "holds," keeps the engineer from entering "lightly" into the process. The ECR number was used until the change passed the check list at "engineer complete." This is done purposely in order to have ECO numbers associated only to changes which are in a "go" or "one way" mode.

Every form must have a form instruction and the ECO form is no exception. Writing a form instruction will reveal problems with the change process and/or the form itself. The form and its instruction are a keystone in the change process.

Change Database

An important element in making good decisions about engineering changes is to have real facts available. Decisions to improve the process will be easier to make and more productive with the "facts in a bank." What portion of your changes affect the BOM? How many affect parts that you purchase? How many changes are class III?

CM people tend to believe that they are so close to the changes, that they intuitively know the answers to these kinds of questions. Many are quite surprised to find that their intuition wasn't as accurate as they believed. Better to get the facts, especially since it is not a huge task.

List all the questions that you or others would like to have answered about your changes. Sample your ECO forms and packages from the last six months or year. Ask your Quality Assurance folks what size sample you need to be "representative." A ten percent sample will probably do. Take care to pull the history at random. Make a matrix on paper or on your PC. Review each change and answer all the questions listed. As you do the first few, you will think of other questions that can easily be asked and answered. Summarize the results. Publish the results. You will become the resident expert on changes.

This facts-bank will be used frequently as you or your team constantly improve your system. Launching "improvements" without the ECO database is a sure way to make many mistakes.

9

Fast Change

Most companies have some kind of a change form. Some have a documented process. ISO 9000 requires a documented process and that you follow that process. ISO and other standards don't care about the speed of the process. DoD and some other agencies find ways to slow the process. Witness that the change approval time for DoD is measured in *months.* Few companies (military or nonmilitary) have a fast process. Yet, this is where the rubber meets the road. This is where the economy is. *This is the most significant strategy in the Configuration Management business.* Let's review some of the reasons why speed is important in the change process:

- Customers see the change or feature they requested much earlier.

- Reduce the amount of Manufacturing rework and scrap costs.

- When retrofitting a change, speed reduces the number of units that Field Support will have to find, disassemble and fix.

- Incorporate real cost reductions earlier.

- Satisfy that frustrated production employee much quicker.

- Prevents the creation of substitute processes.

These are powerful needs! The dollars involved are staggering. If we could magically implement five-day processes in every company in the

USA, the savings would be enormous, and the competition would stagger from the shock. And it is an attainable goal! Small, medium, and large companies have all attained three to five work day CM process time.

About five percent of those companies represented in our University Seminars have attained five work day throughput time. This gives them an enormous advantage over their competition.

I have yet to visit a company that had change control problems that did not also have "bone piles" of down-level material in Manufacturing. Material that was affected by changes. Material that needed to be reworked and put back into the process or scrapped.

Rule: The longer the change throughput time, the bigger the "bone pile."

Reason: Every day, every hour, every minute that manufacturing waits for a change, the more units that are produced which have to be reworked or scrapped.

The typical production operation is oriented to producing new product. Thus, when the design change calls for rework, the tendency is to set them aside to "rework when we're not so busy." Another change comes along that affects the same assembly. The change is implemented as quickly as possible and the units to be reworked are added to the pile. After a while it becomes a major project to sort out what work needs to be done to each unit. The inventory carrying cost of the "bone pile" is substantial.

If the part disposition turns out to be "scrap," how many units are built per day that will be scrapped? Would it be less costly to shut down the production line? Then what will the idle people cost the company?

How many Field Service Engineers or dealers take the heat from customers who are waiting (not too patiently) for a product fix? Is manufacturing building more units to be field retrofitted, risking more unhappy customers? What is one unhappy customer worth?

If we have a true cost reduction, why build any more units than necessary at the higher cost?

What is the cost of creating and maintaining one or more substitute systems? One to make a change fast and another to do it over again "by the formal system." What is then done if there are some differences between the fast fix and the formal fix? How shall we document the different configurations? Why don't we just do it fast and right the first and only time?

All of the above reasons for having a fast change process lead to this golden rule of Engineering Documentation Control:

Golden Rule: The speed with which you process design
                 changes is critical to profitability.

Attaining a single, fast, accurate and well-understood process is easier said than done. There are, however, some methods that will simplify and speed the process.

Measure the Process Time

The first step is to recognize the problem! If it is not known how long it takes to process a design change, then it is not known whether or not there is a problem, nor is it known how serious a problem we have. Without measurement how can one tell if "improvements" in the process are working? Fewer than fifteen percent of the companies attending the University seminars even measure the change process time! The first step is to measure the process time:

Rule: Measure the process throughput time.

Reason: It is necessary to know the throughput time in order to
             know whether or not there is a problem, and the extent of
             the problem.

Many companies assume that the process time is reasonably fast. They are shocked to learn that the measured time is tenfold what they anticipated or would like to have. Sometimes the documentation manager has measured the system and has a drawer full of data. That manager is often frustrated because no one else seems to be concerned with the slow process.

Publish the Results

An old Industrial Engineering axiom says, "Measurement, in and of itself, tends to improve performance." Add to that axiom, "Publish the results."

An example of a measurement chart is shown in Figure 50.

Rule: Publish the results.

Reason: Measurement, in and of itself, tends to improve perfor-
             mance if the results are broadcasted to those who need to
             know.

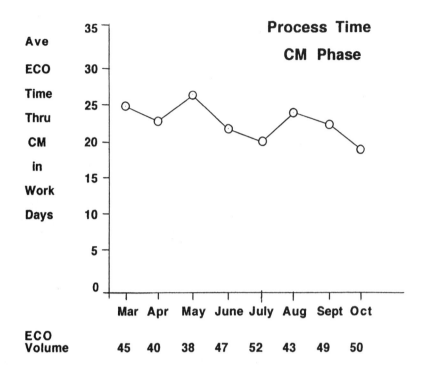

Figure 50. Typical Process Time graph.

Measurement without publishing the results will probably not achieve improvement. The thoughput time should be graphed on a very large chart. A size of two feet by three feet will assure it is seen and considered important. Make several copies. Put one in the CM area, one in the cafeteria, and one outside the "corner" office; in small companies this would be the Presidents office; in larger companies this would be the Division VP or Plant Manager. You might include the VP of Operations and VP of Engineering.This also makes them part of the improvement process. This is a group measurement, not an individual measurement. Properly introduced, it will become a team challenge to reduce the process time.

Rule: Educate those people who need to know why speed is important.

Reason: Understanding will lead to action.

One Configuration Management manager took some of our seminar material and prepared a fifteen minute presentation which she gave to all those involved in the change process and their management. She included higher-level managers. The people responded by coming up with ideas of their own as to how to save time. When she later suggested a small quality improvement team, the idea was welcomed.

Points to Measure

There are five significant points in the process to measure. Begin by measuring these most significant points. A few more points can be added later. Take care not to measure too many activities. The five most important points are shown in the basic flow diagram in Figure 51.

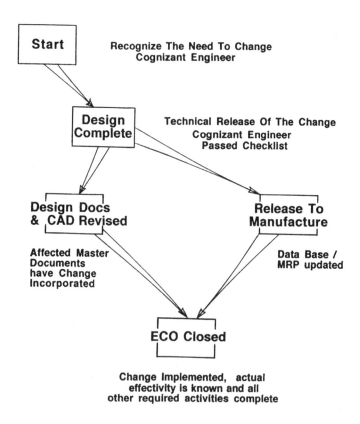

Figure 51. Five most significant points.

The measurement of too many points tends to dilute the importance of the data and to confuse the issue. Too much data tends to increase the possibility that no one will read it. A CM manager with a drawer full of data extracted these five points from the data and proceeded to publish the summary information. Eight work days were taken off the CM time as if by magic. That was their first step toward a world-class process.

A company may not have clearly defined points as shown in this basic flow diagram. The "closest" points in the existing process should be chosen. The points are defined and discussed below:

Start. Identify the time when the problem is first identified and accepted as a problem. This would be the change request "problem accepted date." That is the date the engineer agreed that there was a problem. The first field failure or customer complaint might not be recognized as a problem. If no document exists, ask the engineer (on the ECO form) to indicate when the problem was recognized.

Design Complete. This is the point in the process when the engineer turns in the change *and* CM completes the checklist that verifies it to be complete. (Was the change modeled and tested? Are mark-ups per standard? Etc.) This point can also be called "Technical Release," because it should be a *point of no return.* That is, the only changes which will be made to the ECO package will be to the cover sheet—such as changes to the effectivity plan. After this point, the only way for the engineer to do the fix differently should be to process another change. This causes deliberation early in the process (where it should be) and results in changes done right the first time.

Release. That point in the process wherein Manufacturing is released to buy parts, etc. This point is normally identified by the fact that the CM input to the MRP is complete and verified to be correct. If we are down-loading data to a CNC machine or other forms of CAM, this would be the date that transaction was initialized. Put this date on the ECO.

Design Documents Revised. This is the date that all the master design documents affected by the change have been updated. This point should be done in parallel with the Release of the change. Both the Release and the Design Documents Revised must be completed prior to completing the CM portion of the process.

Implemented / Close. The change is actually incorporated in the product. This point was captured on the ECO when Production Control sent a copy to CM showing the actual effectivity. For class III changes, this would be the date when CM completed incorporation of the change into the master prints. There may be other events that must also be completed prior to closing the change: revision of the Publications, writing of the Field Change Order, etc. When the last one is complete, close the change.

Don't wait! *Measure the throughput time now!* This step is a must, and it should be done prior to taking any other step. This is done in order to know if other improvements achieve the expected throughput time reduction.

Revision of Masters

The best point in time to revise the master drawings and specifications is a much-debated issue. It is done in all three of the change phases! The following is a discussion about doing it in any given phase:

Engineering Phase. Tends to be done by Engineering-directed companies. Tends to make the "Engineer Complete" milestone a definite point of no return. All CM does is add the next revision level. This writer views that as an acceptable approach, providing the design team gets a review of the change prior to incorporation in the masters.

CM Phase. Probably the most common approach. Tends to be required by companies using the part or assembly drawing on the production floor. Often the incorporation operation takes so long to get done that many complaints are received from manufacturing. An edict by management results: "Do it before release to manufacturing." This writer views that as a poor way to fix the problem. The incorporation drafting / CAD process took too long so the solution was to hold up the change until it is done. The solution should have been to find out why the incorporation was so slow and to fix that problem. The change should not be held up one day or one hour by this activity. Shall the production people make one hour's more parts to be scrapped or reworked? Manufacturing should also examine the power of good production processes in lieu of using drawings on the floor.

Implementation Phase. Is typically done by companies that have manufacturing processes used on the production floor and marked prints used at the vendor. They accept the "mark-up" showing the change as an acceptable tool to update the process. This writer views this as an acceptable approach providing it happens fast—after "Engineer Complete."

In fact, no matter where in the process the incorporation effort is done, the key is to assure that it happens fast. That is why it must be separately measured and reported. Less than three work days is a reasonable expectation. This function is often a trouble spot. When it is not a CM function, it often takes a back seat to new design effort.

Set Goals

The first part of the process—from "Start" to "Design Complete"—is very hard to generalize about. I have observed throughput times from one week to ten weeks. People in our seminars have reported design time up to twenty weeks. If a DoD product is involved, an engineering change proposal with customer approval would typically take two months by itself. This is not to say that this is a reasonable period of time, only that it is typical. Don't accept past history as a reasonable time for customer approval. For your company and your product however, identify a goal for this part of the process. Make a separate graph for this portion. Label the graph as Engineering responsibility.

In the middle part of the process, the activities must be thought of and treated together—from "Design Complete" to "Release" or "Up-Date Drawings and CAD," which ever comes later. Three to five work days is an attainable goal. The ability to hand-carry in one-half work day is also important. Label this graph as Configuration Management responsibility.

Measure the revision drafting time separately. A reasonable goal in most companies is two or three work days. Many companies have achieved this time whether they have hand-drafted or CAD or both. Label this graph with the department responsible.

The last segment—from "Release" to "Closed"—is also difficult to generalize about. This is paced by the "effectivity" of the change. Time (effectivity) can vary from "today" to the longest lead time item in the product. Thus a benchmark of implementation time is dependent upon your product. Even here, however, goals can and should be set. This measurement will present a benchmark for future improvement. Label this graph Manufacturing responsibility.

Measure Volume / Reduce Backlog

Next, measure the volume of changes. Measure not just the average rate, but several attributes:

- New problems (changes) per week (at "start")
- Count backlog in Engineering
- ECOs into CM per week (pass check point)
- Count backlog in CM
- ECOs released per week

- Count backlog in Manufacturing
- ECOs closed per week

These volume measurements can be obtained by keeping logs and counting the ECOs in process. Measure these volume figures for several weeks running to make sure that the numbers are representative. Then examine the incoming rate as compared to the outgoing rate.

Example: Lets say that the Loader Company has rates into and out of CM as follows:

- Into CM (pass check point) = 25 ECOs / week
- Out of CM (Released) = 21 ECOs / week

Conclusion: If this pattern persists over several weeks, we can conclude that CM needs long-term help. Without help, the backlog (and throughput time) will grow by 4 ECOs per week. The "help" can be, either to find a way to cut down on the CM workload, or get more manpower into the function.

Reducing the CM workload can be done by adopting some or all of the ideas that have been previously presented, or ideas that are yet to be presented. Reviewing some of the ideas already presented:

- Excessive signatures
- Excessive distribution
- High pages per ECO
- Holding up changes to include manufacturing documents
- Holding up changes to include support documents
- Queuing of changes in other than Design Engineering
- Lack of a standard written process
- Making the same change by a fast process, then again by the formal process
- CM department lacks revision drafting responsibility
- Process time not measured
- Measurement not published

Now examine the backlog and compare that to the throughput time measured previously.

Example: During the same period of time, the backlog was about
125 ECOs constant and the incoming / outgoing rates
were both at 25 changes per week.

Conclusion: Five weeks worth of backlog should equate to five weeks
of throughput time for CM. Check the throughput time
measurement and make sure the throughput time is
about five weeks through CM.

Conclusion: If the incoming and outgoing rates are about the same,
the throughput time can be reduced by working off the
backlog.

At one company, outside temporary help was used to reduce the
backlog. The more effective method is to enlist other department people to
work it off. Engineers, draftsmen and technicians from all affected areas of
the company are asked to come into CM and do a few ECOs apiece.

At another company the Vice President of Design was a volunteer
working side-by-side with the other people asked to help. This was very
effective, as it showed the other helpers and CM people how important the
VP thought it was to have fast ECO time.

If the incoming rate exceeds the outgoing rate, however, reducing
the backlog is a very temporary measure.

In many cases, measurement of the time and volume (with the
appropriate action to reduce the backlog) is all that is needed to reach the
throughput-time goals. A small medical device manufacturer reduced its
process time to one-sixth of original by reducing the backlog. In their case,
measurement, reporting, setting goals, and backlog reduction was all they
needed to achieve four day average time through CM.

Often however, these steps aren't enough to reach the goal. If prior
steps have still not reduced the time to acceptable levels, the next step is
to change the system.

Change The System

Before launching into any system change, especially if significant
changes are contemplated, form an "Improvement Team." The CM
Manager may feel and be competent for the task. The manager probably
is capable of designing a fast system. This is not the issue. The issue will
be to get key other functions to "buy into" the new system.

Rule: Before starting any system improvement program, get Manufacturing, Field Support, and Design Engineering to join CM in an "Improvement Team."

Reason: You want *ownership* in the new system by key functions.

You might want Quality Assurance to join this effort. If they are not under the manufacturing wing, they should probably be added. One key person from each function - no more. Too many cooks can spoil the broth! If CM is under the Design Engineering management, have CM represent all of the design group. This makes a working and workable size team. Each member is required to talk over and review standards with all the key people in their area of responsibility.

You will also want a Management Steering Committee. This group might represent some functions—finance, contracts, etc.—not on the Improvement Team. The Steering Committee should be chaired by a "Top Gun"—the President or VP or GM. The Improvement team should report, about monthly, to the Steering Committee on progress and plans. Get the Steering Committee to buy into your goals. Keep the goal(s) fairly simplistic. For example:

> *Improvement Team Goal:* Design one system which will be the only way to make changes to the product or its design documentation. Attain five work day process time through CM. Improve quality of changes without increasing Design or Manufacturing time. Do this with the existing work force.

Missionary Leader

The leader of the design team must be a person with a high desire to improve the system. The zeal of a missionary is needed. Lukewarm interest will assure failure. The CM manager is probably the correct person to lead the Improvement Team. If the high desire for improvement is not present, another person must be found. A management "champion" should have the same missionary drive. The champion should be on the Steering Committee and probably chair that committee. Between them, they must have the aggressive desire to assure success.

Nine Steps To Success

The Improvement team should follow nine (not so easy) steps:

1. Define the current system
   - Gather any and all existing documentation on the current system.
   - Gather all current forms and form instructions (if any).
   - Assure that time and volume measurements and reporting are in place.
   - Analyze the current ECOs.   Build a "facts bank" (database).
   - Flow-diagram the current system. This need not be done in a "pretty" manner, but it must be done. It will eliminate arguments later, educate the team, and start the teamwork going. Many a CM Manager has commented to me "I thought I knew my own system, but flow-diagraming it opened my eyes!"

2. Flow diagram the proposed system
   - List all the legitimate operations that need to be performed. Break them down into their smallest parts. Don't put them into any order. Determine whether they are required on Class I, II and/or III.
   - Identify required dependencies.   Example: Can't get engineer approvals until modeling and testing is complete.
   - Start each operation as early as possible.   Don't force completion of an operation any sooner than necessary.
   - Do all possible operations in parallel.
   - Use all the "Rules" from this text which apply to your company.
   - Place one "responsible department" on each operation.

3. Define the proposed system in small pieces
   - Policy, Standards, Form, and Form Instructions
   - Keep each to a single subject—should be *three pages or less* (divide and conquer).

4. Team presells the system
   Have each team member review the proposed system with key people, and management, in their area of responsibility. Expect/invite constructive criticism. Iron out the rough spots. Resell as necessary.

5. Trial run the system

> Using the Improvement Team, run a representative set of changes in parallel with the existing system. Debug the system. Run another trial if necessary.

6. Get Steering Committee approval of the system

> Send each standard, as drafted, to the Steering Committee (at least one week prior to their meeting). Discuss each standard at a meeting, revise if necessary, and have the "Top Gun" sign each. With the use of the Implementation Team and the Steering Committee, only one signature is needed. When all the key standards have been reviewed and signed, report to the Steering Committee that it is time for a pilot test.

7. Pilot and Train

> Use the Improvement Team to train key people. Have them pilot run representative (a few of each type) changes by the new process. Don't stop training until all the people in the process have had an adequate exposure to the new system. Nothing can defeat a new system faster than people who haven't been properly trained. Expect criticism, and debug where constructive.

8. Implement

> Get Steering Committee agreement when the time has come to cut over to the new system. Pick a day and start all new changes by the new system. Let the old system changes "flush out." Don't expect immediate improvement. It will take 75 to 150 changes to see peak performance.

9. Follow up

> Assure that all the old methods of making changes have been "extracted," "killed," and "burned." Keep the Improvement Team and the Steering Committee functional until this has occurred and until you have met the goal.

Each step is critical. None can be skipped. Whether you make three or thirty three changes to your system, the only way to assure success is to do all nine steps.

Bootstrap or Reinvent

The question often arises, "Should I make small changes, big changes, or reinvent the system?" A thorough analysis of a company's current processes, documentation, and process time is required to answer that question. A rough guideline might be based on the CM process time:

- Under ten work days   • Improve the process in small steps
- Ten to thirty work days   • Look for logical batches of improvements that can be implemented together
- Over thirty work days   • Design a new process

This guideline is, of course, directed only at the change process. It presumes that a reasonable semblance of order exists in the Release, Request, and BOM processes. What priority is in order if two or more of the major CM processes are in need of improvement? That issue becomes very unique to particular company conditions. If the request process is long and intertwined with the change process, it may not be possible to address them separately. The BOM process is naturally affected by the release and change processes. Attacking them all together is not the answer, however. Find a way to divide and conquer. Remember, you can and should come back to any part of any process again, to make continuous improvement.

The Improvement Team must keep the scope of their first project as small as possible. The management may feel that the entire system needs immediate help. The Improvement Team must take the smallest bite possible for its first improvement. This may be the request process, the change form, or an interchangeability standard. If there is to be an error made in this decision, better to err on the side of small improvement steps.

The most significant of the steps to short process time is to make the Flow Diagram. The flow can then be improved in small bites or in a whole. Before the new or changed process flow diagram is addressed, remember that many of the standards must be in place. Better to have the building blocks in place before starting the structure.

Fast Change Flow

If the Improvement Team has done its job, a complete and crisp flow diagram will result. The diagram will have one responsible function for each operation. It will show where key forms are originated. It will have a method for indicating where time measurement points are. (In the examples to follow, a miniature "clock" will be used.) The operations are joined by arrows. The tail of the arrow indicates the point at which the operation may be started. One or more arrows into an operation indicates "dependencies." The circle indicates the completion of the stated operation. The outgoing arrow(s) indicates where the operations "product" goes.

The flow diagram must be "backed up" by policy, standards, forms, and form instructions. That is, when the flow diagram has an operation which says; "New and Marked-Up Design Documents" the back up will be:

- Design Document standard which defines those documents which are Design Documents and which aren't.

- New Document standard which defines how documents are to be prepared.

- Mark-Up standard which defines the criteria for mark-up.

In this fashion, few if any notes will be required on the diagram and no written "procedure" is needed. This is critical! If many notes or a written procedure is needed, then one of two things have happened:

- The standards are not complete or subjects need to be standardized.

- More operations need to be flow diagramed in order to depict the process.

Several iterations of flow diagram may be necessary to meet each process time goal. Each time a flow diagram is made, ask some hard questions:

- Can the operation be done in parallel with another operation now in series?

- When is the earliest point that the operation can be started?

- When is the latest point the operation can be completed?

- Is there a single function responsible for the operation?

- Is the correct function responsible for the operation? This may not be the department that is currently doing the operation!

- Have provisions for skipping operations depending upon the class of change. For example, class III changes need not go through all the steps that other changes will. Class II cost reductions might not require modeling and testing, etc. If this exception specification becomes very complex, a separate standard may be needed.

- Specify the standard process time expected on all the significant steps in the process. Get the management of the responsible function to agree with the elapsed-time standard. Elapsed-time allowed is generally greater than the actual time to perform the task. For example, inputting a change to MRP might normally be an eight minute job, but you might allow three hours of elapsed time.

Typical Flow Diagram

There is no more a "typical flow" than there is a typical company. A process company will have a different flow than a make-to-print company. The product company might vary depending upon whether it is a make-to-stock or make-to-order or a combination of both. Many features of the change system flow will be similar, however. In order to simplify the flow diagram discussion, we will again use The Loader Company as an example.

Engineering Flow

The "up front' portion of the process is the general responsibility of Engineering. It begins with recognition of the need to change, and ends with the Design Complete operation. The Loader Company flow in engineering is shown in Figure 52

Notice that several operations are done in "parallel." This contributes to quicker throughput time. When the Cognizant Engineer first recognizes the problem, five operations can begin before or at the next Design Team meeting:

- CM looks up the Used On and gives the engineer a list (could be on an ECO form).

- The engineer begins modeling and testing as required.

- New and marked-up prints are prepared and reviewed at the next Design Team meeting.

- The Industrial Engineer is requested to estimate the cost. This is done on a rough basis (because the effectivity hasn't been set) for the engineer's information. The cost will later be up-dated when the design is complete and the effectivity is set.

- The Customer is notified of the impending change. If regulatory agency reviews are required, they are likewise initiated. If the agency or customer has contractual approval rights, the point at which the package is sent might vary from the above.

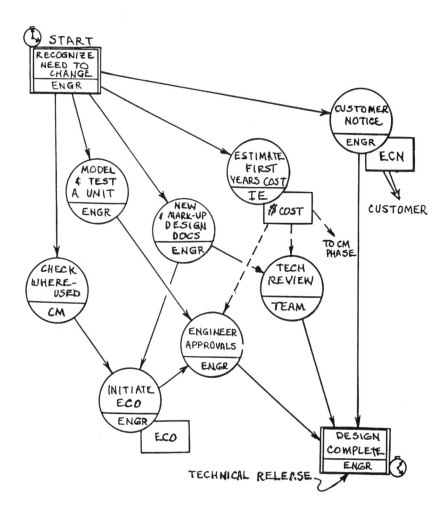

Figure 52. Engineering-phase ECO flow.

The diagram further indicates how the signed and reviewed documents come together when the design effort is complete. It is important to note that Lab Technicians, CAD / Draftsperson, and CM Technician may aid the engineer during this process but that the engineer is still *responsible.* The clock "stops" when the engineer gives the package to CM and it passes the checklist.

It is important to realize that the entire Design Team is aware of the pending change. This happens because each change is discussed at a team meeting. Each member can begin preparations for their implementation operations. For example, the publications writer can identify the manuals affected and even the pages affected.

If a change requires hand-carrying; either the team is called together on an "on call" basis, or the change is hand-carried among the team. One company reported that some hand-carries occurred on the night shift. If the responsible Manufacturing Engineering had to implement that change that night, the ME was responsible to hand-carry the change completely through the system the next morning. Few changes were implemented in that fashion.

Point of No Return

The check point is so significant, it is shown separately to assure proper emphasis. If the engineer's package passes the check, CM will proceed. If the package is deficient, it will be returned (hand delivered) to the Engineer. Each problem will be carefully noted. See Figure 53.

The time required to do this check will be charged to CM if it passes. If not, the time will be charged to the engineer. CM should set a standard to do this operation in one hour.

Policy will indicate that this is a point beyond which the engineer will not be allowed to hold, withdraw, add, delete or change the ECO package. If changes are required a new ECO must be initiated. CM might correct errors found and notify the engineer but the engineer will be unable to make changes. One company that uses this principal, refers to this point as "Technical Release." That term is very expressive of the intent to have a point of no return. After this point, changes may occur on the cover sheet but not in the new or marked prints, specifications, and other design matter attached.

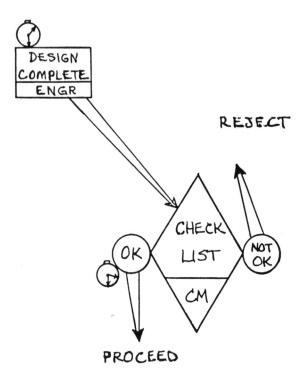

Figure 53. ECO flow point of no return.

Configuration Management Flow

The CM function is responsible for the next part of the process—From Design Complete through Release to Manufacturing and Update of Drawings and CAD. Note these operations in Figure 54.

CM immediately assigns the necessary part numbers, the next revision level, and distributes the change. The cover sheet is distributed to anyone who needs to know (perhaps "on line").The entire package is distributed only to key locations (assuming no "on line" capability for the entire package).

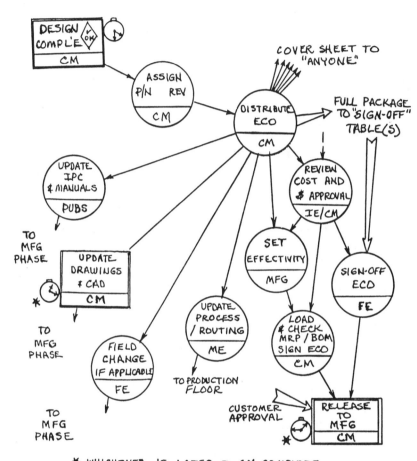

Figure 54. CM-phase ECO flow.

In a small company occupying one building, only one complete package need be available. It would be placed on a "sign-off table" in CM. In larger companies a package might have to be reproduced for the manufacturing people—probably on a table in Production Control. Any recipient of the cover sheet can then go to the sign-off table to review the entire set. In still larger companies, a copy of the entire package might have to go to each building or to the Publications, Field Support and ME functions. A "distribution" standard will be required.

Production Control now coordinates the determination of the effectivity of the change and notifies CM, ME, and the Industrial Engineer (if costs are being estimated).

The Industrial Engineer is now able to finalize the cost and give the cost sheet to CM. CM obtains the required management approvals based on the cost.

As soon as customer approval (if applicable) and the signed cover sheet(s) are in hand, CM can load the change information into the MRP / BOM system, and check the output.

It is very important to note what is <u>not</u> required by this point:

- The update of the publications is not required here.
- Up date (incorporation drafting) of the drawings, specifications and CAD are not required here. The time to do this will be separately tracked, reported and performed in three work day average time.
- The field change form(s), if required, are not needed here.
- Production process / routing changes are not required here.

Waiting for any one or all of those operations to be completed is unnecessary and wasteful. Waiting would cause a delay in ordering the parts required to implement the change. One day, hour, or even a minute can produce more scrap, rework, or an unhappy customer. Thus, these operations go to "Close" or to "Production Floor Implementation."

"Release to Production" is therefore an indication that the MRP has been successfully loaded, and that ordering of parts may proceed. It is accomplished when the cover sheet is redistributed.

Notice that the Update of Drawings and CAD is required to occur before the clock stops on the CM time. It must happen quickly. There is no need to obtain the engineer's signature on the updated drawing. The incorporation of the mark-up correctly is solely the responsibility of CM. The entire CM portion of the process should happen in three to five work days average.

Manufacturing / Implementation Flow

The flow from Release to Manufacturing to ECO Closed is a Manufacturing responsibility. See Figure 55.

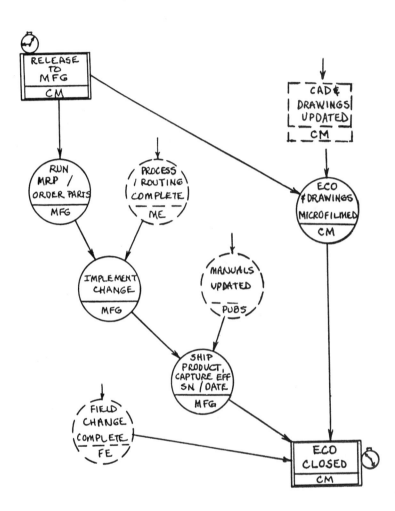

Figure 55. Implementation-phase ECO flow.

When the ECO cover sheet is distributed with the signatures and effectivity plan, the manufacturing people can proceed to order parts, change parts, etc. When the parts and the process/routing are available, manufacturing can implement the change on the production floor. Any changes to the effectivity plan are given to CM and the cover sheet is redistributed.

Thus in order to "Close" the ECO, manufacturing (Production Control) must notify CM of the actual effectivity. The other operations that must be completed in order to close the change need to be defined. In the case of The Loader Company the requirements to close are:

- All master drawings updated and microfilmed.
- The ECO is microfilmed
- The MRP must have been run to "drive" parts to the production floor. The process/routing must have been updated. These things must have occurred in order to implement the change on the production floor. The evidence of this occurring is the actual effectivity feedback.
- Company policy says that manuals that ship with the product must be revised and present or the product cannot ship. Production Control or Publications can notify CM.
- The Field Change Order, if applicable, is completed. A copy of the FCO is sent to CM as evidence that this activity is complete.

After all the listed operations have been completed, CM can close the change. The clock then "stops" on that change. This section is referred to as "manufacturing implementation," but it is obviously implementation on the part of several functions. They must all be tracked to satisfactory completion. One good way of notifying CM of each completion is by copy of the ECO cover sheet.

The flow diagram is a picture the process as we design it, then improve it, train / communicate it, and measure it. The flow diagram is the most powerful tool available to the CM Manager or Systems Analyst. Using the flow diagram as a training tool tends to bridge the gap between Engineering and the rest of the world.

The system must also be managed, just as the people involved must be managed.

Management for Fast Change

The management at the highest levels must be motivated to achieve a fast, accurate change system. They must participate in the steering committee, form an improvement team, set goals and follow up on the entire process. Once the time is measured, the volume is measured, the backlog is reduced, and the new or revised system is in place, the management task passes to the CM Manager.

Some of the things that the CM Manager can do to assure the speed and accuracy of the system are:

- Be dedicated to continuous improvement with or without an improvement team.

- Establish *one* ECO "basket" (Just-In-Time "Kanban") for each work station. Do not have and "in" *and* "out" basket. The single basket will be an "in" basket for work in process.

- One ECO can be worked on at a time at each work station—others stay in the basket.

- Do not allow ECOs to be put into files or desk drawers. The manager needs to be able to walk around and see the total ECOs in process at each work station.

- Require each person to hand deliver a completed ECO to the next workstation. If the next station is very far away, examine the alternatives. Another basket for hand carrying by anyone who is making a trip may be practical. A special mail arrangement may be necessary. The manager may carry them.

- CM does not hand-carry changes. The person who "thinks hand-carry is required" does the hand-carrying.

- Each CM technician must be instructed to drop what they are doing to do "hand-carries" ahead of all other changes. If the person doing the hand-carry is not familiar with the process, show him or her to the next work station.

- Train all cognizant engineers and others in the change process.

- Establish a limit on the number of changes that will be allowed to accumulate in each basket (kanban) before help will be obtained. The limit may be fairly high in the beginning, then reduced over time to very few changes.

Example: The average volume of changes is 18 per week. The current goal is fifteen days (three weeks) turn around time. There are six work stations in the process. Conclusion: No more than nine ECOs can be in any one work station (18x3÷6=9). After the fifteen work day goal is met, a ten work day goal can be set. This would translate into six ECOs per work station. Then set a five work day goal which would be three ECOs per work station.

- Look for help from other workstations where the kanban is low. The manager may have to step in to help a work station when needed. Temporary help may be in order.

Help must come quickly or the people will sense that speed isn't that important. Once the CM people have been trained to help each other, they will generally begin to do this on their own.

- Cross train the people. The ideal, is to have all people trained in every work station. This would allow organizing the people by product or customer or mirror the engineering organization. A quantum leap in communications is possible. Cross training is needed to fill the sick or absent person's work station. *Remember: If you think training is expensive—Try Ignorance!* Larger CM departments should consider a subgroup breakdown. Pair a "beginner" with a "fully-learned" or a "teacher."

- The manager holds an informal "continuous improvement / department meeting" for ten minutes at the same time each day. The manager and the CM Technicians explore ways to improve the system, its accuracy and its speed. Don't be negative about any idea. Merely sort out the best ones for implementation. Invite other people on occasion.

- When a mistake is made on a change, make sure that the mistake is corrected by the person who made it. If someone else corrects the mistake, chances are that the mistake will be repeated. Do on-the-spot training to assure that the person knows how to do it right.

- Train the manufacturing and field service people on the workings of the change process. They will come up with improvements, too.

When the Manager is absent, a temporary leader should hold the department improvement team meeting. Continuous improvement needs to become a habit. The Flow Diagram will be the primary tool for discussion of ideas and for implementing process changes.

A Case Study

A fast growing corporation in the computer products business. Fast reaction is a necessity for survival. The company's largest division processed about one hundred changes each month. Their OEM contracts routinely required customer approval.

That division was experiencing many of the symptoms of an engineering documentation control problem. Fixes took too long. Customers were impatient. Sometimes the paper got lost! The division Executive Vice President recognized the challenge.

We started our analysis by properly defining the problem. The people involved measured the actual throughput time. It soon became apparent that the 100 changes per month were taking an average of *120 work days.* The time broke down into roughly equal parts:

- 40 work days to design and develop the changes.
- 40 work days to process the paper work and update the BOM / MRP.
- 40 work days to implement the change in production.

It was determined to attack the middle forty first. We set a five work day goal. We assigned one person from Engineering, Materials, and Manufacturing (Materials did not answer to Manufacturing) to a "task force." A steering committee was formed. The division Executive VP chaired that group. The task force started by making a plan:

- Analyze the current process
- Brainstorm and document changes to (or reinvent) the process
- Document the process
- Trial run
- Approval of the process
- Train
- Implement

Analysis of the current system included:

- Continuing measurement and large-graph reporting (see Figure 56).
- Sampling of over one hundred changes from the prior year. A data bank was formed with over 10,000 bits of information about their changes.
- Flow-diagramed the current process.
- Gathered all the current system forms, policies, and procedures.

The result was filled with surprises, even for those who considered themselves very knowledgeable about the process. The middle forty work days included the following events:

- Translate a messy engineer's mark-up into "Was-Now" drafted ECO
- Set effectivity
- Occasionally estimate costs
- Revise all drawings, specifications, and field support document master.
- Obtain an engineer's signature on each updated master.
- Stop, hold, change, or reverse the process at the engineer's whim.
- Make copies totaling over one million sheets of paper per year.

We divided the entire process into small subjects and wrote standards about each. One to five pages per standard/subject. The task force then brainstormed improvements. It was determined to reinvent the process.

In the meantime, the CM process time had been reduced to thirty-two work days. Large throughput-time charts were posted. The task force and the steering committee were ever present. The people involved realized, for the first time, that process time was important. They took the first eight work days out by individual action. The task team wasn't sure how it happened!

Training and implementation of the new process took hold. The process time continued downward. See Figure 56. In about twelve months, a new process was designed, training was complete, the new process in place, debugged, and the time reached the goal—five work day average.

This reinvention took over three man years of total effort. That company considered it worth every hour. The surprises continued:

- It was done without any change in the number of people involved in the process. Two fewer people in CM were offset by two "new" people: an IE to estimate the cost of all Class I and II changes, and carry over of one team member to facilitate continuous improvement.
- The design and development time went down a few days. This happened even in the face of requiring modeling, testing and design team meetings in the Engineering Phase. Why? The only explanation seemed to be that measurement and reporting, in and of themselves, made it happen.

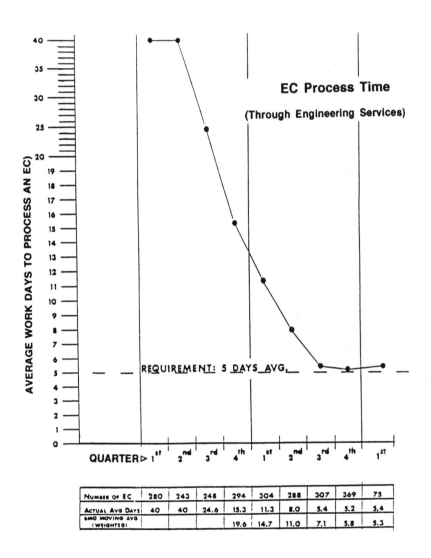

Figure 56. Case Study Process-Time graph.

- The Manufacturing / Implementation phase time also went down a few days. Same apparent explanation!
- The teamwork in the CM area visibly increased.
- They obtained a one-day average hand-carry time. Only four percent of their changes were hand carried.

They had no good way to measure the reductions in rework, scrap, "bone pile" effort, field support savings, earlier cost reductions, or customer happiness. Judgments were that all of these factors had, likewise, improved.

Significance of Speed

We have already discussed the benefits resulting from having a fast and accurate change process. We did this on the basis of identifiable results—reduce rework, etc. It is interesting to note that speed is important as a *strategy*. Consider the following quote from the *Harvard Business Review* in a July / Aug 1988 article, "Time - The Next Source Of Competitive Advantage." In this article, author George Stalk, Jr. states; *"As a strategic weapon, time is the equivalent of money, productivity, quality, even innovation"*

This is why the Engineering Documentation Control or Configuration Management must have a:

Golden Rule: The speed with which you process design changes is critical to profitability.

10

Process Standards and Audits

CM process specifications are referred to by many different names. Some call them policy and procedure. Sometimes the word "documentation" is used. This writer prefers the term "standards." The word "procedures" seems to be a generally used term, much like this writer uses the word "standards." The term procedure would imply step by step instructions, but it does not exclude forms, form instructions or the use of flow diagrams to depict the processes. As emphasized before, the flow diagram is a better tool than step by step procedure because it is easier to display parallel activities and to yield a training "picture."

Regardless of what they are called, every company needs to develop a set of standards for their CM processes. This is necessary because they:

- Make it easy to train new people.
- Give people a uniform method to follow.
- Leave those who are creative a foundation on which to improve.
- Provide a tool for training people in process changes.
- Give people the baseline from which to take exceptions.
- Give management, customer, or regulating agency something to audit "against."

For all of these reasons, the standards are a significant part of the CM task. As our policy statement points out, it is the CM Manager's responsibility to see that they are created and kept up to date. The CM manager may enlist some help in developing the standards. The "Improvement Team" can, and should, take some of the burden for their development. A CM department "teacher" should develop some. No matter who does the development, they must be done if the CM processes are to be carried out in some form of "sanity."

No one should be embarrassed if the standards need to be changed. In fact, just the opposite should be true. If the standards are to be useful, they will be constantly corrected and improved. Kaoru Ishikawa in his 1985 *"What Is Total Quality Control? The Japanese Way"* writes, "...if newly established standards and regulations are not revised in six months, it is proof that no one is seriously using them."

CM Policy

The first standard written should be a policy statement. It must be brief but precise. A good example of a CM policy is shown in Figure 57.

The policy should be signed by a high company officer. In small companies, the president should sign them. In larger companies, the Chief Engineer or Executive Vice President should sign. This officer should also be the signer of each standard.

Typical Standard

The standards must be short. They should cover only one subject. The typical standard should be one to three pages in length. If a standard is much longer than that, it probably covers more than one subject. It probably also won't be read. The goal is to divide the total subject of Engineering Documentation Control into its logical processes and then to develop standards on each subject in that logical process. The logical processes, you will recall, are:

- Product and Documentation Release
  - Bill Of Material
    - Request for Change
      - Change

EC³ Corp   **C M POLICY**   Standard # 001

PURPOSE:
To assure the lowest total product life cycle cost as a systematic and minimally controlled product & documentation Release, Change Request, Design Change, and Bill of Material processes.

POLICY:
- To have an organized, fast, accurate, consistent, well understood and minimally controlled method for controlling the configuration of hardware and software products.

- This system of Configuration Management shall consist of planning, control, identification, traceability, and reporting.

- This system of Configuration Management shall consist of a Release, Change Request, Change Control and Bill of Material processes.

- To be used for control of design documentation by Engineering, Manufacturing, Field Support and other affected organizations.

- To assure the maintenance of a single Bill Of Material data base.

RESPONSIBILITIES:

C M MANAGER:
- Design and documentation of the CM Process by appropriate Flow Diagram, Form, Form Instruction, and other Standards.

- To manage and audit the process and to report to senior staff as to its speed, accuracy and volume.

- To educate those involved as to good CM practices and in the company processes.

V P ENGINEERING:
- To assure that the C M function has the necessary resources and authority to perform its functions.

Figure 57. Configuration Management Policy.

The standards will take the form of:

- Forms
    - Form Instructions
        - Policy Statement
            - Flow Diagrams
                - Standardized Definitions and Methods

The "Standardized Definitions and Methods" allow the flow diagrams to be clear and crisp. As previously discussed, they keep the words on a flow diagram to an absolute minimum. While preparing a flow diagram, if lengthy operation statements or notes are needed, chances are that a separate standard is called for.

Subjects to Standardize

The particular subjects that would be candidates for a standard will vary from company to company. Some guidance can be given, however. By process, subjects to consider are shown below.

Product and Document Release Process Standards

- Product / Model numbers
- Release Form
- Release Form Instructions
- Drawing and Specification Formats
- Drawing and Specification Preparation
- Part Numbering
- Release Phases / Stages
- Release Flow Diagram
- Checklist for Release
- Release Team Meetings
- Management Review in the Release Progress
- End Item Configuration and Identification
- Serial Number Assignment

Bill Of Material Process Standards

- BOM Content
- BOM Structuring
- BOM / Engineering Parts List
- Item Master Input and Verification
- Parts List Input and Verification
- MRP Codes
- Spares List
- Units of Measure and Quantities
- Modular BOM and Shopping List Drawing

Request for Change Process Standards

- Cognizant Engineer List
- Request Form
- Request Form Instruction
- Request Flow Diagram

Change Control Process Standards

- Engineering Change Order Form
- Change Form Instruction
- Change Cost Form
- Change Cost Form Instruction
- Definition of Interchangeability
- Part Number Change Logic
- Mark-Up of Engineering Documents
- ECO Number
- ECO Classes
- Dispositioning
- Design Team in the Change Process
- Effectivity of Changes
- Checklist for Technical Completion of Changes
- Implementing the Change in Manufacturing
- Closing the Change
- Field Changes

Breaking down the processes in this manner allows each standard to be short. This brevity will make them easier to develop, review, agree upon and approve. Divide and conquer! An example of a one page standard for "Mark-Up of Engineering Documents" is shown in Figure 58.

EC³ Corp   **Standard # 100**

MARK UP OF ENGINEERING DOCUMENTS

PURPOSE:
To encourage the use of the mark up technique for communication of the old and new designs. This saves time and improves the clarity of design change over the "from - to" drafting method. To specify the acceptable conditions for mark ups.

OVERVIEW:
* Use of the mark up technique is encouraged since it affords the fewest possibilities for transposition errors. The master mark up (in red) will be used by the draftsperson to revise the master or the CAD.

* Mark ups must be clearly and neatly done since they will be used in the ECO "as is".

* Printed documents must be double spaced in order to be properly marked up.

* Mark up of the new condition must be in <u>red pen or pencil</u>, bold and printed (not cursive). It should be in a different "style" than the original lettering however.

* A CAD overlay may be made to serve as the mark up or "TO" condition.

* Both the print and the mark ups must be capable of being readable after three generations of reproduction . . . . to silver microfilm, to diazo microfilm, to print.

* A very high quality latest revision print can be obtained from the Drawing Center on a "while you wait" basis. Just ask for a "print for mark up".

* Portions of a document may be used by providing;

    * Standard drawing sizes are used (multiples of 8 1/2" x 11")

    * The print is the latest revision level in the portion used.

    * The title block is included.

* The "old" (or "was") (or "from") condition shall <u>not</u> be obliterated in part or in total. Underlining or circling of the portion to be deleted are the acceptable methods.

* Mark ups can be changed at or before the Technical Review meeting.

* The mark up technique <u>can</u> be used for the "make from" (same as except) situations.

* Encouraging use of mark ups does not preclude the use of "from - to" documents.

AUTHORIZATION:

_____   _____
sign   **date**

Figure 58. Typical Standard.

Several miscellaneous standards may be necessary. They might address such subjects as Definitions, Auditing, Distribution, Security, etc. If a company is seeking ISO 9000 certification, definitely add a topic: "Disposal of Down-Level Prints." These standards need not be developed all at once. Start with the process which is highest priority and with the subjects that most need clarifying.

Standards Manual

The standards should be placed in a book or in a computer file. They may be under the CM managers control, in a company manual, or in the quality manual. Given a choice, opt for a CM manual under CM's control. If they are in a separate manual, the company manual or quality manual should reference the CM manual. One good way to do this would be to place an overall policy statement into the company manual. In the policy statement, place a reference to the CM manual.

Each standard should be given a number and be date controlled. They should not be given an engineering part or document number. Doing so might lead one to believe that they are under the CM process control. The forms should be numbered from a log. The form number should be on the form - typically in the lower left hand corner. A simple numbering system should be developed, such as:

CM 001	A size drawing
CM 002	B size drawing
CM 003	Release form
CM 004	Change form
CM 005	Checklist - changes
CM 006	Request form

Larger companies may choose to put engineering part numbers on their forms and to stock them in the warehouse. If that is a consideration, it may be an ideal time to put the most-used forms "on line," save the paper cost and improve communications.

Training

The necessity for training has been pointed out several times. It cannot be over emphasized. Train before implementing. Train before "finalizing" a standard. Train before implementing any continuous improvement. It is a "pay me now, or pay me later" situation. The investment in training will pay back many times in the future.

The process of continuous improvement must mean continuous training. Even well-conceived and documented processes can fail for lack of training. Don't just call a group of people into a room and tell them what is happening. Use a real world company assembly to develop your training tools. Document that assembly, release it, structure the parts list / BOM, request a change to it, and change it. Develop the new form(s) for that company assembly. Walk people through the process. Go "on line" when applicable.

Different levels of training may be appropriate. A good place to start is with generic CM training for the team(s) and related people. A "system overview" training session might be good for the general population. Specific training for the Design Engineers, Manufacturing Engineers, Production Control / Materials, CM, or the production floor management. You may want to develop a specific class for your customers or agency people.

Just as the standards develop with continuous improvement, your training will develop over time. Training will be the key to bridging the gap between Engineering and the rest of the world.

Auditing the CM Processes

If the CM discipline is to bridge the gap between Engineering and the rest of the world, it must be subject to audit. Outside audit, inside audit, self audit, or all of the above. Rather than looking at the idea of audit with fear, the CM manager must view audit as an opportunity. In fact, start with a self-audit in order to find out how useful they can be. Perform one or more of the "sanity tests" later described. You will be surprised that all parts of the process aren't working quite as planned.

Outside Auditor's View

It is only human to look for standardized methods of doing business. Auditors are only human. Lack of standards gives the impression of chaos. Whether your customer or governing agency require it or not, having standards is a real necessity to world-class CM. Some institutions require them. ISO 9000 series states: " The supplier shall establish and maintain procedures to control and verify the design of the product in order to ensure that the specified requirements are met." Engineering Documentation Control (CM) is at the heart of "verify the design" and "specified requirements." In this writer's judgment, CM is the heart of a vast majority of ISO 9000 requirements. CM is also the heart of many other agency requirements. And, after all, having standards is just good business. They provide a baseline for normal activities and a baseline for "management by exception."

Internal Audit

The ideal internal audit should be done with the Quality Assurance or Internal Audit Department. If you have no such organization, or they are not able to do a system audit, the CM manager should do the auditing. Either way, it must not be taken lightly. It is a necessary step to attain world-class recognition.

Without written standards, auditing the CM processes is a somewhat limited effort. Still, some of the following "sanity tests" can be done. With written standards, the task makes more sense. The approach is then to verify that what is said in the standards, is in fact, followed.

Audit Plan

Make sure that there is a plan for performance of the audit before it starts. The plan should address several issues:

- Why is the audit being done?
- Who will do the audit? Will CM be free to work with the auditor?
- When will it be done?
- What documents will be audited?
- What processes?
- What sample size will be taken? How will the sample be chosen?
- How will a discrepancy be defined?
- Will a report be written? By whom? When?

The detail with which each issue is answered will vary depending upon whether the CM Manager is performing his / her own audit, whether the customer is involved, etc. Regardless of the type of audit, it will be a waste, even counter-productive, unless the CM Manager is dedicated to proper follow up.

Audit Follow-Up

Every audit must have a conclusion. The conclusion should be to have each discrepant item resolved and closed. Each discrepancy must be followed to find out the root cause of the problem. Effort must be expended to fix the root cause of each problem. A few "anomalies" are allowed, but most problems must be traced and fixed. The "fix" might be training, revising a standard, etc.

If this follow up is not done, the people involved in the process will quickly figure out that it was a "white wash." This can affect their moral and even increase the errors made. Issue a final report that closes the audit and informs the people and the management of the root cause fixes.

Auditing the CM processes can take a number of different routes. The audit plan should determine which route(s) will be followed. Some possibilities for "sanity tests" are shown.

Release Process Audit

- Sample drawings, specifications, and other design documents:
  - Were the documents prepared according to the standard?
  - Were the documents signed according to the standard?
  - Was the revision level assigned by CM as part of the release process?
  - Is the release form number in the revision "ECO" number block?
  - Is the release document readily available?
- Sample purchase orders:
  - Were purchases for prototype, pilot, and production made from documents released for that or a "higher" release level?
  - Were the drawings "modified" by the purchase order?

- Sample a product:
  - Is it obvious as to what release level (prototype, pilot, or production) the product was made for?
  - Does the product match the documentation for that release level.
- Sample recent release forms:
  - Were the forms apparently completed per the standard?
  - Do the forms cross-check to the logs?
- Walk through the process:
  - Are the people aware of what the standards say and are they following them?
  - Does the form appear as it should at each step in the process?
  - Can all the release form numbers be accounted for?

BOM Process Audit

- Sample recent Parts Lists:
  - Do they cross-reference (find number or balloon number) to the pictorial drawing?
  - Is there an item for item match to the pictorial?
  - Do they use units of measure and quantities per the standard?
  - Are the units of measure the correct ones for purchasing purposes?
  - Are any assemblies at a higher release level than its lowest level part?
  - Are referenced documents properly noted?
  - Is the parts list a product of the MRP / database?

- Sample a product:
  - Does the product contain all the parts in the BOM and no more?
  - Does the product contain the quantity of parts per the BOM?
  - Given the nameplate data, can the non-interchangeable changes be identified?

- Sample a current BOM:
  - Does it contain the ECOs that it should?
  - Is the effectivity in the BOM per the ECO?
  - Is there only one BOM database which is universally used?
  - If more than one BOM, do they agree?

Request Process Audit

- Sample recent request forms:
  - Does the requester receive an answer to each request?
  - Are requests answered on a timely basis?
  - Are the reasons given for rejection reasonable?
- Walk through the process:
  - Are the people aware of what the standards say, and are they following them?
  - Does the form appear as it should at each step in the process?

Design Change Process Audit

- Sample recent ECOs:
  - Do the ECOs contain the information required by the standards?
  - Does the average process time agree with the report?
  - Do the forms cross check to the logs?
  - Are the ECOs properly delineated on the traceability reports?
  - Does the product contain the change per the actual effectivity?
- Sample Wavers and Deviations:
  - Were they done according to standard?
  - Are non-interchangeable ones reflected in the traceability reports?
  - Are deviations being used to make design changes?

- Sample traceability reports:
  - Do they contain all the class I ECOs closed?
  - Is the stated effectivity per the ECO?
- Sample a finished product:
  - Does the product contain what the ECO effectivity says it should?
  - Does the product contain what the traceability report says it should?
- Walk through the process:
  - Do the people understand what is required by the standards and do they follow them?
  - Does the form appear as it should at each step in the process?
  - Can all the ECO numbers be accounted for?

These may not be the correct questions for your company. If troublesome conditions have been known to exist, those error conditions should be added to your audit. If prior audits found little problem in a given area, the current audit may not check that area.

Audit Frequency

Most quality department folks say that an audit should be performed about once a year. I would be happy to see most folks do their first audit. Too often, the first audit occurs when the customer or his representative shows up.

Start by developing the standards on the most troublesome process. Then set about doing an audit on one or two aspects of that process once a year. Then, move to the next most-troublesome process. Audit that process and follow with a yearly audit of one or two suspected problem areas. Depending upon the results, a different set of aspects might be chosen each year.

Train Without a Whistle

Publish the results of the audit. Publish the follow up resolution of all discrepancies. The occurrence or recognition of problems should not be viewed as a weakness. The failure to follow each to its root cause and fixing the problem is a weakness. Let folks know that you not only recognized the problems, but that you fixed them.

An old timer used to say; "A train don't run by its whistle, but you never saw a train without a whistle!" The meaning was clear—when you achieve something good, you should toot your own whistle. You want a world-class CM system that you can toot your whistle about. World-class CM systems don't get that way, or stay that way, without regular auditing. Nor do they get that way without hard work and often considerable pain. This is true because creating a new system has always been a difficult task. Witness what Machiavelli "The Prince" wrote in the year 1513:

> "It must be remembered that there is nothing more difficult to plan, more doubtful of success, nor more dangerous to manage than the creation of a new system. For the Initiator has the enmity of all who would profit by the preservation of the old institutions and merely lukewarm defenders in those who would gain by the new ones."

11

CM in the Future

It is somewhat presumptive to predict the future, however it may be more permissible as a wish, rather than a forecast. What should the future hold? The following is a result of a mixture of ideas from engineering, repair and manufacturing experience; consulting experience; holding seminars; discussion with peers; as well as researching and writing this book.

System Standards

Documentation of the system will not be viewed as merely a way to satisfy an agency or ISO 9000 requirement. Standards will be viewed as the first step toward constant improvement, and a necessity to management-by-exception. Appreciation for single subject, brief standards will evolve.

Part Numbers

There will be a gradual movement away from smart part numbers except for simplistic products. Small companies are tending to use less significant part numbers. Classification coding systems will be developed or purchased to fill the needs of significance. The "ideal" part number will have minimum significance. The part number will have the document number embedded in it. It will also have a tab in order to facilitate part number changing on non-interchangeable changes.

Interchangeability

The significance of interchangeability and part number changing will be "rediscovered." Reliance on the product specification to interpret form and function interchangeability will be the norm. There will be a recognition that changing the part number is the least painless way to track non-interchangeable changes in the long run.

Engineering functions will come to realize that the manufacturing systems depend upon revision levels being interchangeable, and therefore relatively insignificant in their processes. The revision level will be reserved for interchangeable changes to the document which represents the revised item. The parts will not be identified by revision level. The relationship between Purchasing, Receiving Inspection, and Suppliers will be on the basis of purchase order and purchase order revision (design change).

Traceability of non-interchangeable changes to the end-product will be recognized as a task that needs the full co-operation of Engineering and Manufacturing. It will not be done by use of the drawing revision.

The BOM

The design portion of the Bill Of Material will be recognized as a key *configuration management process*. The singular BOM will become a significant way to bridge the gap between engineering and the rest of the company. It will be recognized as a process that needs to be jointly developed by Engineering and Manufacturing to be mutually beneficial.

More simplified BOMs will emerge—fewer structure levels—driving toward one, two or three level bills.

There will be more wide-spread use of modular BOMs as a better method of documenting features and options and, more importantly, as a powerful tool in responding quickly to customer orders.

Clear and Crisp Release Process

The design development and the documentation release process will be recognized as a marriage of necessity. Clear, crisp, fast, accurate, and well-understood methods will result. Small companies will develop a process where none existed before. Larger companies will simplify their processes.

The major emphasis will be on encouraging a part-by-part, assembly-by-assembly evolution rather than today's tendency toward massive batching of the documentation for release.

The release process will be complemented by increased use of concurrent engineering (design team) practices.

Simplified Request Process

There will be a tendency to more quickly recognize the need for change. There will be a gradual recognition that the simpler the request process, the better. Companies will abandon the tendency to process the request as though it were already a change. The process time savings will translate into competitive advantage and cost savings.

One Fast Change Process

If for no other reason, the competition will force the abandonment of multiple formal and informal systems in favor of one fast, accurate and well-understood process.

The fast change process will allow the horse (documentation) to get in front of the cart (the product).

The trend will be away from boards and committees, replaced by a process with "up front" design teams (concurrent engineering).

Process design for the "rule" as opposed to the "exception" will evolve. This will free management time to handle exceptions.

More methods for avoiding and eliminating some changes will be devised; development of "smart" checklists and use of design teams early in the processes are the most significant.

Many "myths" apparent in change processes will be exposed. Primary among the disappearing myths will be the queuing of changes to master documents.

This fast change process time-saving will also translate into competitive advantage and cost-savings.

Automation

Putting the release, request, and change forms "on line" will be the rule. Putting the rest of the package on line will come somewhat slower.

There is and will be a tendency to measure every operation in the process because computers make it so "easy." Eventual recognition that "no one can use all that data," will be followed by a movement to measuring only a few key points.

An increased use of database information in the CM discipline will occur. An explosion of "cure all" automated CM system software is occurring. It will not, unfortunately, be very well integrated with either MRP or CAD.

Almost no software exists to allow "interaction" of CAD and MRP. This is a necessity for companies to achieve one integrated Bill Of Material. As that need is recognized, applications will follow to fill that gap. The key element—security on the revision field for CM—will come with some of those packages.

Government Agencies

A very gradual movement toward simplification of agency standards will occur, probably directly proportional to budget cuts. This movement will be akin to watching an iceberg melt.

The Discipline

There will be an increased recognition of Configuration Management / Engineering Documentation Control as a teachable *discipline.* Several certification groups will eventually unite just enough to merge the certification requirements.

Significant increases in CM societies and society membership will occur. Their influence will force common certification requirements.

The dominance by DoD-oriented organizations and societies will give way to local society memberships who will find a significant majority of their members are interested in generic CM. The International Standards Organization may be the driving force here.

The discipline will gradually shift from the traditional "Identification, Control, Accounting, and Planning" to emphasis on the processes involved.

There will be an increased use of operative Design Teams in the CM processes—Release, BOM, Request, and Change. There will be a recognition that poor implementation of concurrent engineering / design team practices does not negate the power of the concept.

There will be increased emphasis on the product specification as the key procurement tool. Companies will realize that approval of design changes is a poor substitute for well thought-out product specifications. A move to limit and to place stringent time controls on customer approval requirements will occur and is occurring.

Increased emphasis on costing changes will occur. There will be gradual recognition that not costing changes results in creeping elegance and profit erosion.

Academia

Colleges, universities, business and trade schools will increase CM course offerings. The courses will become a part of the required engineering curriculum at forward-looking colleges and universities. There will eventually be degrees offered in Engineering Documentation Control / Configuration Management.

Industry in General

Functions that are now dispersed in the organization will be brought together into meaningful CM departments. There will be a tremendous demand for CM managers who have proven that they can "bridge the gap." There will be an ever-increasing emphasis on CM as a practical way to bridge the gap between Engineering and the rest of the company. The discipline will be recognized as the key way to eliminate the "throw it over the wall" syndrome.

American industry will lead the world in developing simplistic methods to handle the CM processes, integrated with CAD and MRP, in a systematic approach.

Recommended Reference and Reading List

Design Assurance for Engineers and Managers
> By: John A. Burgess, Marcel Dekker, Inc., New York (1984)
>> Well presented quality design considerations for research and development people.

Implementing Configuration Management Hardware, Software and Firmware
> By: Fletcher J. Buckley, IEEE Press, New York (1993)
>> A must-read for anyone interested in DoD / Military contracting Configuration Management. Includes excellent reference lists.

CIM Applications List
> By: Grayme Bartuli, 12685 Dodd Court, Rosemount, MN
>> Included in University of Wisconsin, Milwaukee, Continuing Engineering Education program seminars on Engineering Documentation Control.
>> An excellent, evolving listing of Conputer Integrated Manufacturing (CIM) software application programs including Configuration Management and Product Data Management programs.

ISO 9000: The World Quality Standard
> By: Donald R. Stovicek, Senior Ed., *Tooling & Production,* April (1993)
>> Puts the ISO 9000 specifications into perspective, explains them, and will help formulate your company's strategy.

Group Technology
> By: Frederick B. Ingram, APICS Journal, Fourth Quarter, (1982)
>> This international student award program winning article explains Group Technology / Classification Coding systems, concepts, structures and uses.

Engineering Changes: A Case Study
> By Frank B. Watts, APICS Journal, Fourth Quarter, (1984)
>> The story of how one company drove its configuration management process time on engineering changes from forty work days to five.

Index

257